WONDER WOMAN

Love and Murder

WON

Jodi Picoult
Writer

Drew Johnson & Ray Snyder with Rodney Ramos *(chapters 1 & 2)*
Terry Dodson & Rachel Dodson *(chapters 3 & 4)*
Paco Diaz *(chapter 5)*
Artists

Alex Sinclair Lee Loughridge Dave McCaig
Colorists

Rob Leigh Travis Lanham
Letterers

Terry Dodson & Rachel Dodson with Alex Sinclair
Original covers

DER WOMAN

Love and Murder

Wonder Woman created by William Moulton Marston

Dan DiDio
Senior VP-Executive Editor

Matt Idelson
Editor-original series

Nachie Castro
Associate Editor-original series

Anton Kawasaki
Editor-collected edition

Robbin Brosterman
Senior Art Director

Paul Levitz
President & Publisher

Georg Brewer
VP-Design & DC Direct Creative

Richard Bruning
Senior VP-Creative Director

Patrick Caldon
Executive VP-Finance & Operations

Chris Caramalis
VP-Finance

John Cunningham
VP-Marketing

Terri Cunningham
VP-Managing Editor

Alison Gill
VP-Manufacturing

Hank Kanalz
VP-General Manager, WildStorm

Jim Lee
Editorial Director-WildStorm

Paula Lowitt
Senior VP-Business & Legal Affairs

MaryEllen McLaughlin
VP-Advertising & Custom Publishing

John Nee
VP-Business Development

Gregory Noveck
Senior VP-Creative Affairs

Sue Pohja
VP-Book Trade Sales

Cheryl Rubin
Senior VP-Brand Management

Jeff Trojan
VP-Business Development, DC Direct

Bob Wayne
VP-Sales

Cover by Terry Dodson &
Rachel Dodson with Alex Sinclair

WONDER WOMAN:
LOVE AND MURDER

DC Comics, 1700 Broadway,
New York, NY 10019
A Warner Bros. Entertainment Company
Printed in China. First Printing.

HC ISBN: 1-4012-1487-8
HC ISBN: 978-1-4012-1487-6
SC ISBN: 1-4012-1708-7
SC ISBN: 978-1-4012-1708-2

⌒ JODI PICOULT

introduction

When DC Comics first approached me to write the Wonder Woman comic book series, my immediate thought was that I didn't have time to devote to it, given the fact that I was supposed to be writing a novel. My second thought was that it was far too cool an opportunity to pass up (something my children immediately reiterated). I decided to undertake the challenge for a few reasons — because it was something I'd never done before; because I'd always been a fan of Wonder Woman (who hasn't?); because I'd admired other writers who'd seamlessly moved between fiction and comic books (Brad Meltzer foremost); and because I would be only the second woman to write the comic book in its long history.

I have never had so much fun writing — nor worked so hard. The chance to flex my comedic muscles, the balance of fitting a story into twenty-two pages, and the task of keeping Wonder Woman's long history as a character intact all weighed heavily upon me. Most daunting of all: how could I put my fingerprint on Wonder Woman? Why, of all the writers in the world, had DC Comics asked ME to take her on?

My first attempt to effect subtle change was to take her out of her bustier, as any woman writer would know it's impossible to fight crime without straps. I was soundly rejected. But when I seriously began to think of Wonder Woman and my own impressions of her, I knew what I'd have to do: create a storyline that captured her wide demographic of fans — from young women looking for a role model to adults who'd grown up with her, male and female — and create a richness and depth of character that had previously been missing. Like Superman, Wonder Woman's larger than life. But unlike Clark Kent, Wonder Woman's "human" identities have been underdeveloped. It was easy for readers to admire her, and hard for them to relate to her. To that end, I began to think about today's term, "wonder women," which is used to refer to women who do it all...and usually feel like they're not doing any of it well enough! What if Wonder Woman continued to be the strongest, smartest female on this planet...but had some doubt in other areas of her life? Not in a way that weakened her...but that made her, well, more human? What if she were worried, like the rest of us, about not fitting in with the people we like the most? What if she struggled with being who she wanted and needed to be...and not just who her parents intended? These are universal battles, and it seemed to me that Wonder Woman was plenty strong enough to undertake them.

I chose to bring back Circe because she was my favorite villain — a smart, savvy woman, whose motivation for wreaking havoc is not as simple as it seems, but is actually also related to the people she loves the most. And I also chose to bring back Wonder Woman's mother, Hippolyta, because I wanted Wonder Woman to have a psychological foil just as strong as she is. Even those of us who command complete control, after all, usually bow to our parents' wishes. But what if our parents' wishes strike at the core of who we are?

The cliffhanger in LOVE AND MURDER was important to me. Not only was it a fantastic ending that would leave people gasping — it also was a wonderful starting point for the next writer who'd inherit the series after me. But most of all, it illustrated what I wanted in my arc: a Wonder Woman who reflects upon her previous actions and realizes that what we convince ourselves is right might now, in hindsight, be as innocent as we believed at the time; a Wonder Woman who is strong enough psychologically as well as physically to stand up to her mother and say that there's a difference between love and duty — and who is willing to put her own life at stake to teach her mother that lesson as well.

This series has been one of the high points of my writing career; I hope you enjoy it as well.

Jodi Picoult
June 2007

Previously in Wonder Woman

Maxwell Lord, the "Black King" of the government agency known as Checkmate, had been secretly gathering sensitive information on the world's super-heroes. Using his mental powers, Lord was able to take control of the mind of the world's most powerful hero, Superman, and used the Man of Steel to beat up Batman and attack Wonder Woman. The Amazing Amazon eventually bound Lord in her "lasso of truth," forcing Lord to tell her how to stop the rampaging Superman from potentially causing countless deaths and massive destruction. Lord replied with the only solution available: "Kill me."

Seeing no other choice, Wonder Woman snapped Lord's neck, freeing Superman. But both the Man of Steel and the Dark Knight could not condone Wonder Woman's actions — believing that there could have been another way to stop Lord. Following this tragic event, Wonder Woman took a year off from her duties to do some soul-searching, and also adopted the identity of Diana Prince — a special agent for the Department of Metahuman Affairs. Diana is partnered with Nemesis, a master of disguise, and the two report to Sarge Steel. She now divides her time between her government job and her original mission of bringing peace to "Man's World" as Wonder Woman.

But that peace is about to be shattered...

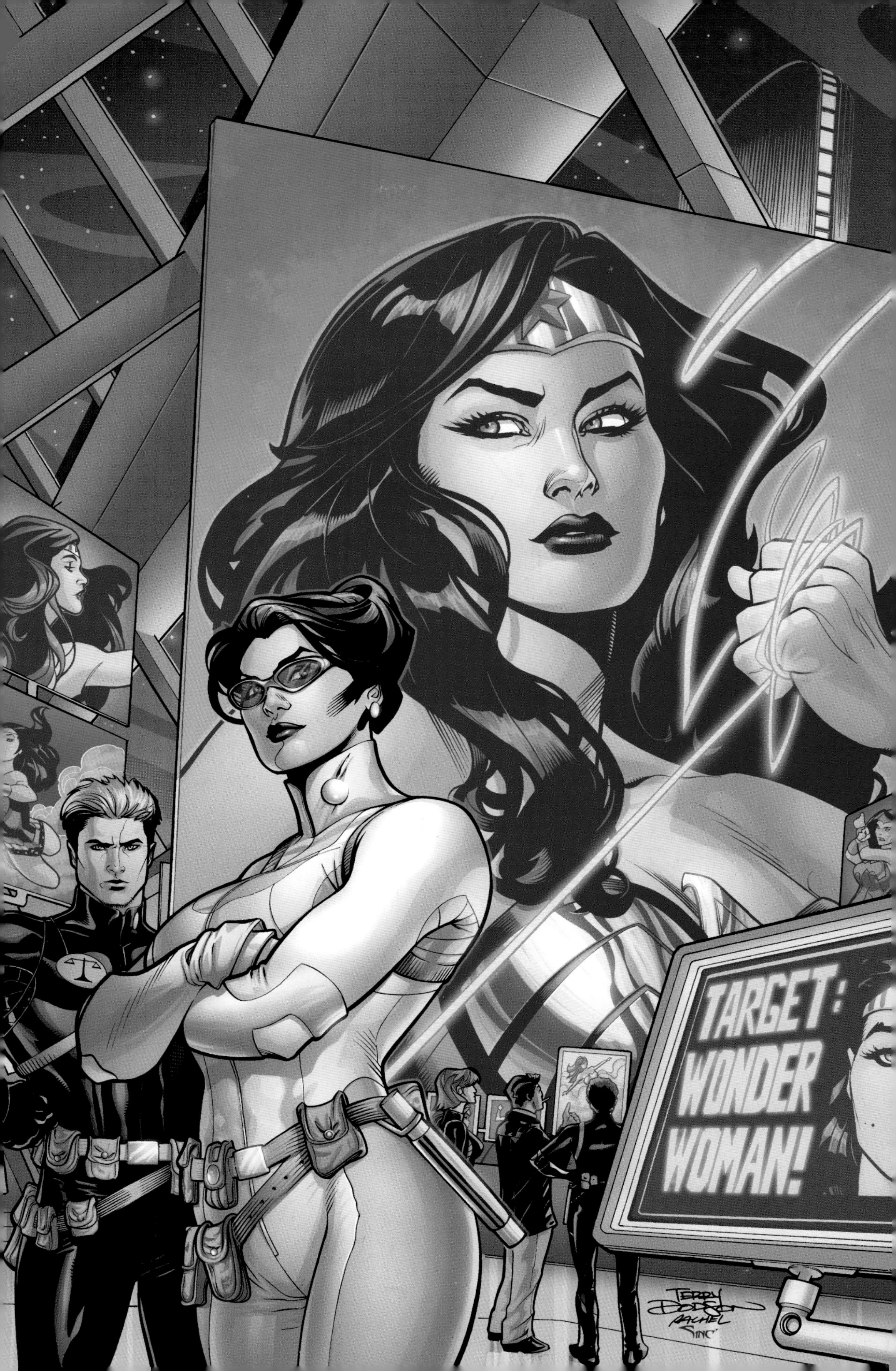
TARGET:
WONDER
WOMAN!

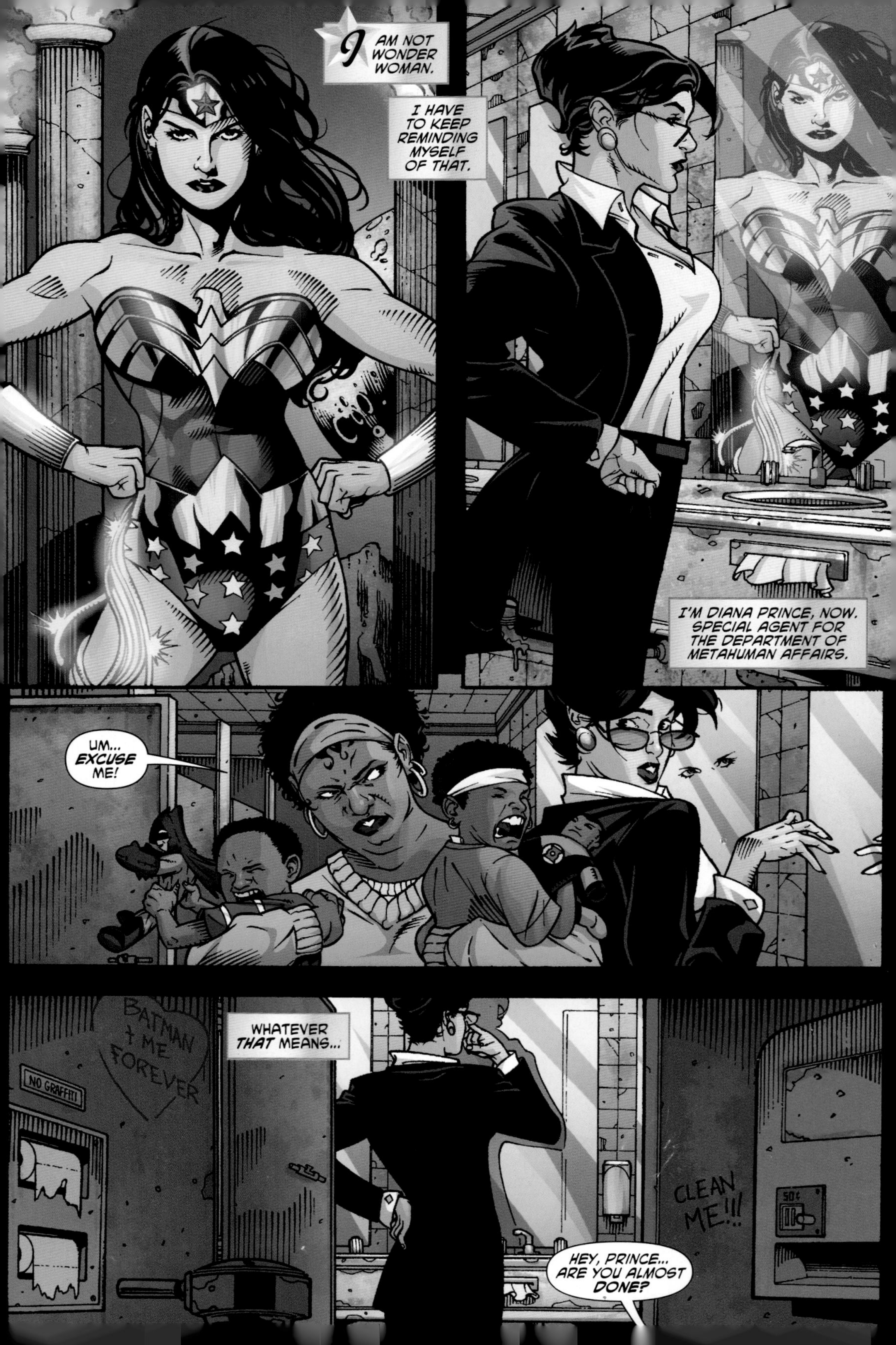
I AM NOT WONDER WOMAN.
I HAVE TO KEEP REMINDING MYSELF OF THAT.
I'M DIANA PRINCE, NOW. SPECIAL AGENT FOR THE DEPARTMENT OF METAHUMAN AFFAIRS.
UM... EXCUSE ME!
BATMAN + ME FOREVER
NO GRAFFITI
WHATEVER THAT MEANS...
CLEAN ME!!!
50¢
HEY, PRINCE... ARE YOU ALMOST DONE?

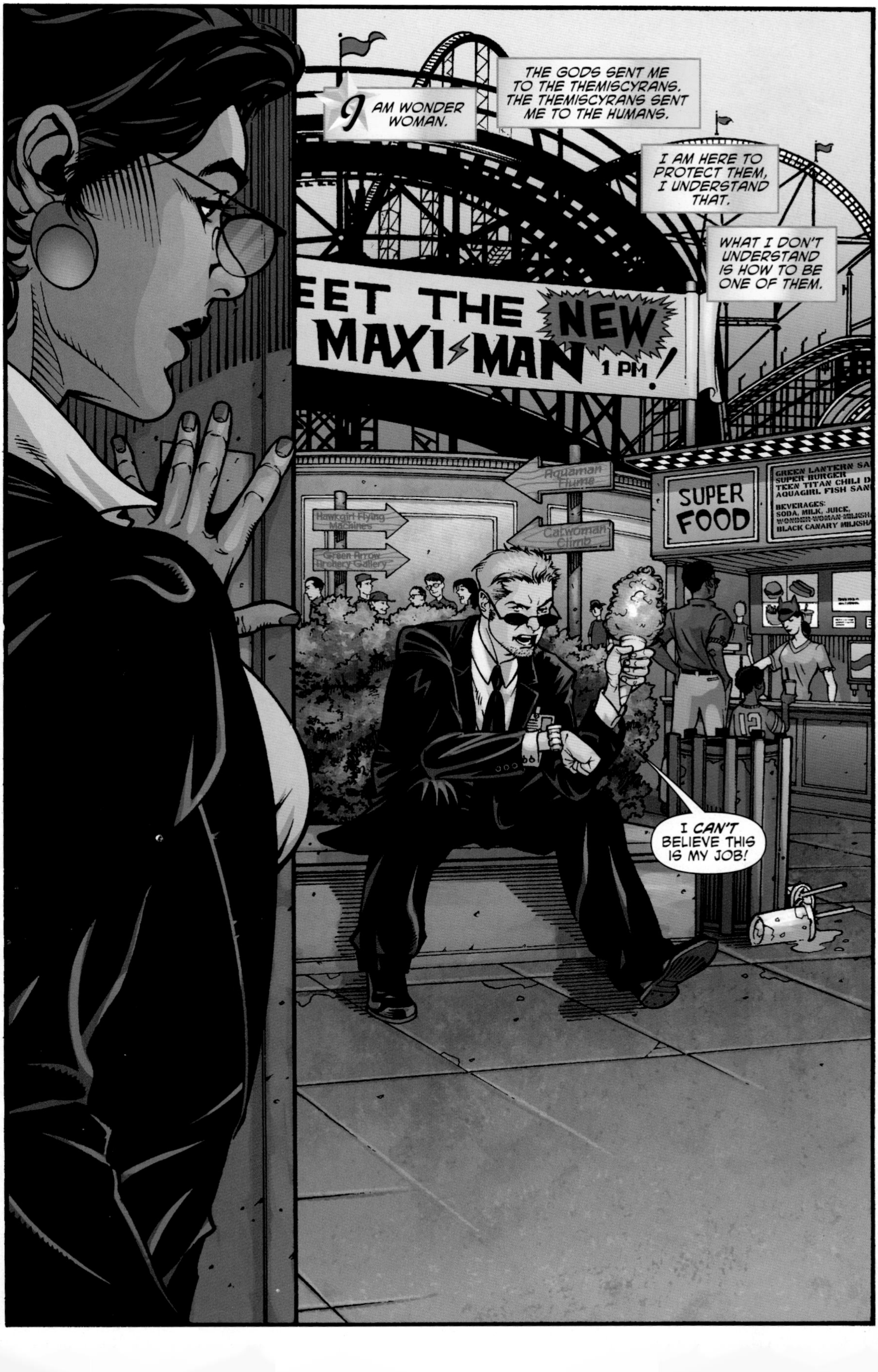
I AM WONDER WOMAN.
THE GODS SENT ME TO THE THEMISCYRANS. THE THEMISCYRANS SENT ME TO THE HUMANS.
I AM HERE TO PROTECT THEM, I UNDERSTAND THAT.
WHAT I DON'T UNDERSTAND IS HOW TO BE ONE OF THEM.
EET THE NEW MAXI-MAN 1 PM!
Aquaman Flume
Hawkgirl Flying Machines
Green Arrow Archery Gallery
Catwoman Climb
SUPER FOOD
SUPER BURGER
BEVERAGES:
SODA, MILK, JUICE,
I CAN'T BELIEVE THIS IS MY JOB!

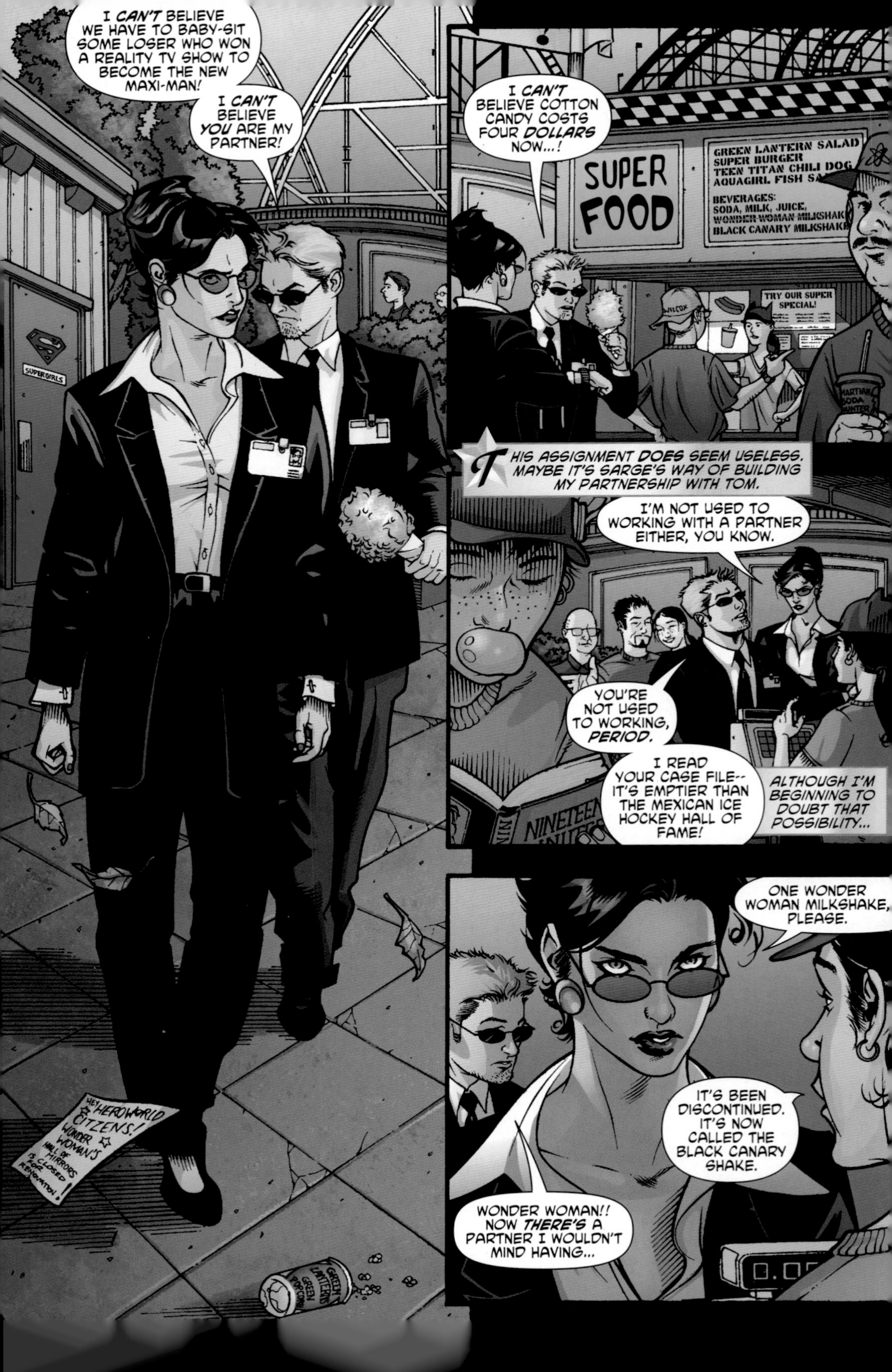
I CAN'T BELIEVE WE HAVE TO BABY-SIT SOME LOSER WHO WON A REALITY TV SHOW TO BECOME THE NEW MAXI-MAN!
I CAN'T BELIEVE YOU ARE MY PARTNER!
SUPERGIRLS
HEY, HEROWORLD CITIZENS! WONDER WOMAN'S HALL OF MIRRORS IS CLOSED FOR RENOVATION!
GREEN LANTERN'S GREEN POPCORN
I CAN'T BELIEVE COTTON CANDY COSTS FOUR DOLLARS NOW...!
SUPER FOOD
GREEN LANTERN SALAD
SUPER BURGER
TEEN TITAN CHILI DOG
BEVERAGES:
SODA, MILK, JUICE,
WONDER WOMAN MILKSHAKE
TRY OUR SUPER SPECIAL!
THIS ASSIGNMENT DOES SEEM USELESS. MAYBE IT'S SARGE'S WAY OF BUILDING MY PARTNERSHIP WITH TOM.
I'M NOT USED TO WORKING WITH A PARTNER EITHER, YOU KNOW.
YOU'RE NOT USED TO WORKING, PERIOD.
I READ YOUR CASE FILE-- IT'S EMPTIER THAN THE MEXICAN ICE HOCKEY HALL OF FAME!
ALTHOUGH I'M BEGINNING TO DOUBT THAT POSSIBILITY...
ONE WONDER WOMAN MILKSHAKE, PLEASE.
IT'S BEEN DISCONTINUED. IT'S NOW CALLED THE BLACK CANARY SHAKE.
WONDER WOMAN!! NOW THERE'S A PARTNER I WOULDN'T MIND HAVING...

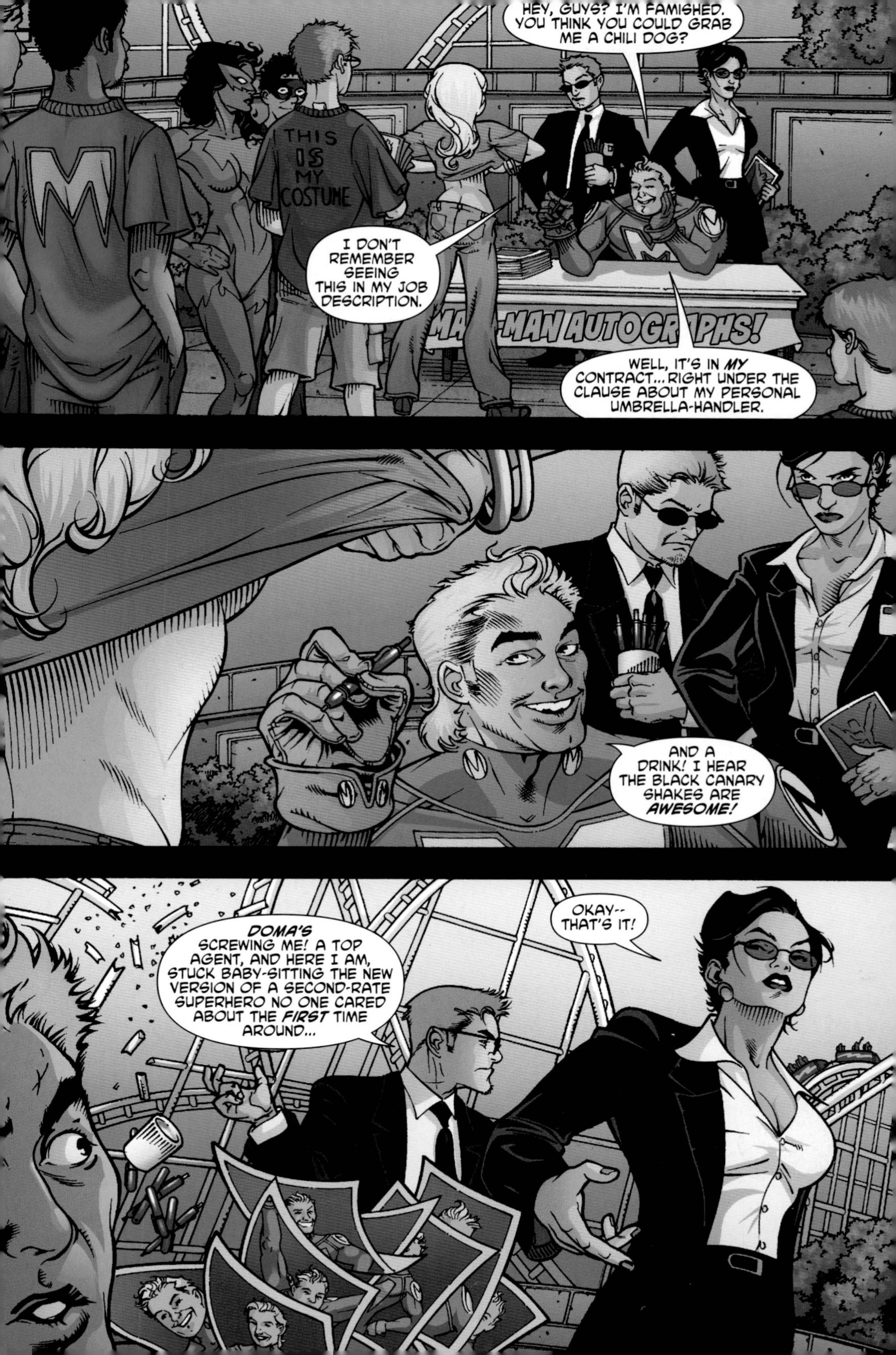
HEY, GUYS? I'M FAMISHED. YOU THINK YOU COULD GRAB ME A CHILI DOG?
THIS IS MY COSTUME
I DON'T REMEMBER SEEING THIS IN MY JOB DESCRIPTION.
MA -MAN AUTOGR PHS!
WELL, IT'S IN MY CONTRACT... RIGHT UNDER THE CLAUSE ABOUT MY PERSONAL UMBRELLA-HANDLER.
AND A DRINK! I HEAR THE BLACK CANARY SHAKES ARE AWESOME!
DOMA'S SCREWING ME! A TOP AGENT, AND HERE I AM, STUCK BABY-SITTING THE NEW VERSION OF A SECOND-RATE SUPERHERO NO ONE CARED ABOUT THE FIRST TIME AROUND...
OKAY-- THAT'S IT!

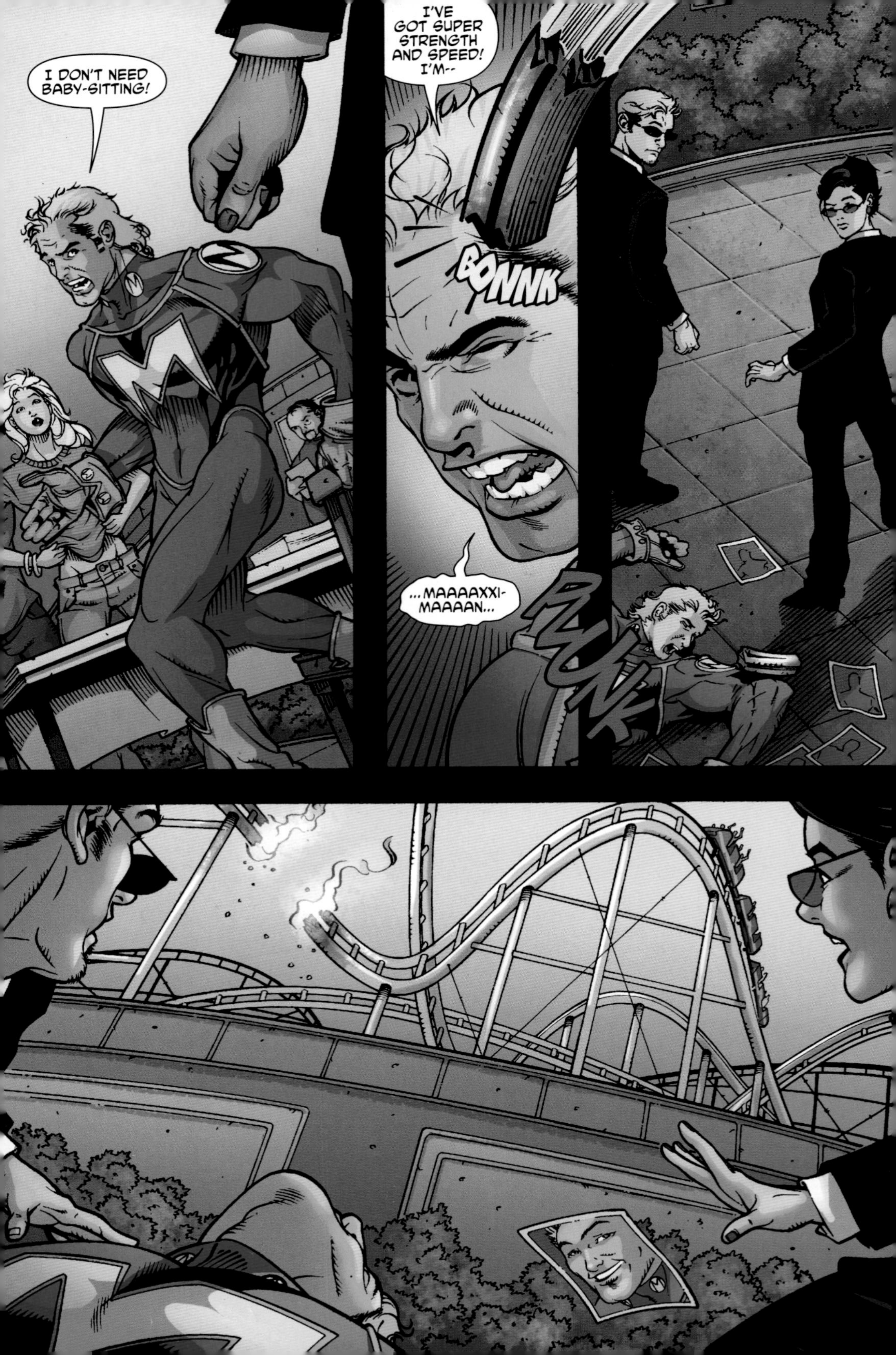

I DON'T NEED BABY-SITTING!
I'VE GOT SUPER STRENGTH AND SPEED! I'M--
BONNK
...MAAAAXXI-MAAAAN...

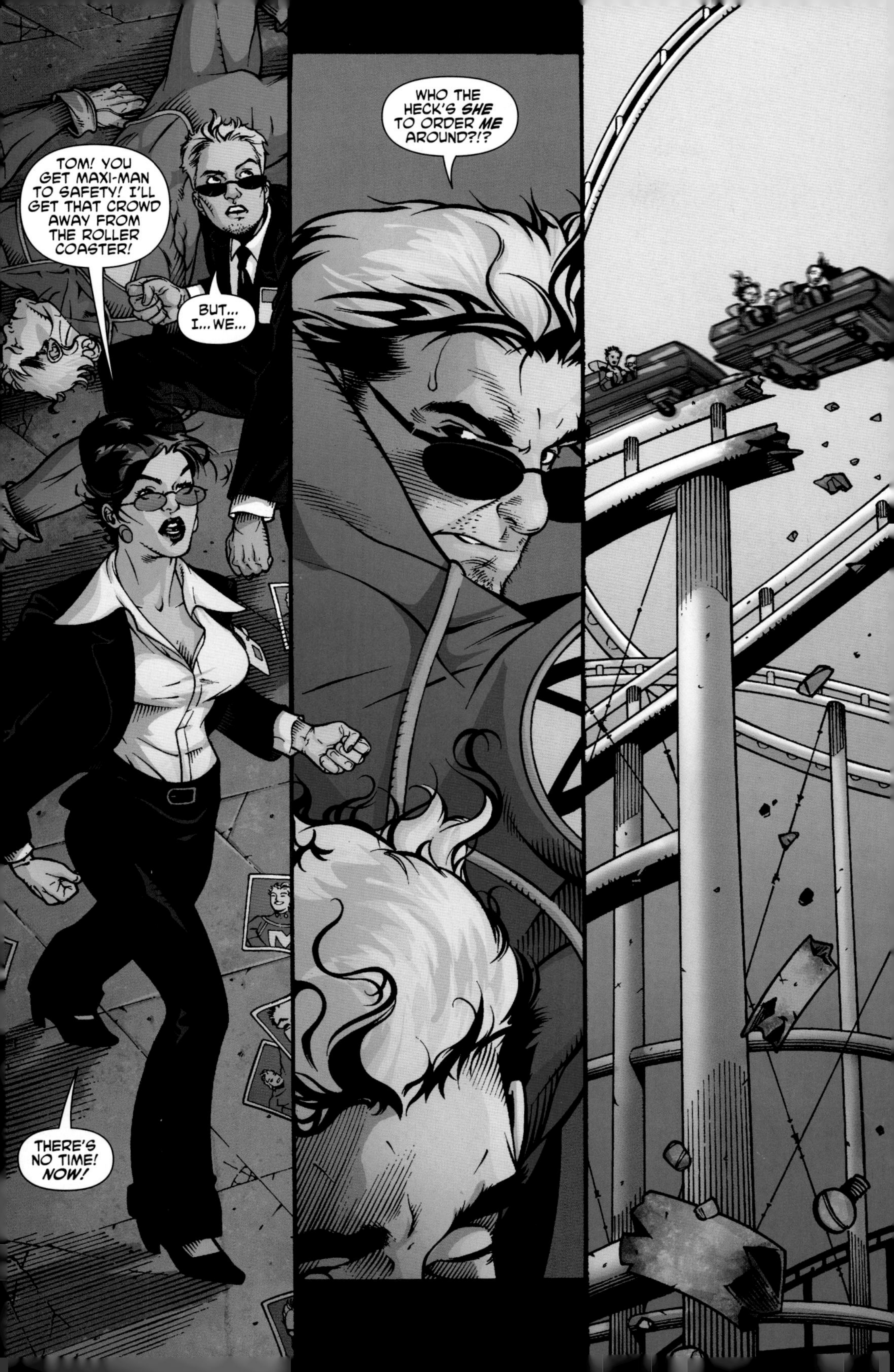
TOM! YOU GET MAXI-MAN TO SAFETY! I'LL GET THAT CROWD AWAY FROM THE ROLLER COASTER!
BUT... I...WE...
THERE'S NO TIME! NOW!
WHO THE HECK'S SHE TO ORDER ME AROUND?!?

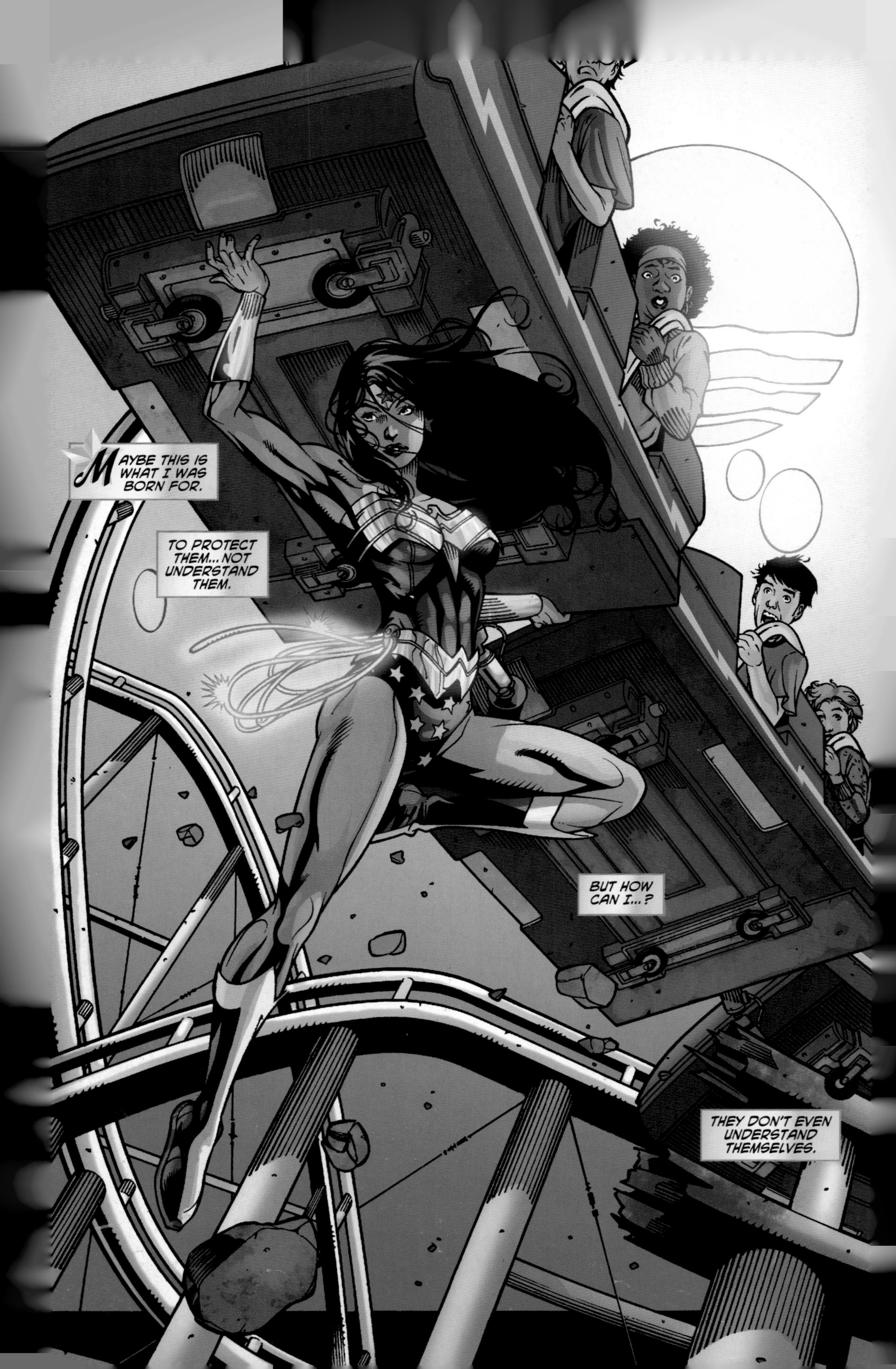
MAYBE THIS IS WHAT I WAS BORN FOR.
TO PROTECT THEM... NOT UNDERSTAND THEM.
BUT HOW CAN I...?
THEY DON'T EVEN UNDERSTAND THEMSELVES.

LATER...

I CAN'T BELIEVE I MISSED WONDER WOMAN!... I BET SHE LOOKED HOT.

WHAT ARE YOU, TWELVE?

THANKS FOR SHOPPING AT T THE HERO S

BE A HERO! BUY HERO STUFF!

I THOUGHT SARGE WANTED US BACK AT HEADQUARTERS.

RELAX, I JUST NEED TO GET MY NIECE A BIRTHDAY GIFT.

THE BATMAN ONE'S BETTER. LOOK--IT'S GOT A DETACHABLE BATARANG... BUT MY--ER, WONDER WOMAN'S LASSO DOESN'T EVEN COME OFF.

TRUST ME, MY NIECE'LL LOVE IT...

I THOUGHT YOU WERE AN ONLY CHILD...?

ALL WONDER WOMAN STUFF IS 75% OFF.

BE A HERO! BUY HERO STUFF!

SWEET!

UM... WHY?

WONDER WOMAN'S NOT COOL, I GUESS.

DOESN'T SAVING THE WORLD ALL THE TIME MAKE YOU COOL?

DEP OF A

ALL I KNOW IS SHE'S NEVER SOLD AS WELL AS SUPERMAN OR BATMAN...

75% OFF! SWEET!

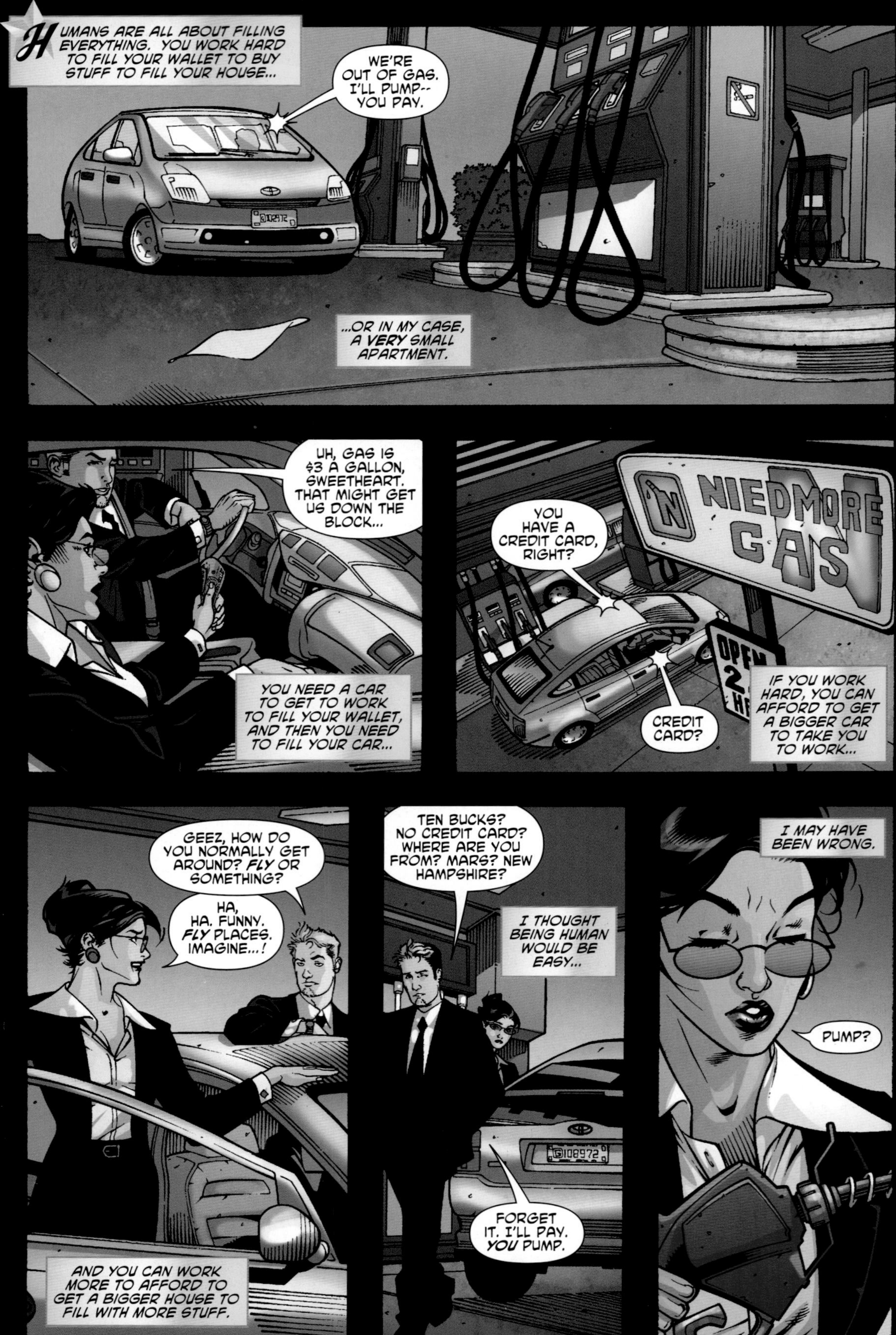
HUMANS ARE ALL ABOUT FILLING EVERYTHING. YOU WORK HARD TO FILL YOUR WALLET TO BUY STUFF TO FILL YOUR HOUSE...
WE'RE OUT OF GAS. I'LL PUMP-- YOU PAY.
...OR IN MY CASE, A VERY SMALL APARTMENT.
UH, GAS IS $3 A GALLON, SWEETHEART. THAT MIGHT GET US DOWN THE BLOCK...
YOU NEED A CAR TO GET TO WORK TO FILL YOUR WALLET, AND THEN YOU NEED TO FILL YOUR CAR...
NIEDMORE GAS
YOU HAVE A CREDIT CARD, RIGHT?
CREDIT CARD?
IF YOU WORK HARD, YOU CAN AFFORD TO GET A BIGGER CAR TO TAKE YOU TO WORK...
GEEZ, HOW DO YOU NORMALLY GET AROUND? FLY OR SOMETHING?
HA, HA. FUNNY. FLY PLACES. IMAGINE...!
AND YOU CAN WORK MORE TO AFFORD TO GET A BIGGER HOUSE TO FILL WITH MORE STUFF.
TEN BUCKS? NO CREDIT CARD? WHERE ARE YOU FROM? MARS? NEW HAMPSHIRE?
I THOUGHT BEING HUMAN WOULD BE EASY...
FORGET IT. I'LL PAY. YOU PUMP.
I MAY HAVE BEEN WRONG.
PUMP?

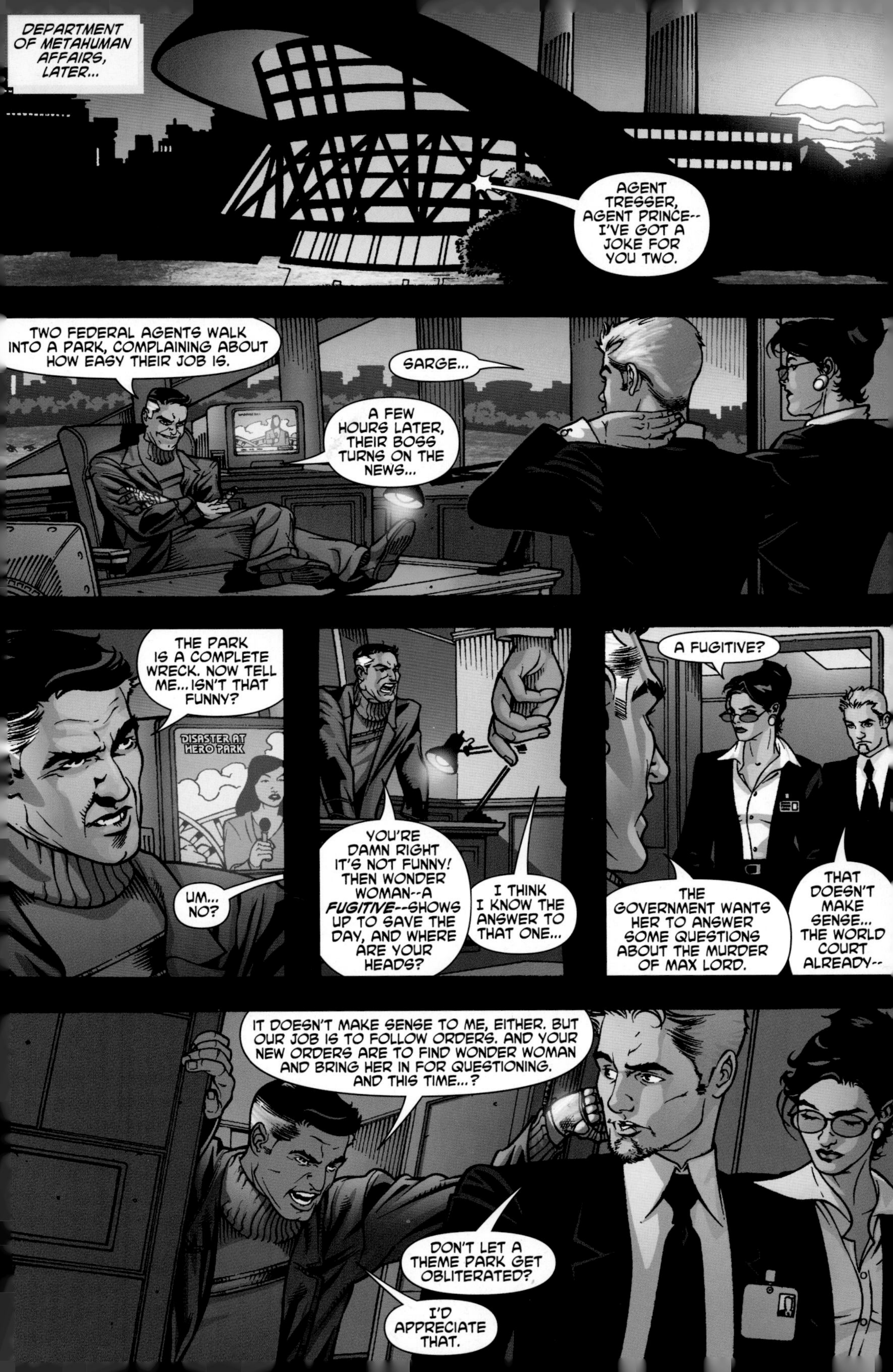
DEPARTMENT OF METAHUMAN AFFAIRS, LATER...
AGENT TRESSER, AGENT PRINCE-- I'VE GOT A JOKE FOR YOU TWO.
TWO FEDERAL AGENTS WALK INTO A PARK, COMPLAINING ABOUT HOW EASY THEIR JOB IS.
SARGE...
A FEW HOURS LATER, THEIR BOSS TURNS ON THE NEWS...
THE PARK IS A COMPLETE WRECK. NOW TELL ME... ISN'T THAT FUNNY?
DISASTER AT HERO PARK
UM... NO?
YOU'RE DAMN RIGHT IT'S NOT FUNNY! THEN WONDER WOMAN--A *FUGITIVE*--SHOWS UP TO SAVE THE DAY, AND WHERE ARE YOUR HEADS?
I THINK I KNOW THE ANSWER TO THAT ONE...
A FUGITIVE?
THE GOVERNMENT WANTS HER TO ANSWER SOME QUESTIONS ABOUT THE MURDER OF MAX LORD.
THAT DOESN'T MAKE SENSE... THE WORLD COURT ALREADY--
IT DOESN'T MAKE SENSE TO ME, EITHER. BUT OUR JOB IS TO FOLLOW ORDERS. AND YOUR NEW ORDERS ARE TO FIND WONDER WOMAN AND BRING HER IN FOR QUESTIONING. AND THIS TIME...?
DON'T LET A THEME PARK GET OBLITERATED?
I'D APPRECIATE THAT.

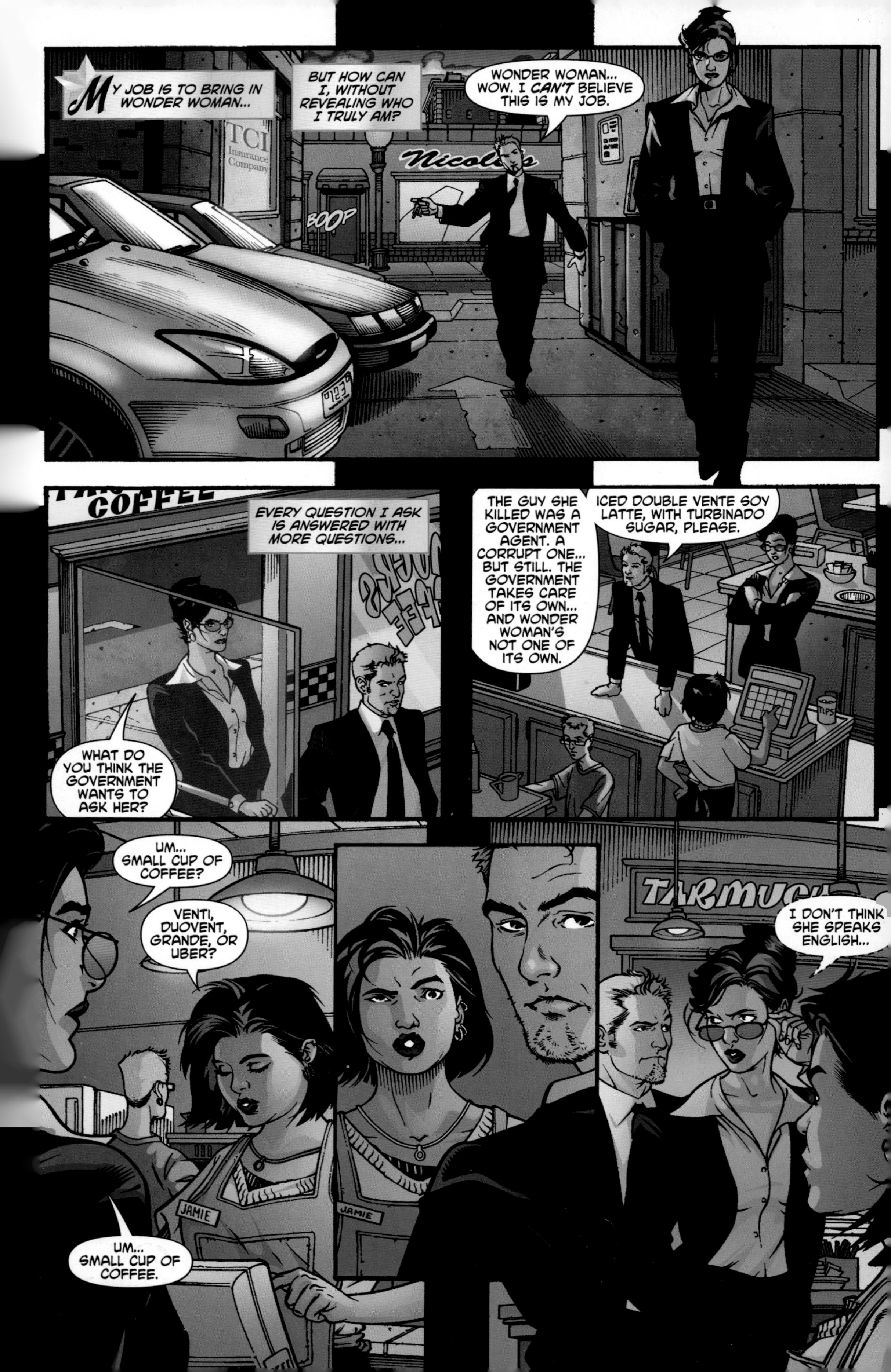

MY JOB IS TO BRING IN WONDER WOMAN...
BUT HOW CAN I, WITHOUT REVEALING WHO I TRULY AM?
WONDER WOMAN... WOW. I CAN'T BELIEVE THIS IS MY JOB.
TCI Insurance Company
Nicolo's
BOOP
COFFEE
EVERY QUESTION I ASK IS ANSWERED WITH MORE QUESTIONS...
WHAT DO YOU THINK THE GOVERNMENT WANTS TO ASK HER?
THE GUY SHE KILLED WAS A GOVERNMENT AGENT. A CORRUPT ONE... BUT STILL. THE GOVERNMENT TAKES CARE OF ITS OWN... AND WONDER WOMAN'S NOT ONE OF ITS OWN.
ICED DOUBLE VENTE SOY LATTE, WITH TURBINADO SUGAR, PLEASE.
TIPS
UM... SMALL CUP OF COFFEE?
VENTI, DUOVENT, GRANDE, OR UBER?
UM... SMALL CUP OF COFFEE.
JAMIE
JAMIE
TARMUCK
I DON'T THINK SHE SPEAKS ENGLISH...

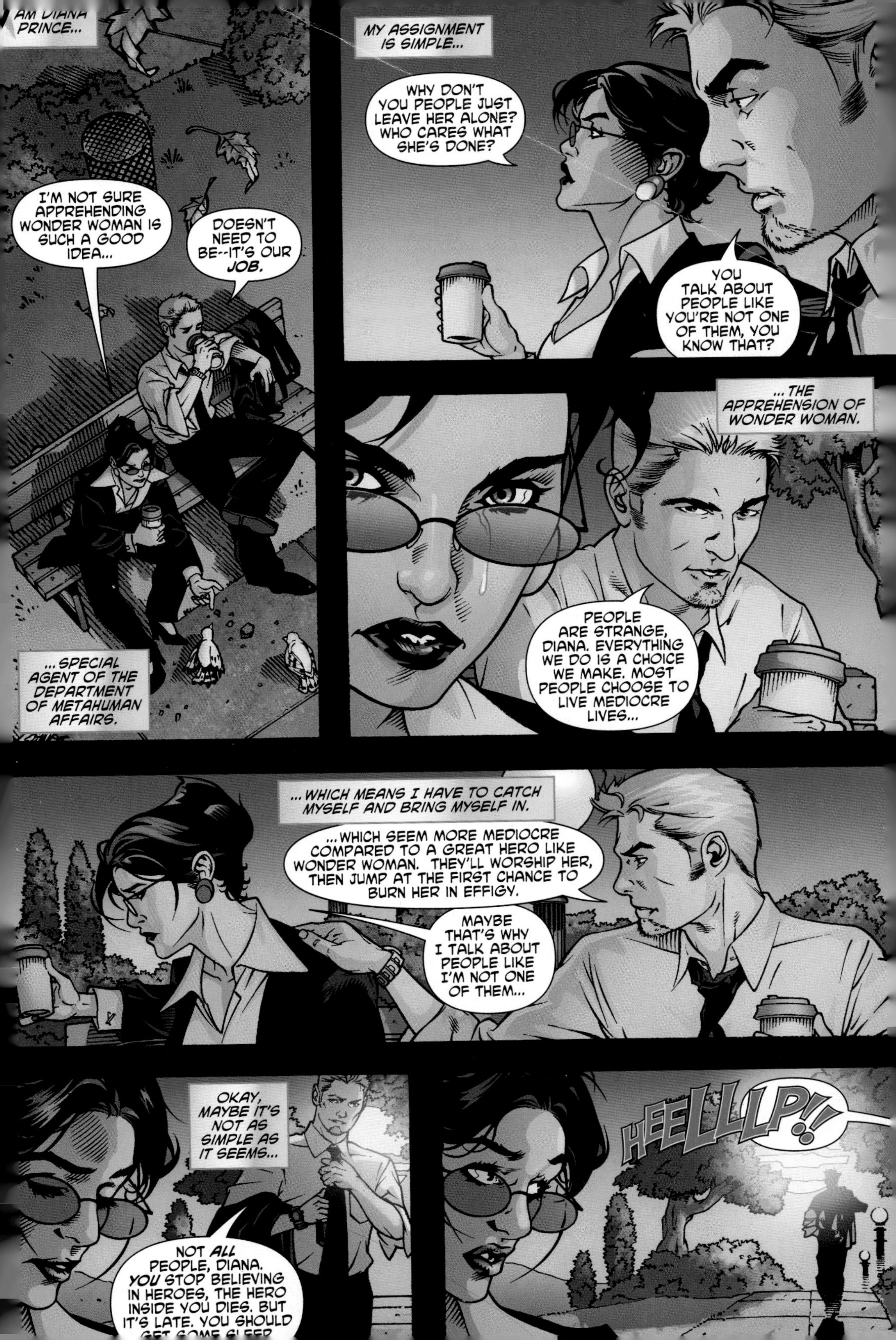
AM DIANA PRINCE...
I'M NOT SURE APPREHENDING WONDER WOMAN IS SUCH A GOOD IDEA...
DOESN'T NEED TO BE--IT'S OUR JOB.
...SPECIAL AGENT OF THE DEPARTMENT OF METAHUMAN AFFAIRS.
MY ASSIGNMENT IS SIMPLE...
WHY DON'T YOU PEOPLE JUST LEAVE HER ALONE? WHO CARES WHAT SHE'S DONE?
YOU TALK ABOUT PEOPLE LIKE YOU'RE NOT ONE OF THEM, YOU KNOW THAT?
...THE APPREHENSION OF WONDER WOMAN.
PEOPLE ARE STRANGE, DIANA. EVERYTHING WE DO IS A CHOICE WE MAKE. MOST PEOPLE CHOOSE TO LIVE MEDIOCRE LIVES...
...WHICH MEANS I HAVE TO CATCH MYSELF AND BRING MYSELF IN.
...WHICH SEEM MORE MEDIOCRE COMPARED TO A GREAT HERO LIKE WONDER WOMAN. THEY'LL WORSHIP HER, THEN JUMP AT THE FIRST CHANCE TO BURN HER IN EFFIGY.
MAYBE THAT'S WHY I TALK ABOUT PEOPLE LIKE I'M NOT ONE OF THEM...
OKAY, MAYBE IT'S NOT AS SIMPLE AS IT SEEMS...
NOT ALL PEOPLE, DIANA. YOU STOP BELIEVING IN HEROES, THE HERO INSIDE YOU DIES. BUT IT'S LATE. YOU SHOULD
HEELLLP!!

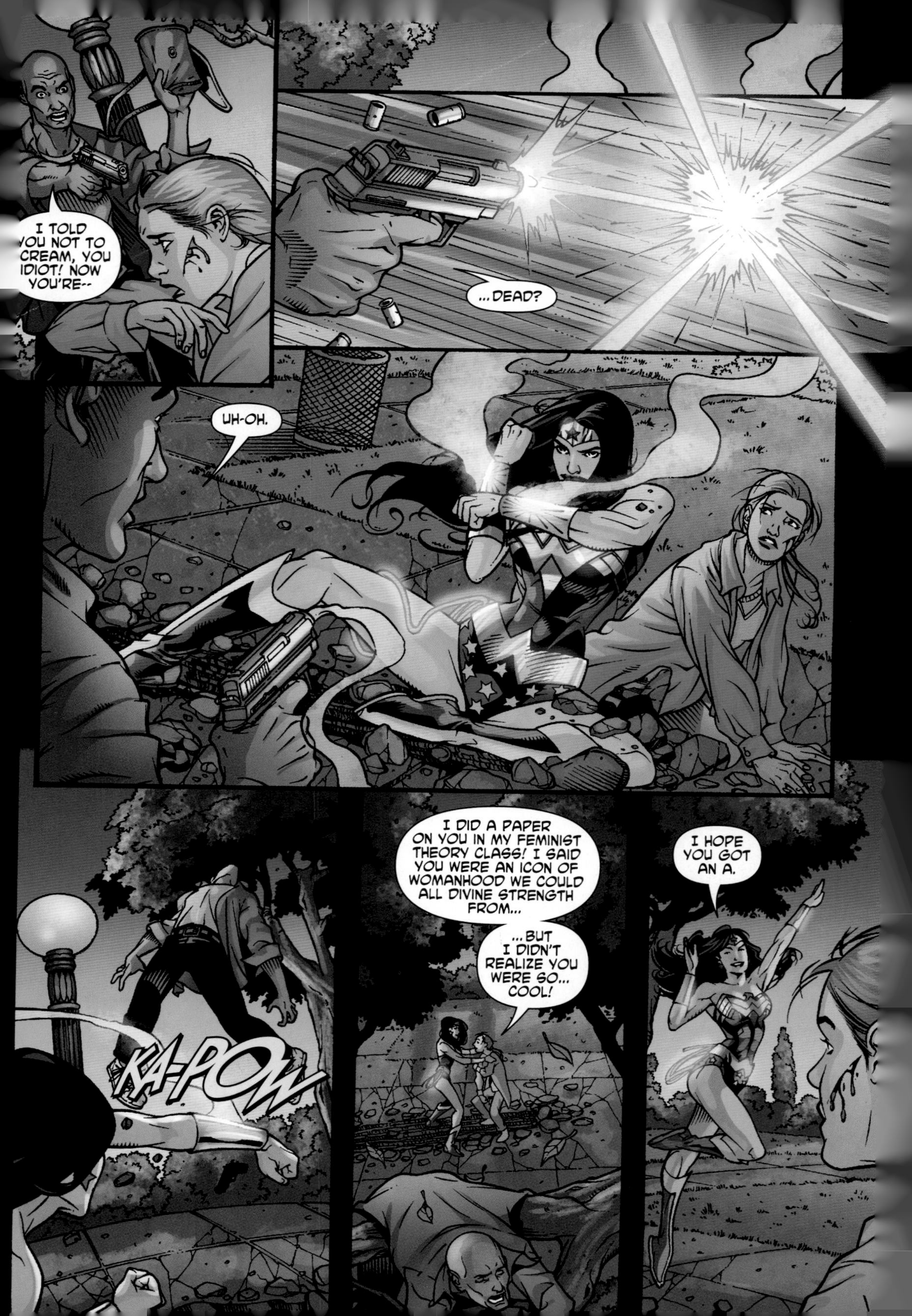
I TOLD YOU NOT TO SCREAM, YOU IDIOT! NOW YOU'RE--
...DEAD?
UH-OH.
KA-POW
I DID A PAPER ON YOU IN MY FEMINIST THEORY CLASS! I SAID YOU WERE AN ICON OF WOMANHOOD WE COULD ALL DIVINE STRENGTH FROM...
...BUT I DIDN'T REALIZE YOU WERE SO... COOL!
I HOPE YOU GOT AN A.

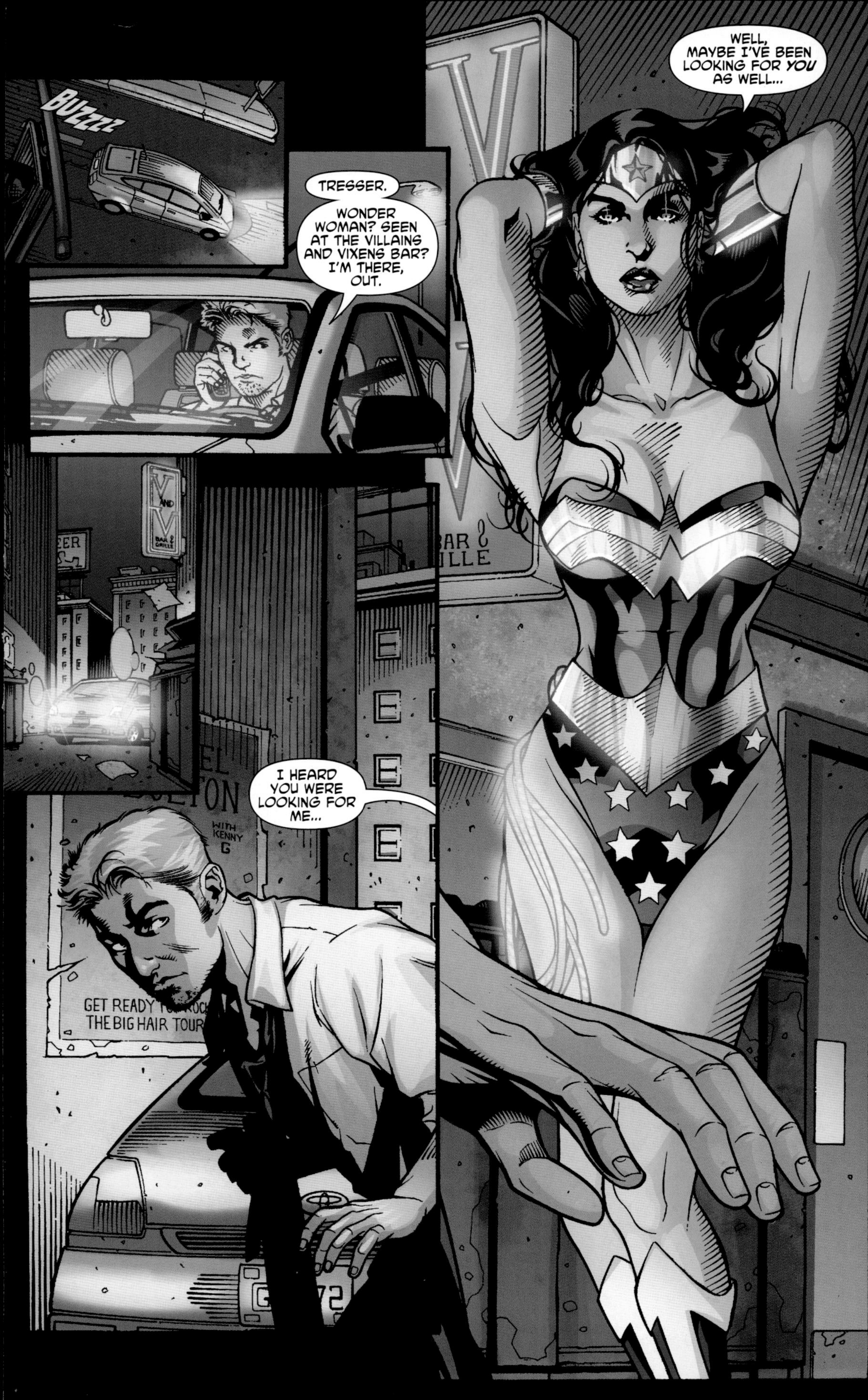
BUZZZZ
TRESSER.
WONDER WOMAN? SEEN AT THE VILLAINS AND VIXENS BAR? I'M THERE, OUT.
I HEARD YOU WERE LOOKING FOR ME...
WITH KENNY G
THE BIG HAIR TOUR
WELL, MAYBE I'VE BEEN LOOKING FOR *YOU* AS WELL...

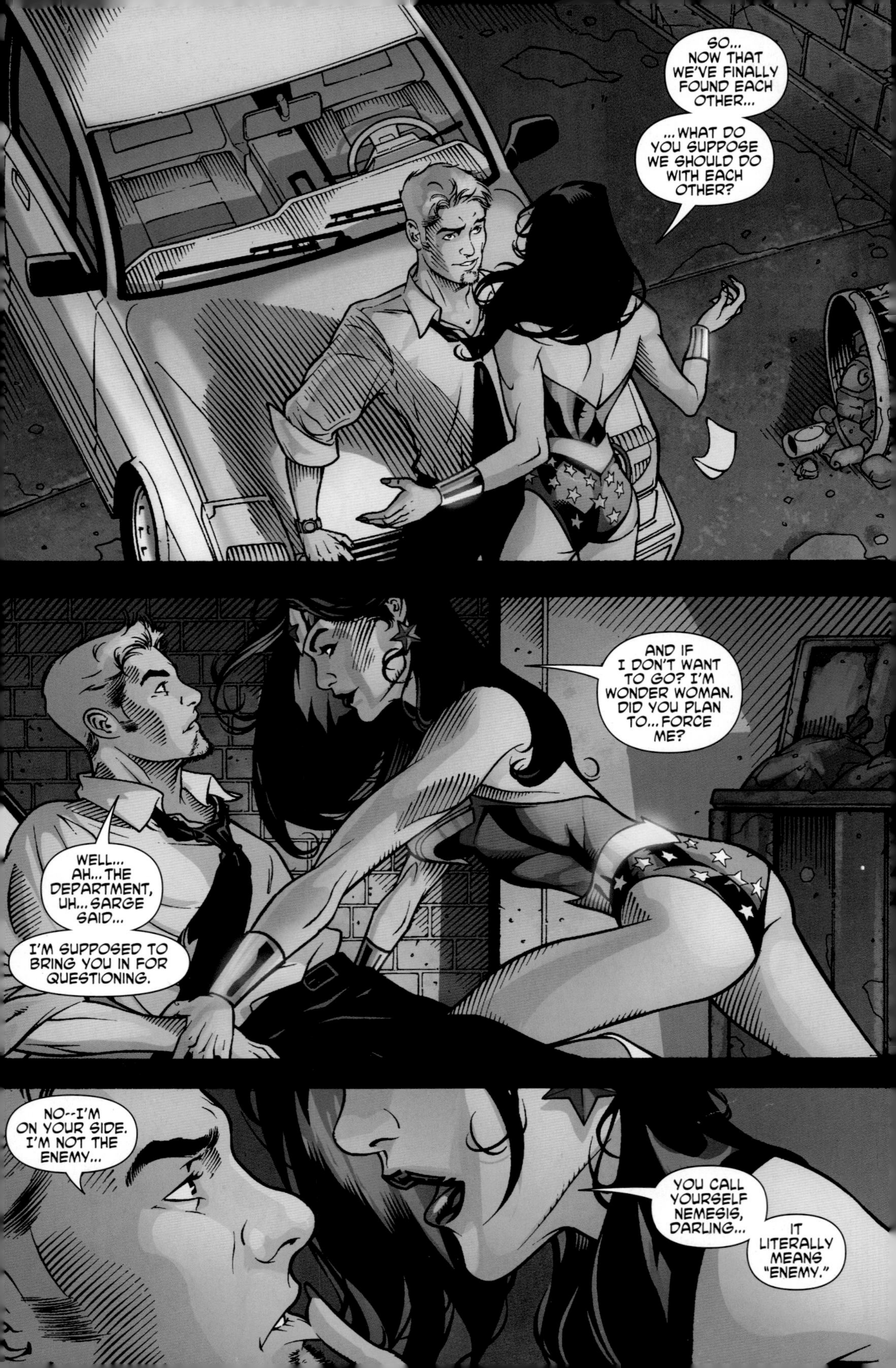
SO... NOW THAT WE'VE FINALLY FOUND EACH OTHER...
...WHAT DO YOU SUPPOSE WE SHOULD DO WITH EACH OTHER?
AND IF I DON'T WANT TO GO? I'M WONDER WOMAN. DID YOU PLAN TO...FORCE ME?
WELL... AH... THE DEPARTMENT, UH...SARGE SAID...
I'M SUPPOSED TO BRING YOU IN FOR QUESTIONING.
NO--I'M ON YOUR SIDE. I'M NOT THE ENEMY...
YOU CALL YOURSELF NEMESIS, DARLING...
IT LITERALLY MEANS "ENEMY."

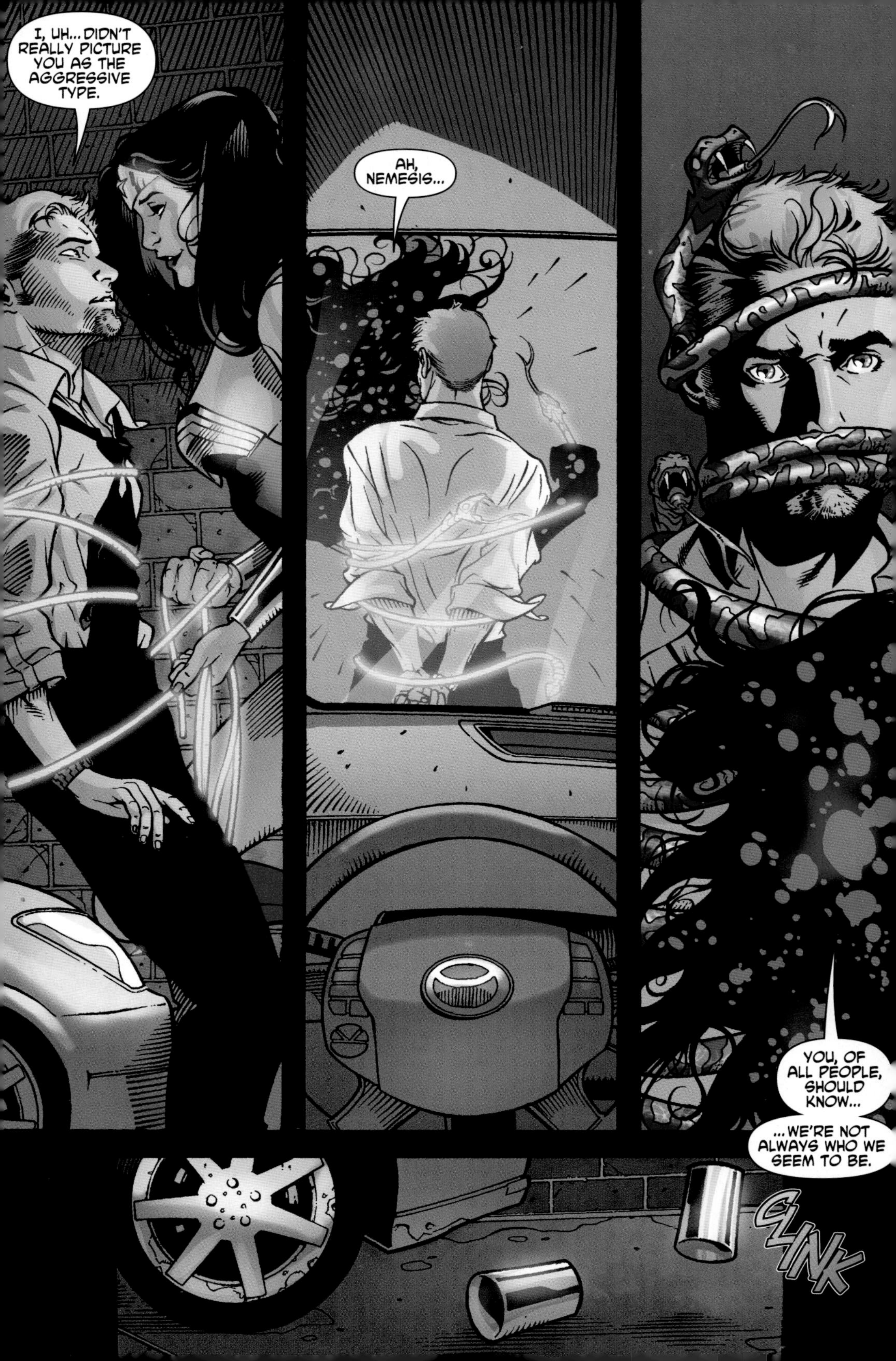
I, UH...DIDN'T REALLY PICTURE YOU AS THE AGGRESSIVE TYPE.
AH, NEMESIS...
YOU, OF ALL PEOPLE, SHOULD KNOW...
...WE'RE NOT ALWAYS WHO WE SEEM TO BE.
CLINK

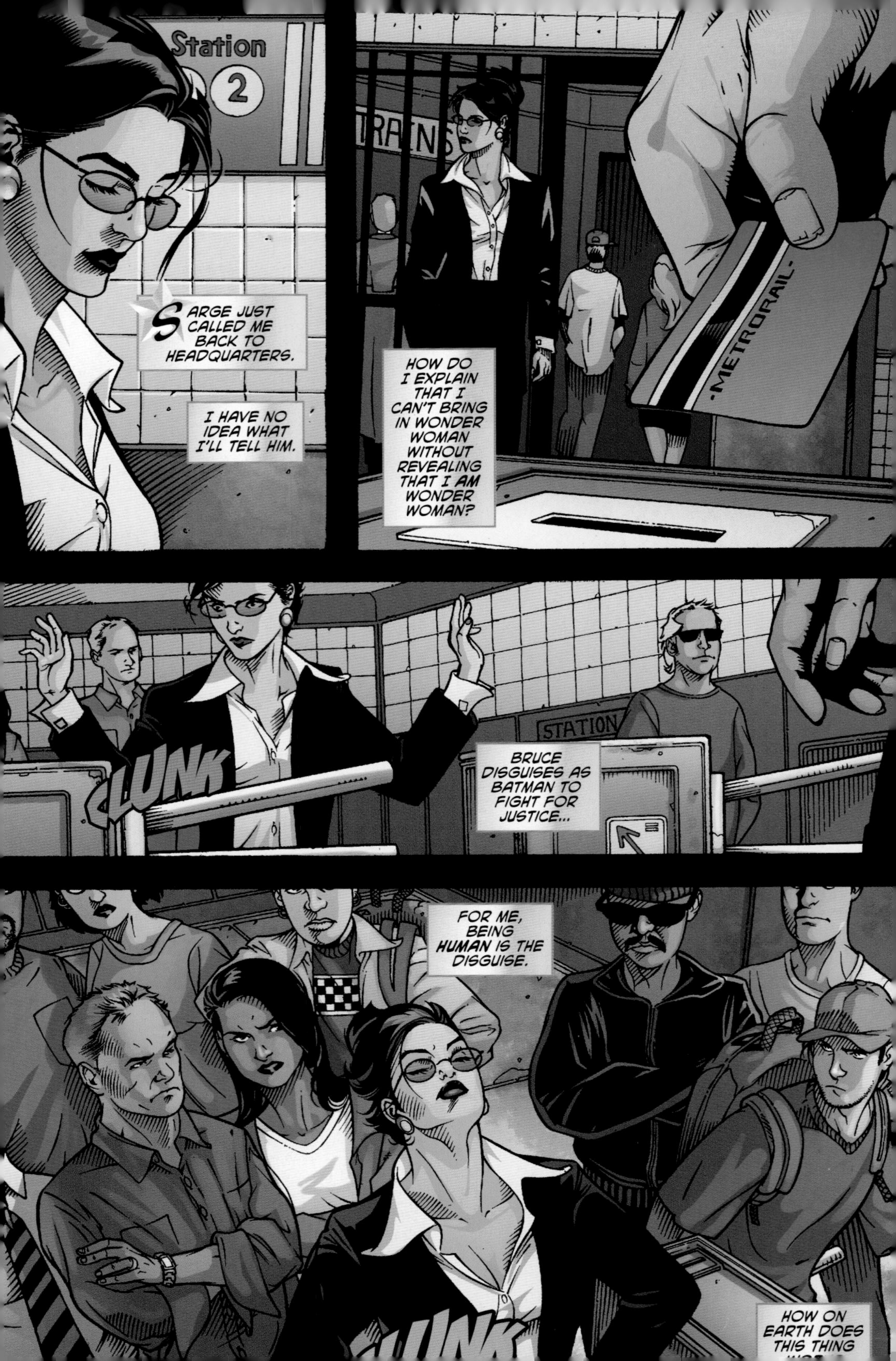
Station
2
SARGE JUST CALLED ME BACK TO HEADQUARTERS.
I HAVE NO IDEA WHAT I'LL TELL HIM.
TRAINS
HOW DO I EXPLAIN THAT I CAN'T BRING IN WONDER WOMAN WITHOUT REVEALING THAT I AM WONDER WOMAN?
·METRORAIL·
CLUNK
STATION
BRUCE DISGUISES AS BATMAN TO FIGHT FOR JUSTICE...
FOR ME, BEING HUMAN IS THE DISGUISE.
HOW ON EARTH DOES THIS THING

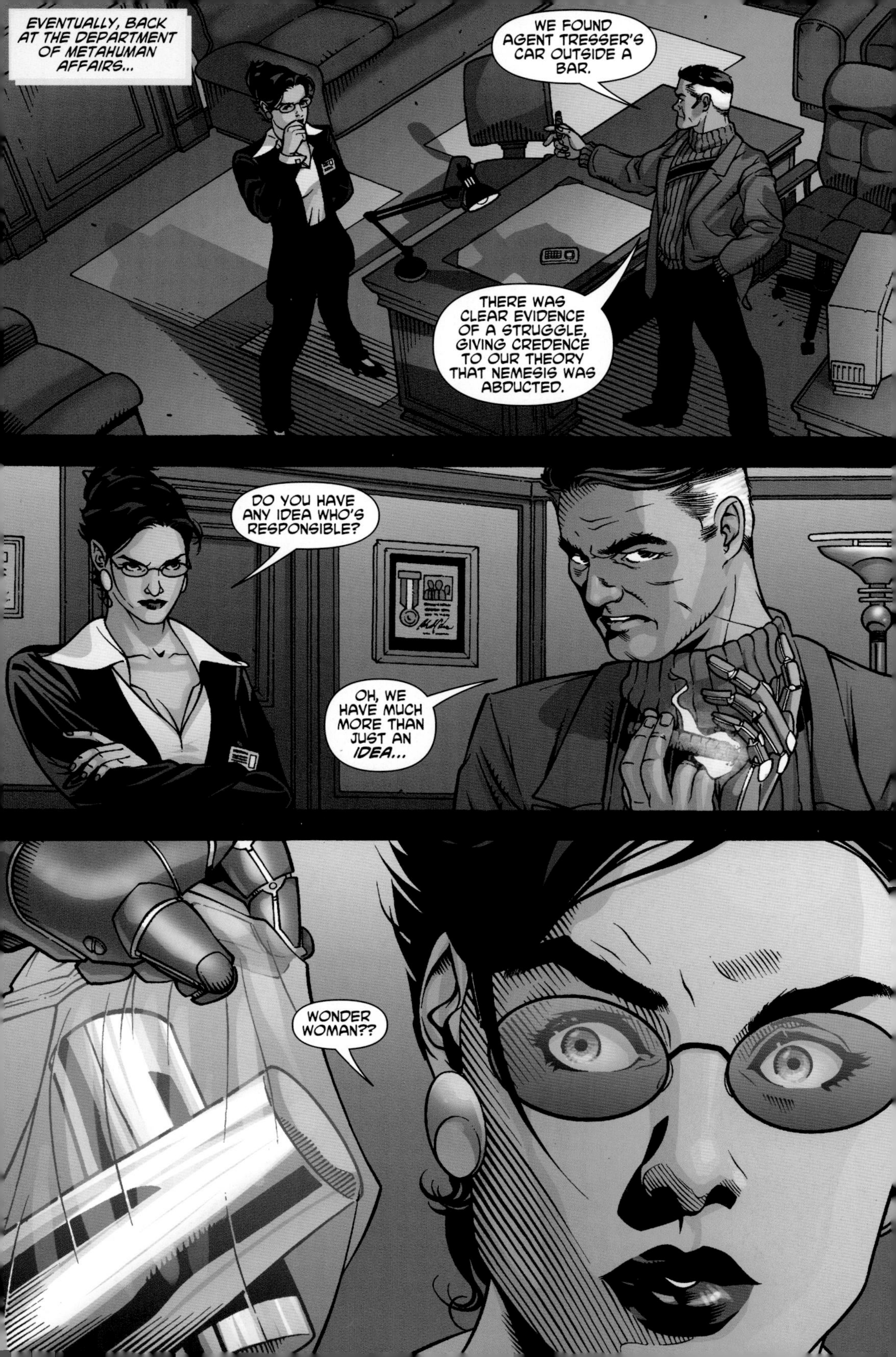
EVENTUALLY, BACK AT THE DEPARTMENT OF METAHUMAN AFFAIRS...
WE FOUND AGENT TRESSER'S CAR OUTSIDE A BAR.
THERE WAS CLEAR EVIDENCE OF A STRUGGLE, GIVING CREDENCE TO OUR THEORY THAT NEMESIS WAS ABDUCTED.
DO YOU HAVE ANY IDEA WHO'S RESPONSIBLE?
OH, WE HAVE MUCH MORE THAN JUST AN *IDEA*...
WONDER WOMAN??

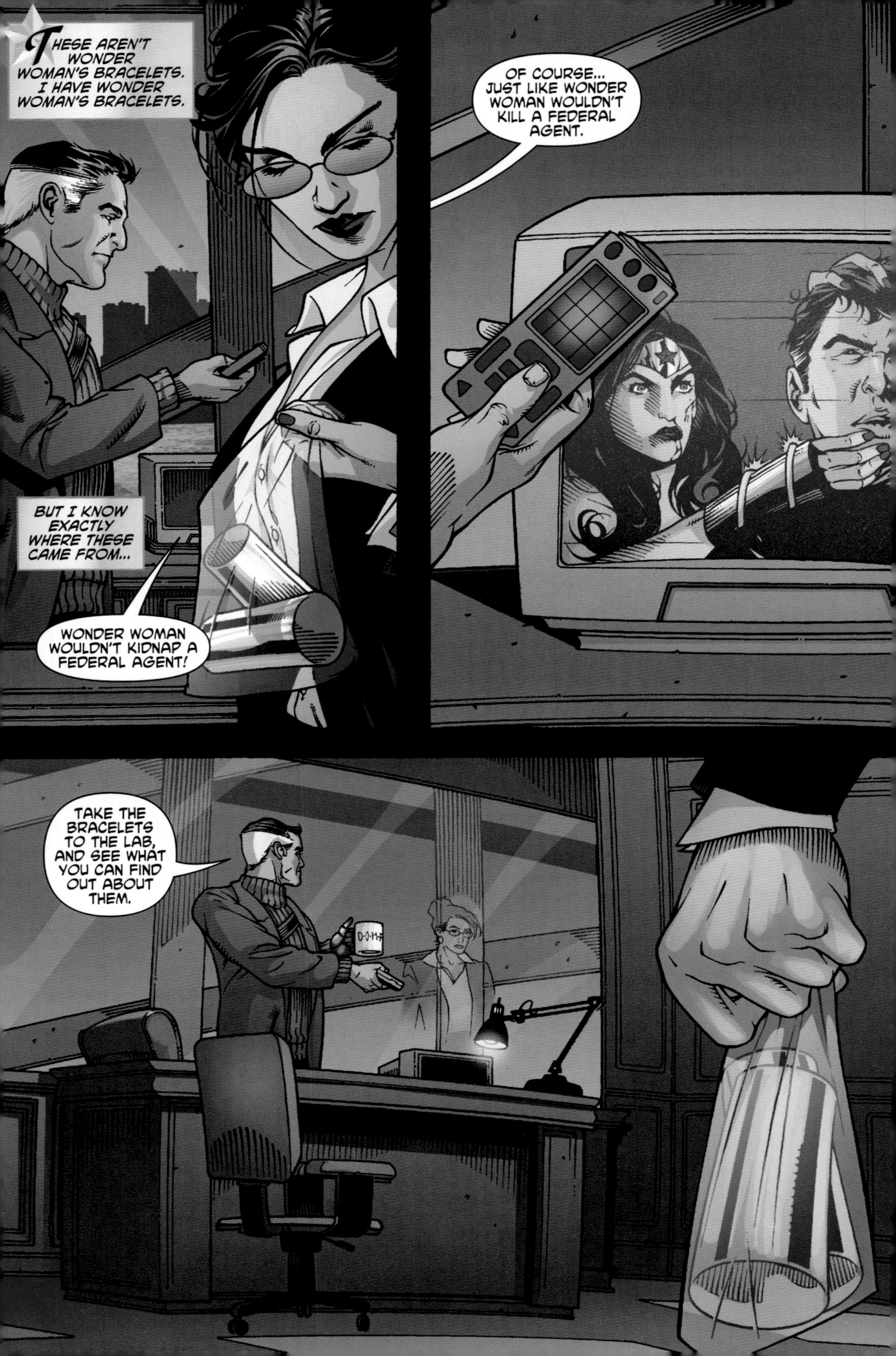
THESE AREN'T WONDER WOMAN'S BRACELETS. I HAVE WONDER WOMAN'S BRACELETS.
BUT I KNOW EXACTLY WHERE THESE CAME FROM...
WONDER WOMAN WOULDN'T KIDNAP A FEDERAL AGENT!
OF COURSE... JUST LIKE WONDER WOMAN WOULDN'T KILL A FEDERAL AGENT.
TAKE THE BRACELETS TO THE LAB, AND SEE WHAT YOU CAN FIND OUT ABOUT THEM.

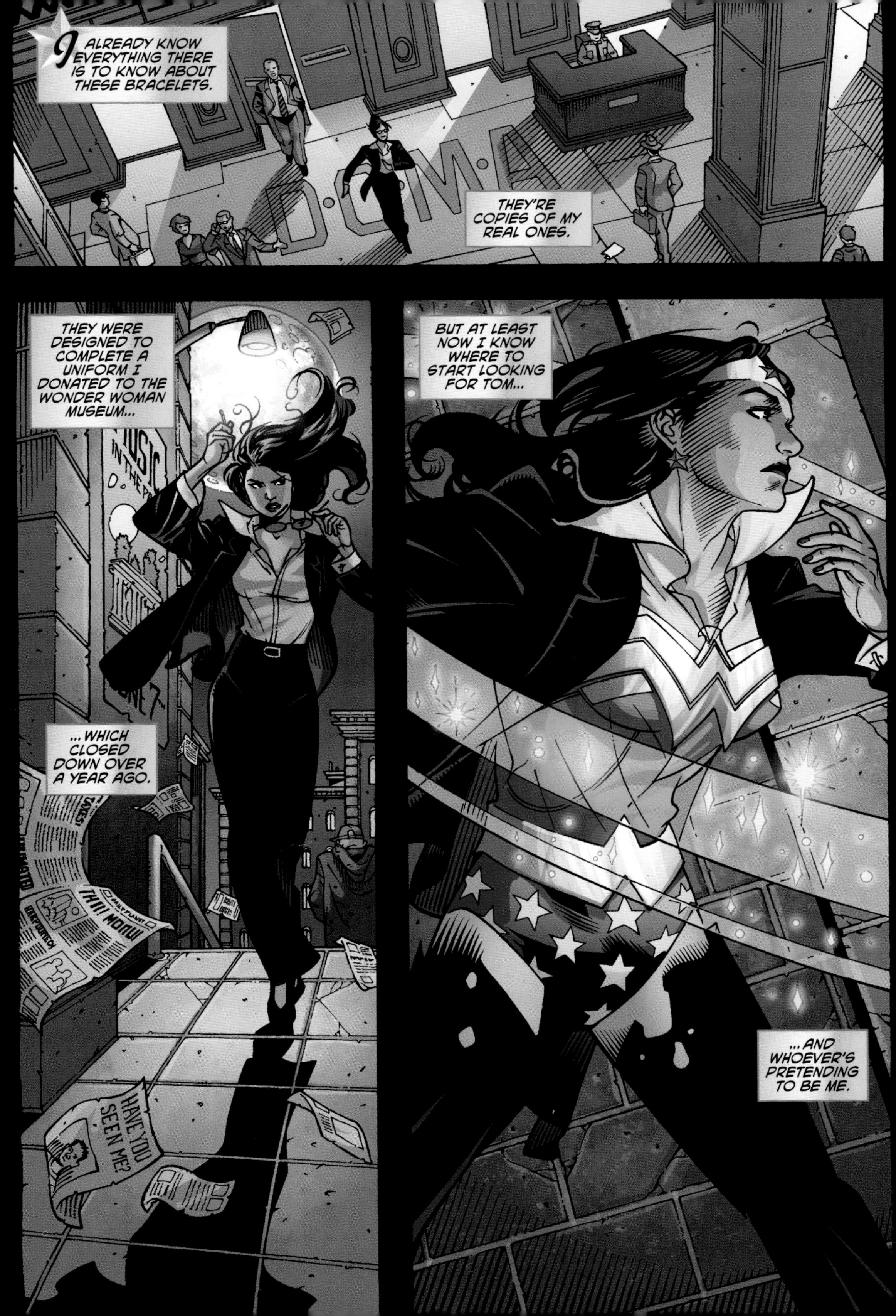
I ALREADY KNOW EVERYTHING THERE IS TO KNOW ABOUT THESE BRACELETS.
THEY'RE COPIES OF MY REAL ONES.
THEY WERE DESIGNED TO COMPLETE A UNIFORM I DONATED TO THE WONDER WOMAN MUSEUM...
...WHICH CLOSED DOWN OVER A YEAR AGO.
HAVE YOU SEEN ME?
BUT AT LEAST NOW I KNOW WHERE TO START LOOKING FOR TOM...
...AND WHOEVER'S PRETENDING TO BE ME.

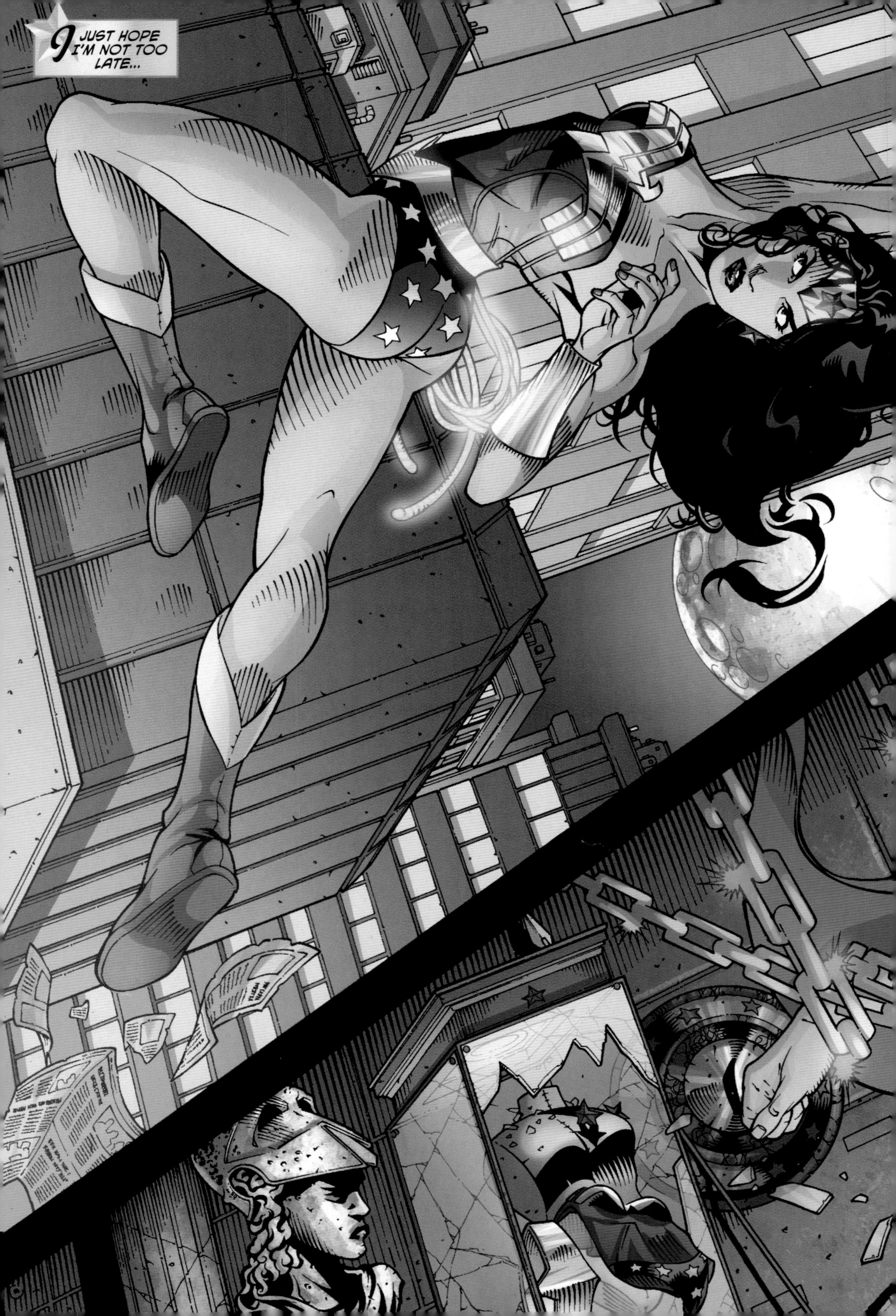
I JUST HOPE I'M NOT TOO LATE...

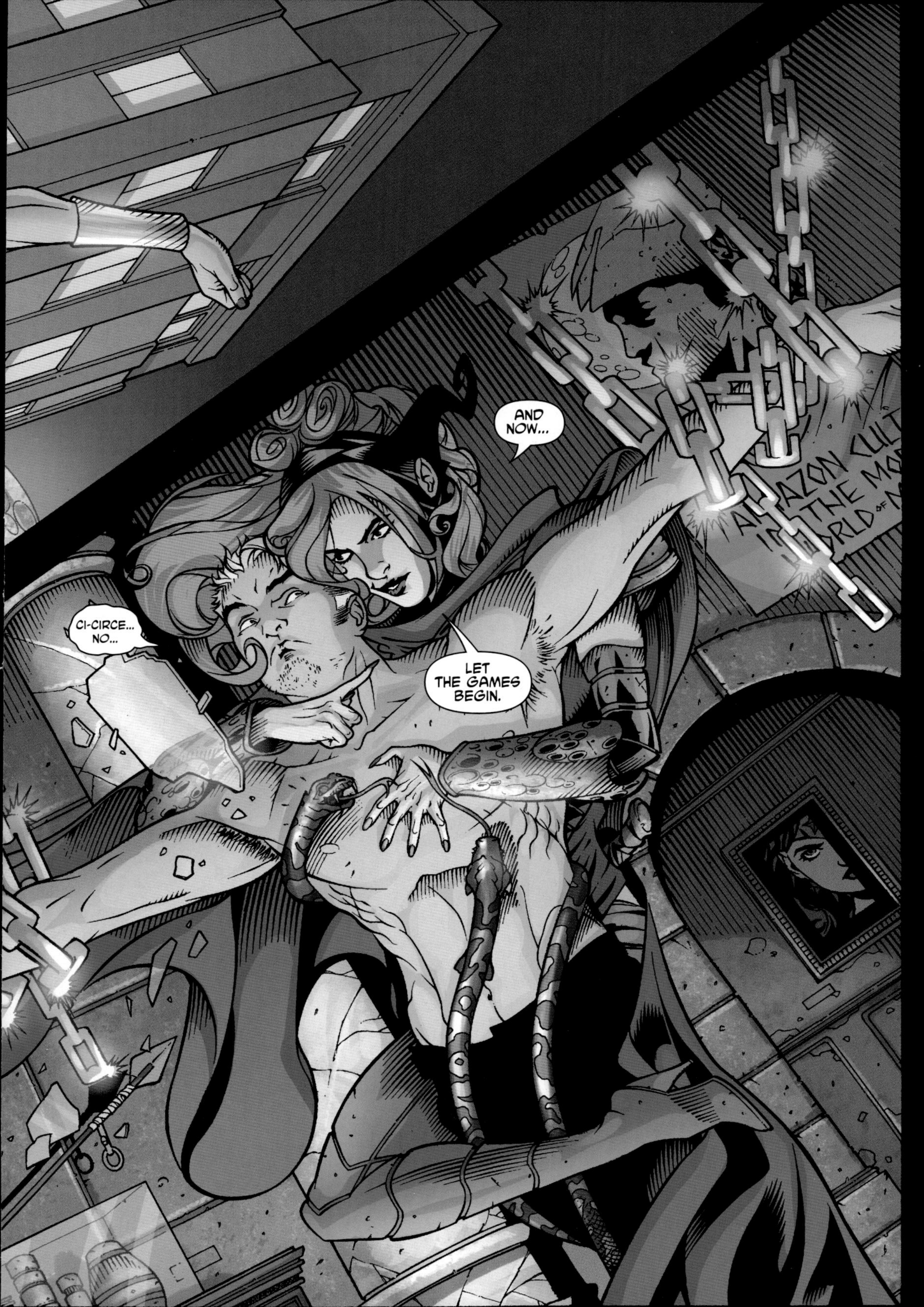
AND NOW...
CI-CIRCE... NO...
LET THE GAMES BEGIN.

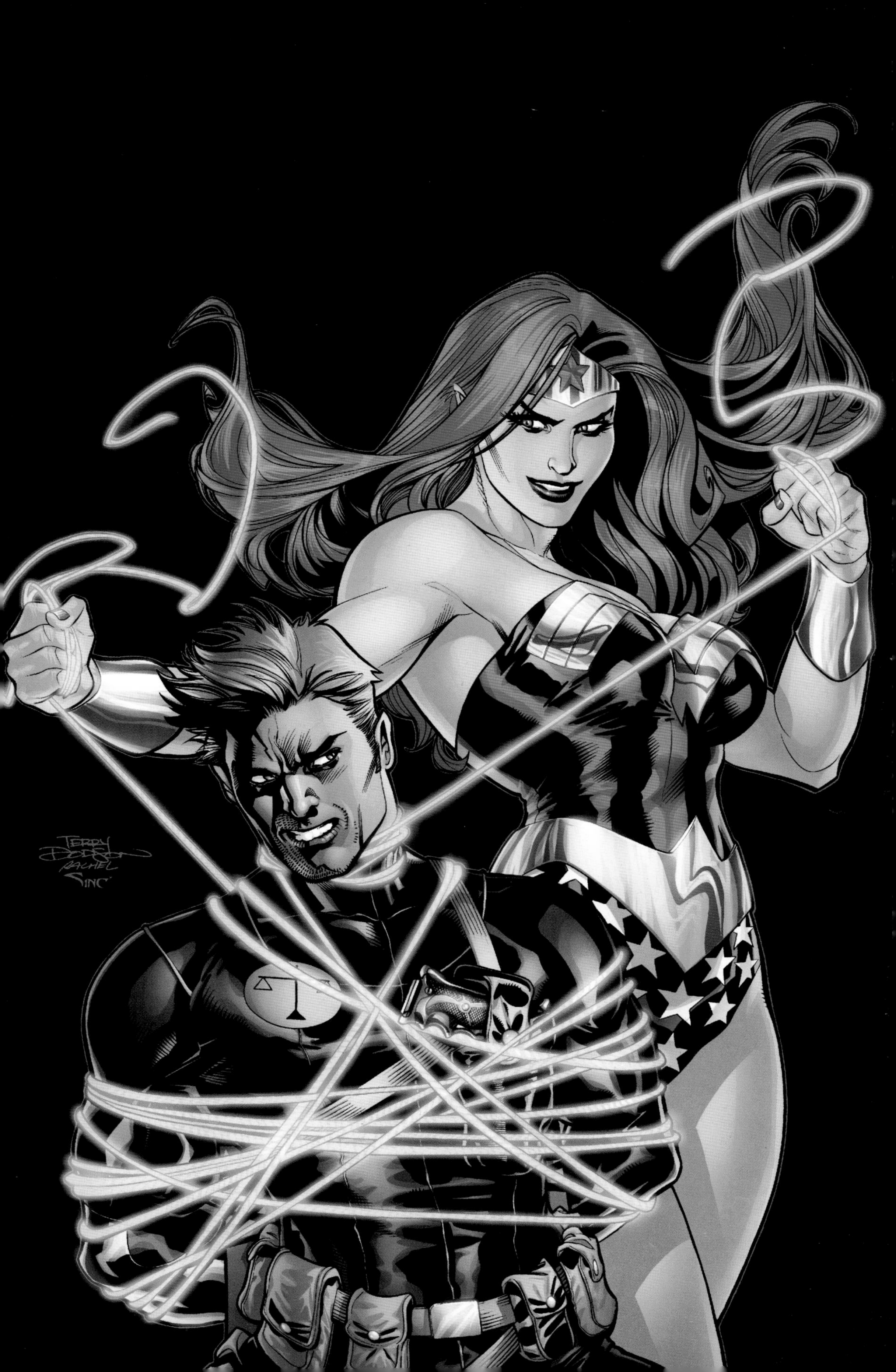
TERRY
DODSON
RACHEL

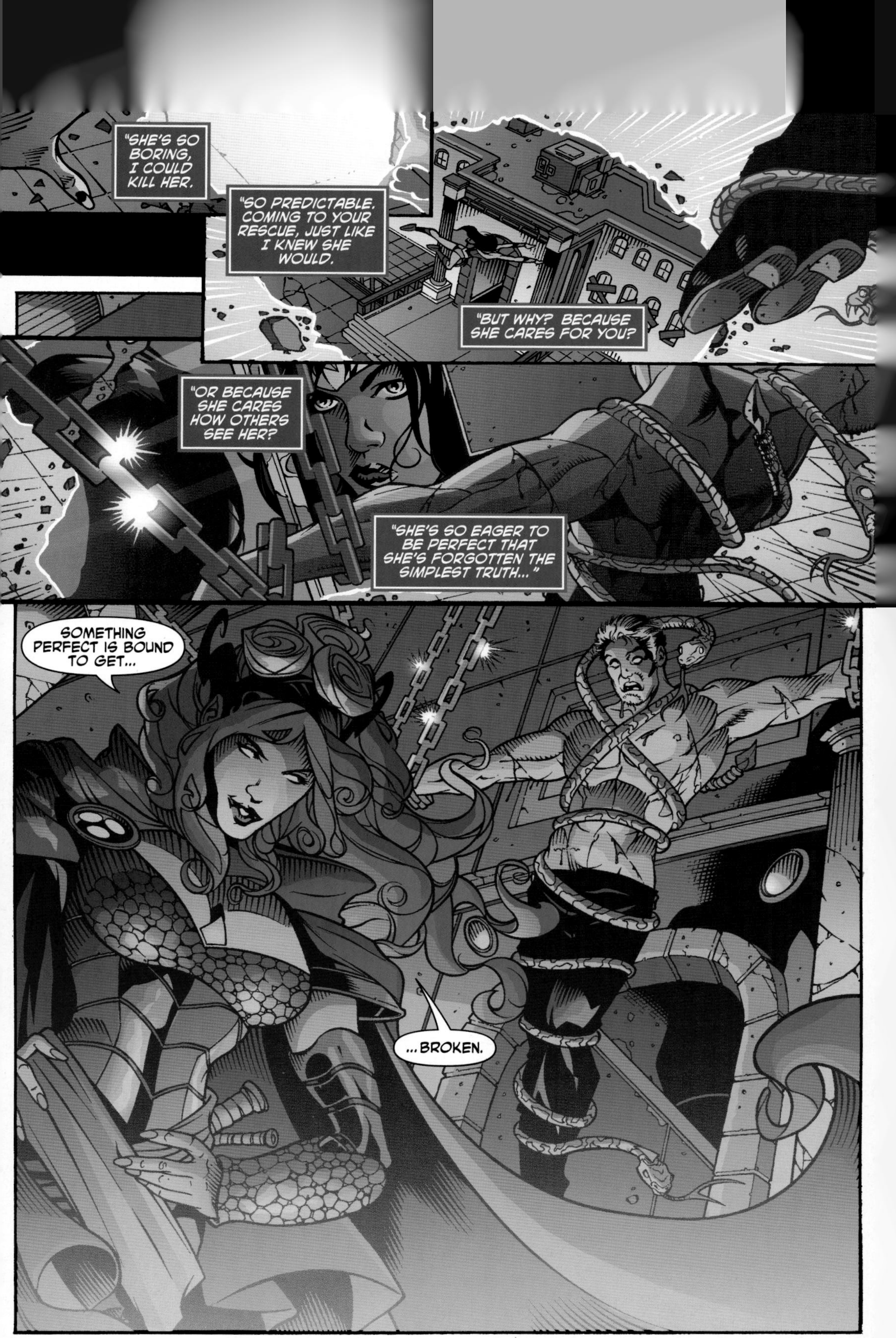
"SHE'S SO BORING, I COULD KILL HER.
"SO PREDICTABLE. COMING TO YOUR RESCUE, JUST LIKE I KNEW SHE WOULD.
"BUT WHY? BECAUSE SHE CARES FOR YOU?
"OR BECAUSE SHE CARES HOW OTHERS SEE HER?
"SHE'S SO EAGER TO BE PERFECT THAT SHE'S FORGOTTEN THE SIMPLEST TRUTH..."
SOMETHING PERFECT IS BOUND TO GET...
...BROKEN.

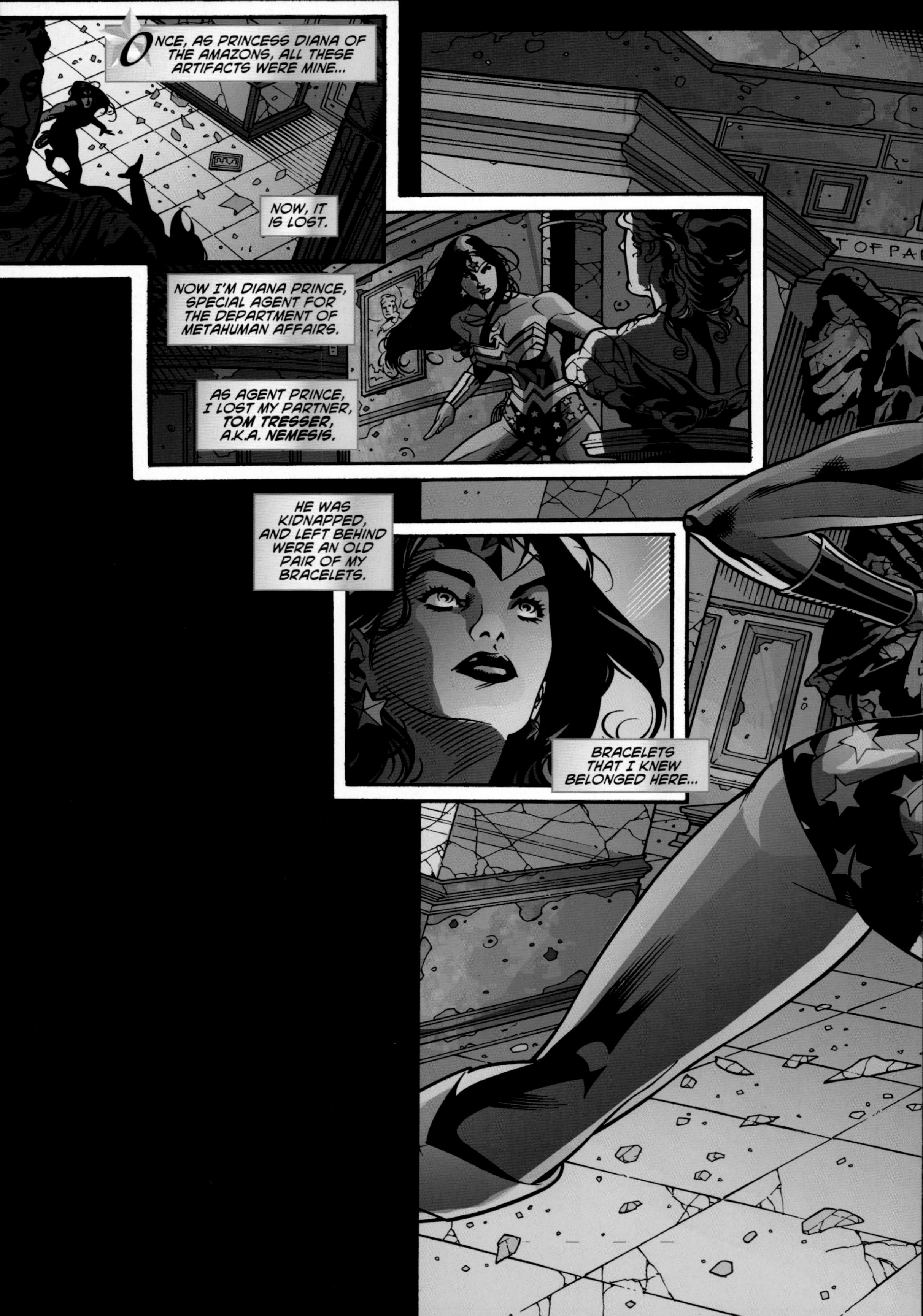
ONCE, AS PRINCESS DIANA OF THE AMAZONS, ALL THESE ARTIFACTS WERE MINE...
NOW, IT IS LOST.
NOW I'M DIANA PRINCE, SPECIAL AGENT FOR THE DEPARTMENT OF METAHUMAN AFFAIRS.
AS AGENT PRINCE, I LOST MY PARTNER, TOM TRESSER, A.K.A. NEMESIS.
HE WAS KIDNAPPED, AND LEFT BEHIND WERE AN OLD PAIR OF MY BRACELETS.
BRACELETS THAT I KNEW BELONGED HERE...

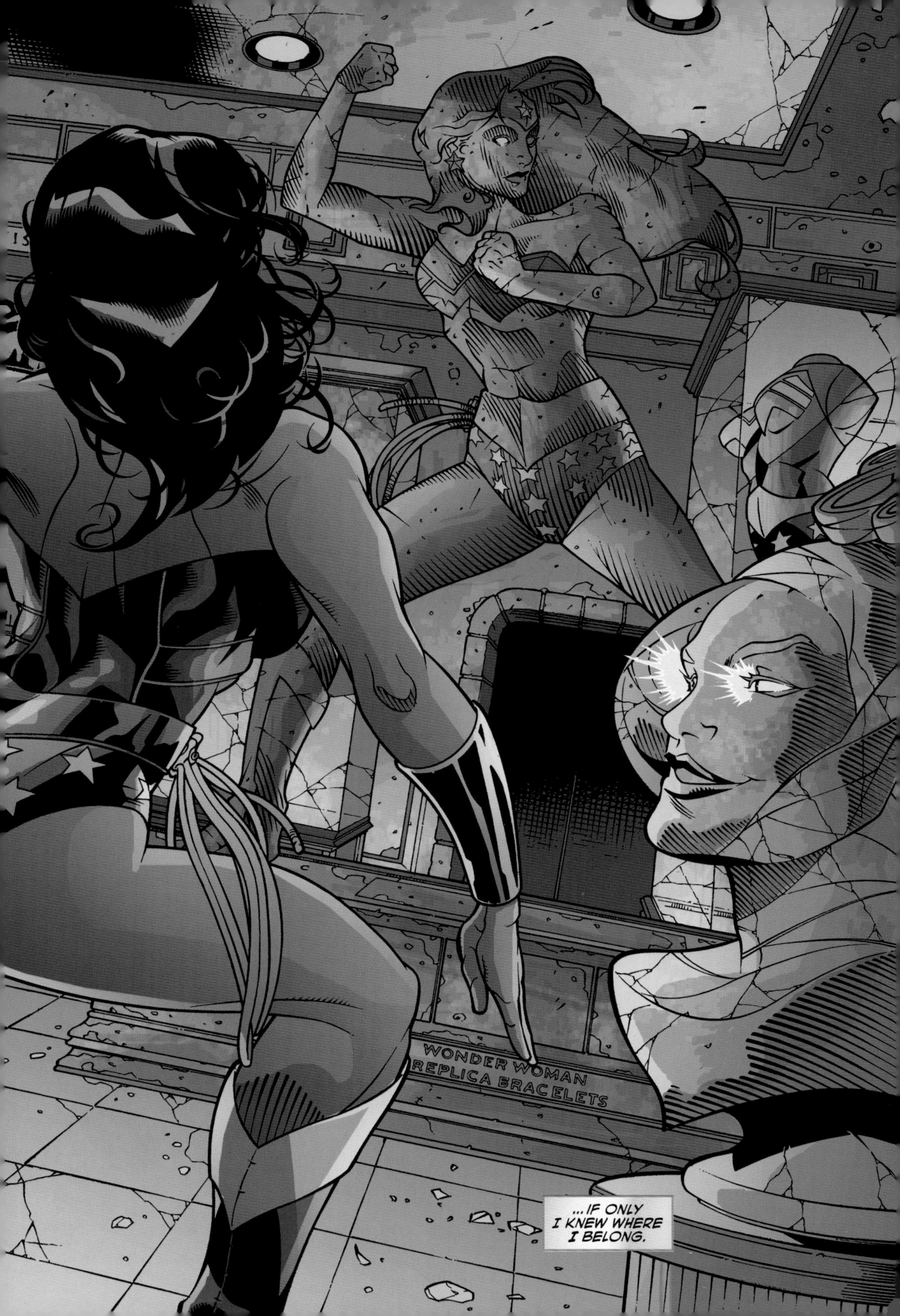
WONDER WOMAN
REPLICA BRACELETS
...IF ONLY
I KNEW WHERE
I BELONG.

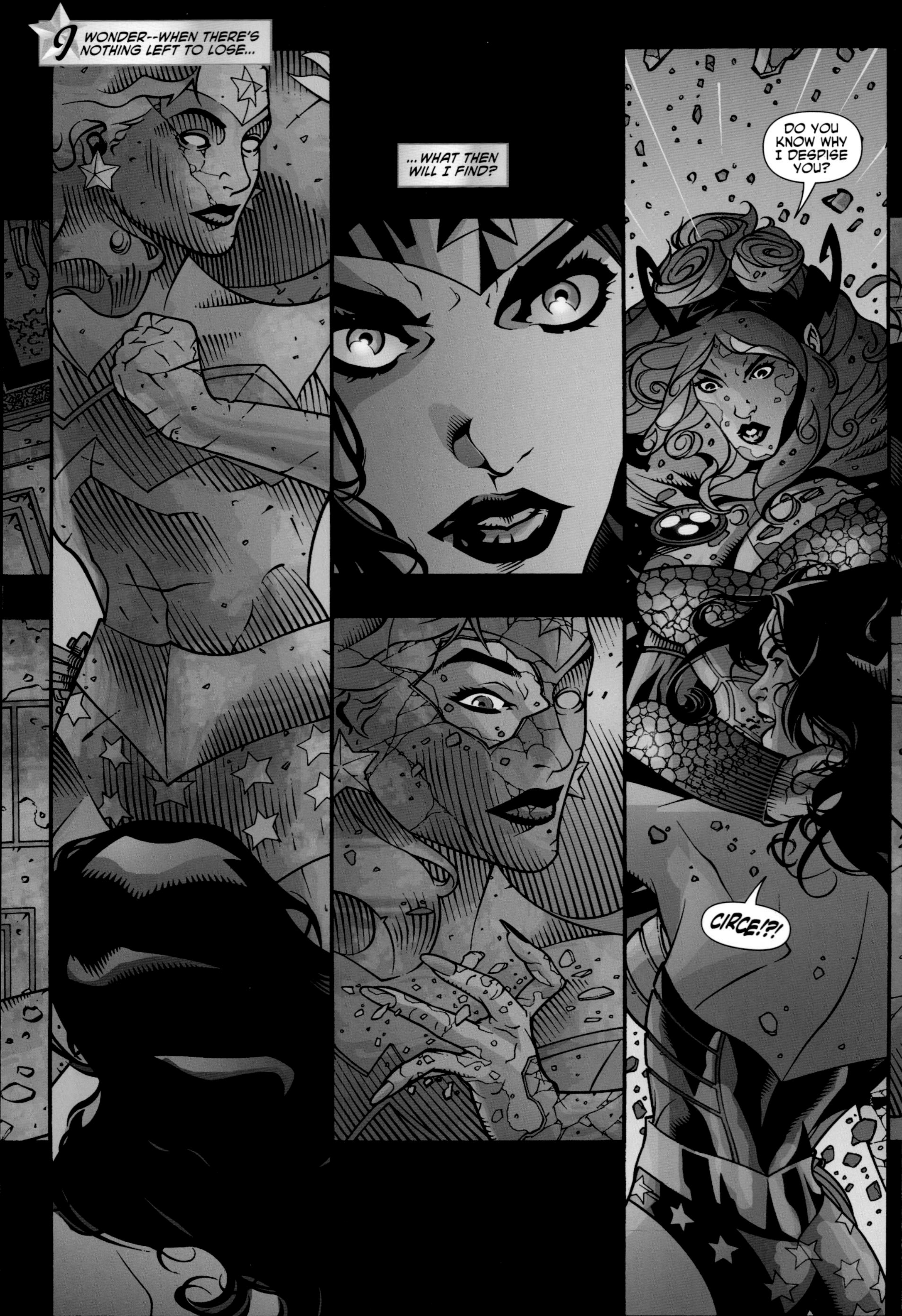
I WONDER--WHEN THERE'S NOTHING LEFT TO LOSE...
...WHAT THEN WILL I FIND?
DO YOU KNOW WHY I DESPISE YOU?
CIRCE!?!

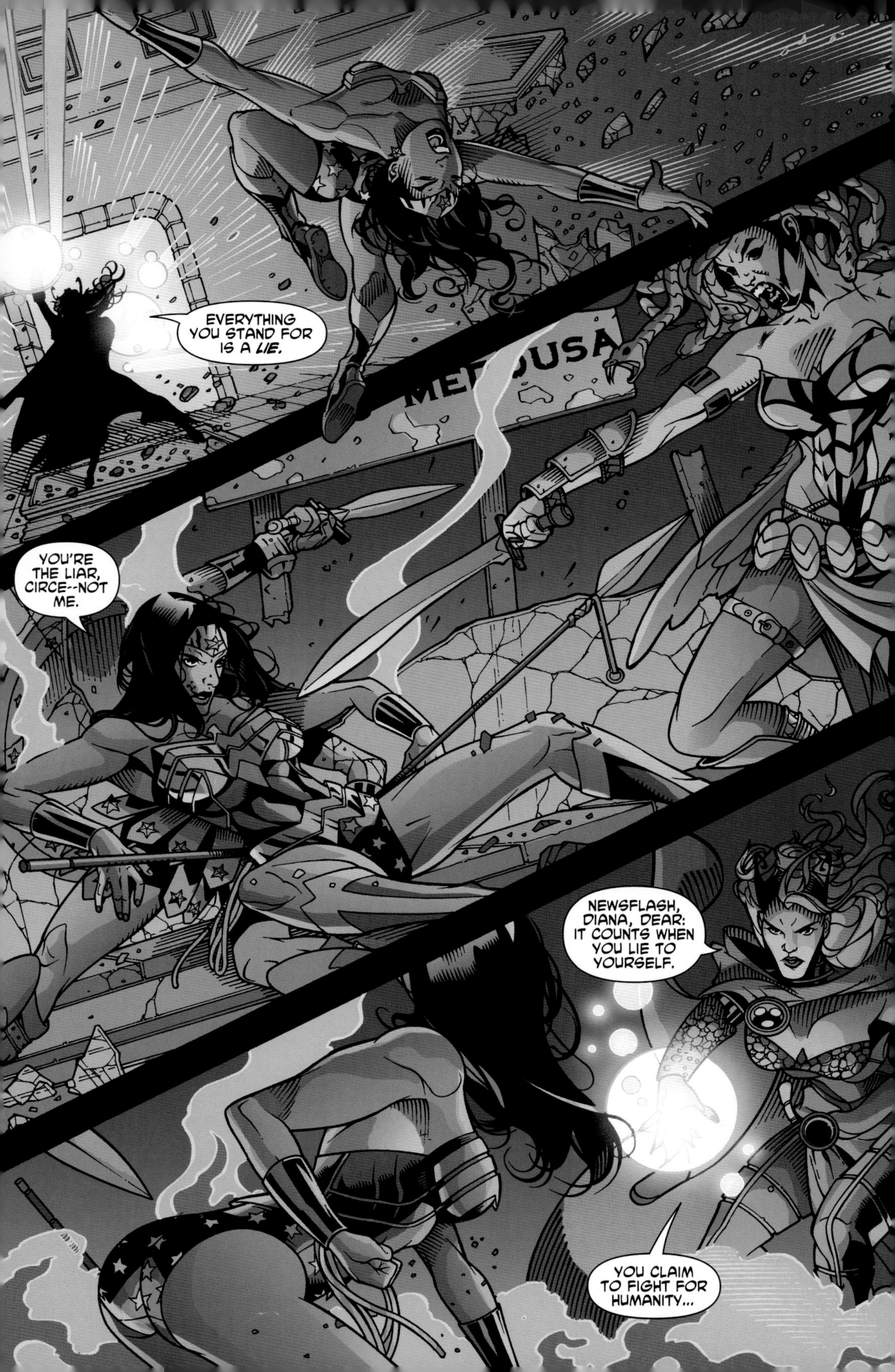
EVERYTHING YOU STAND FOR IS A *LIE.*
MEDUSA
YOU'RE THE LIAR, CIRCE--NOT ME.
NEWSFLASH, DIANA, DEAR: IT COUNTS WHEN YOU LIE TO YOURSELF.
YOU CLAIM TO FIGHT FOR HUMANITY...

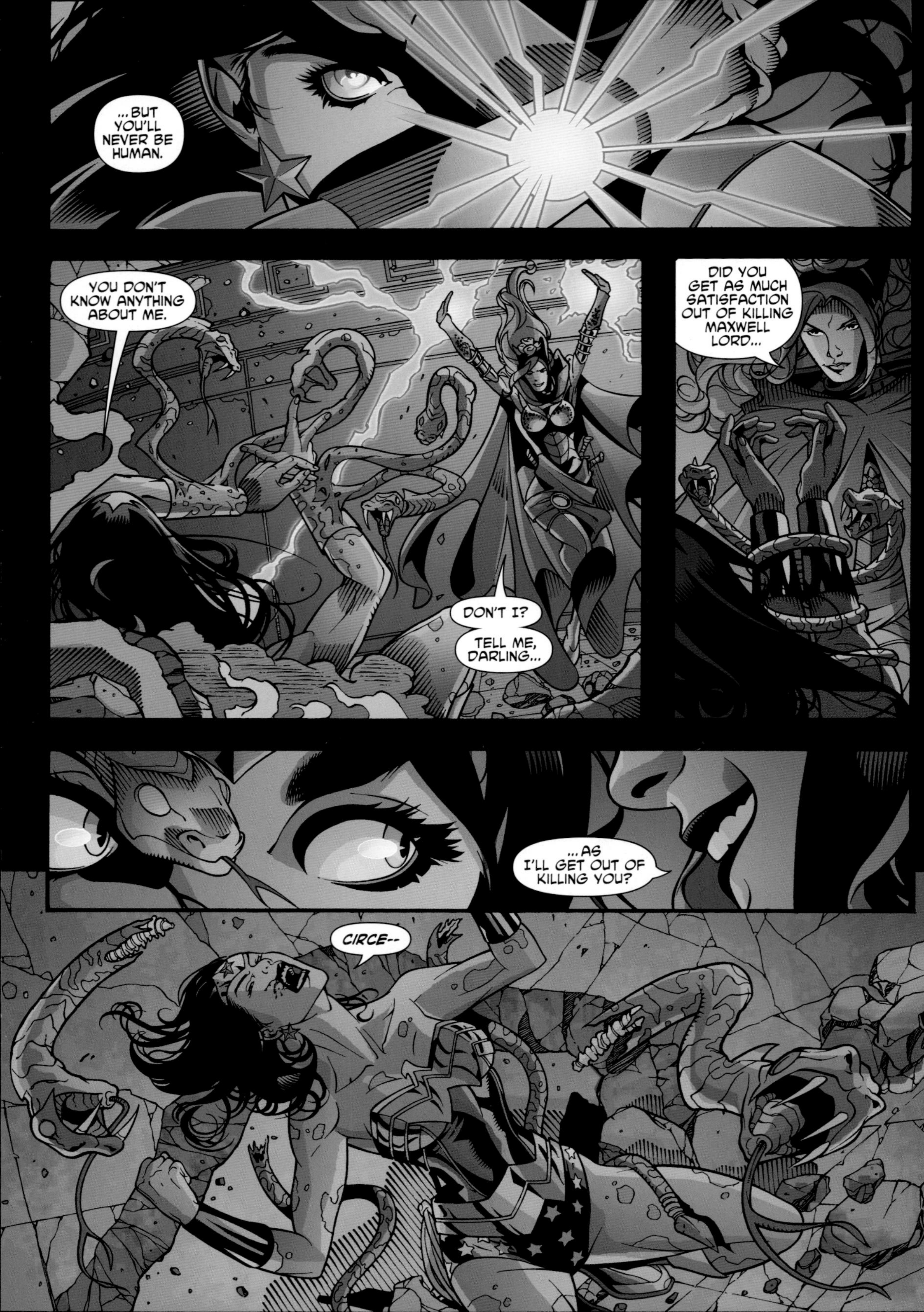
...BUT YOU'LL NEVER BE HUMAN.
YOU DON'T KNOW ANYTHING ABOUT ME.
DON'T I?
TELL ME, DARLING...
DID YOU GET AS MUCH SATISFACTION OUT OF KILLING MAXWELL LORD...
...AS I'LL GET OUT OF KILLING YOU?
CIRCE--

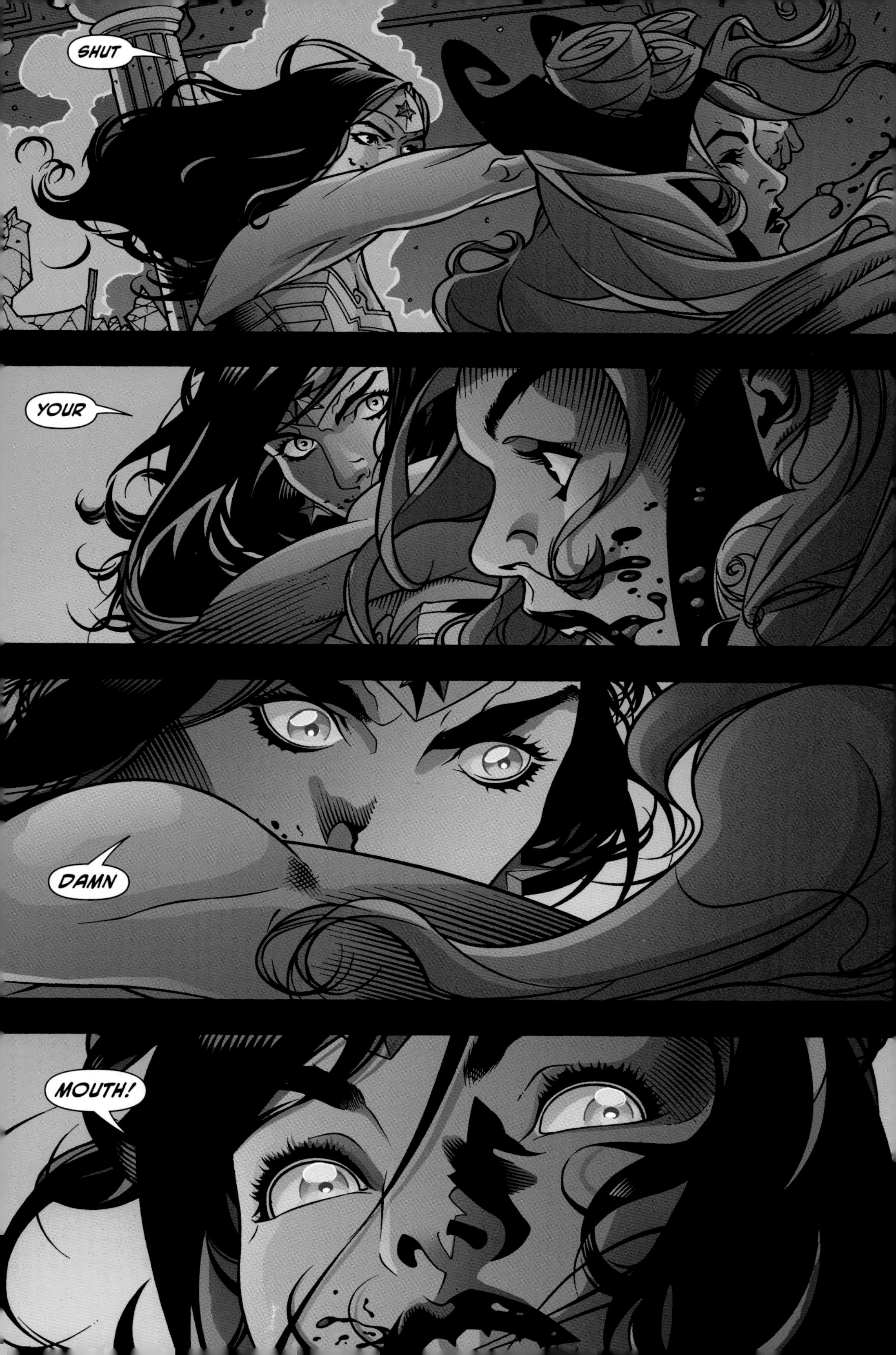
SHUT
YOUR
DAMN
MOUTH!

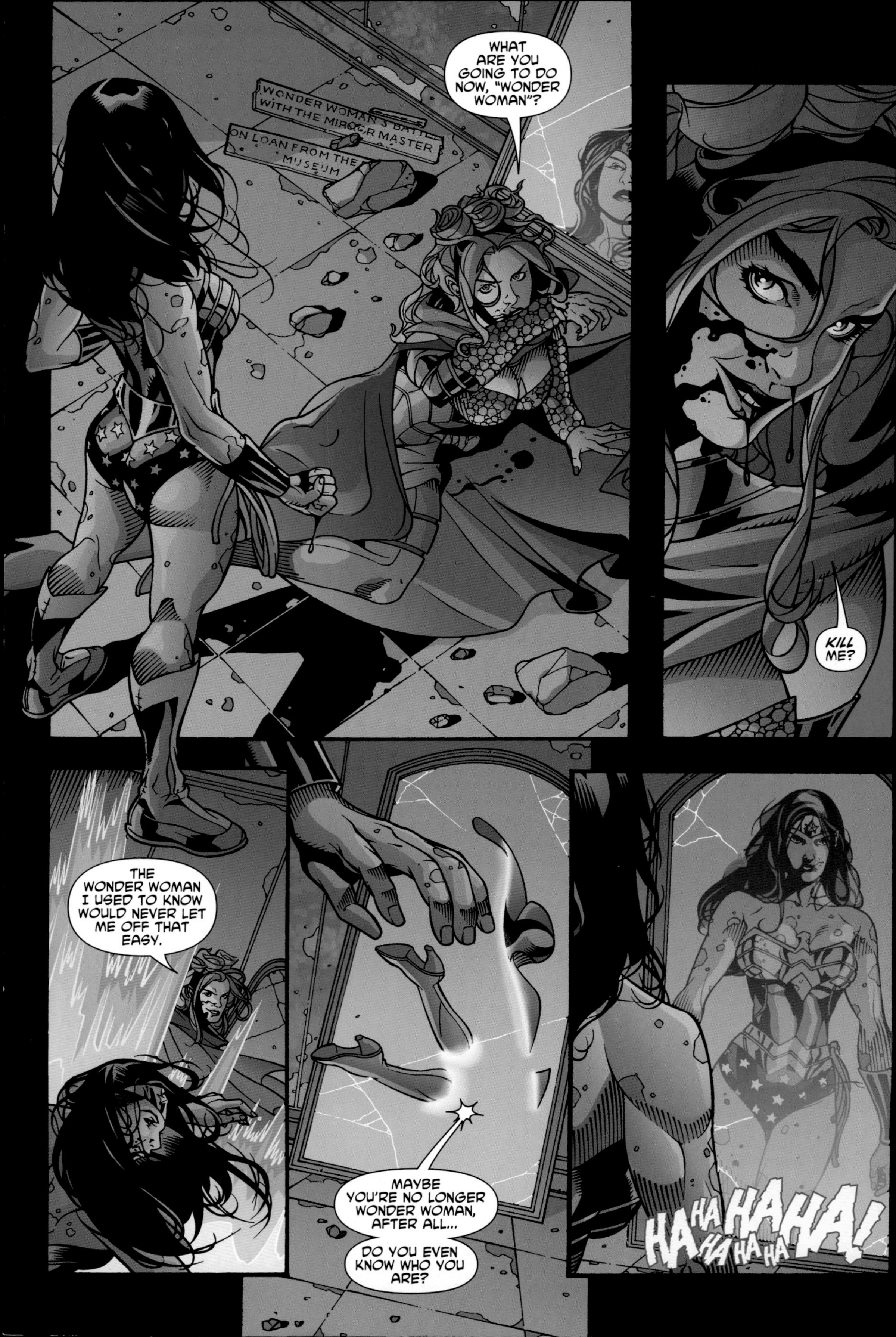
WONDER WOMAN'S BATTLE WITH THE MIRROR MASTER
ON LOAN FROM THE MUSEUM
WHAT ARE YOU GOING TO DO NOW, "WONDER WOMAN"?
KILL ME?
THE WONDER WOMAN I USED TO KNOW WOULD NEVER LET ME OFF THAT EASY.
MAYBE YOU'RE NO LONGER WONDER WOMAN, AFTER ALL...
DO YOU EVEN KNOW WHO YOU ARE?
HA HA HAHA! HA HA HA HA

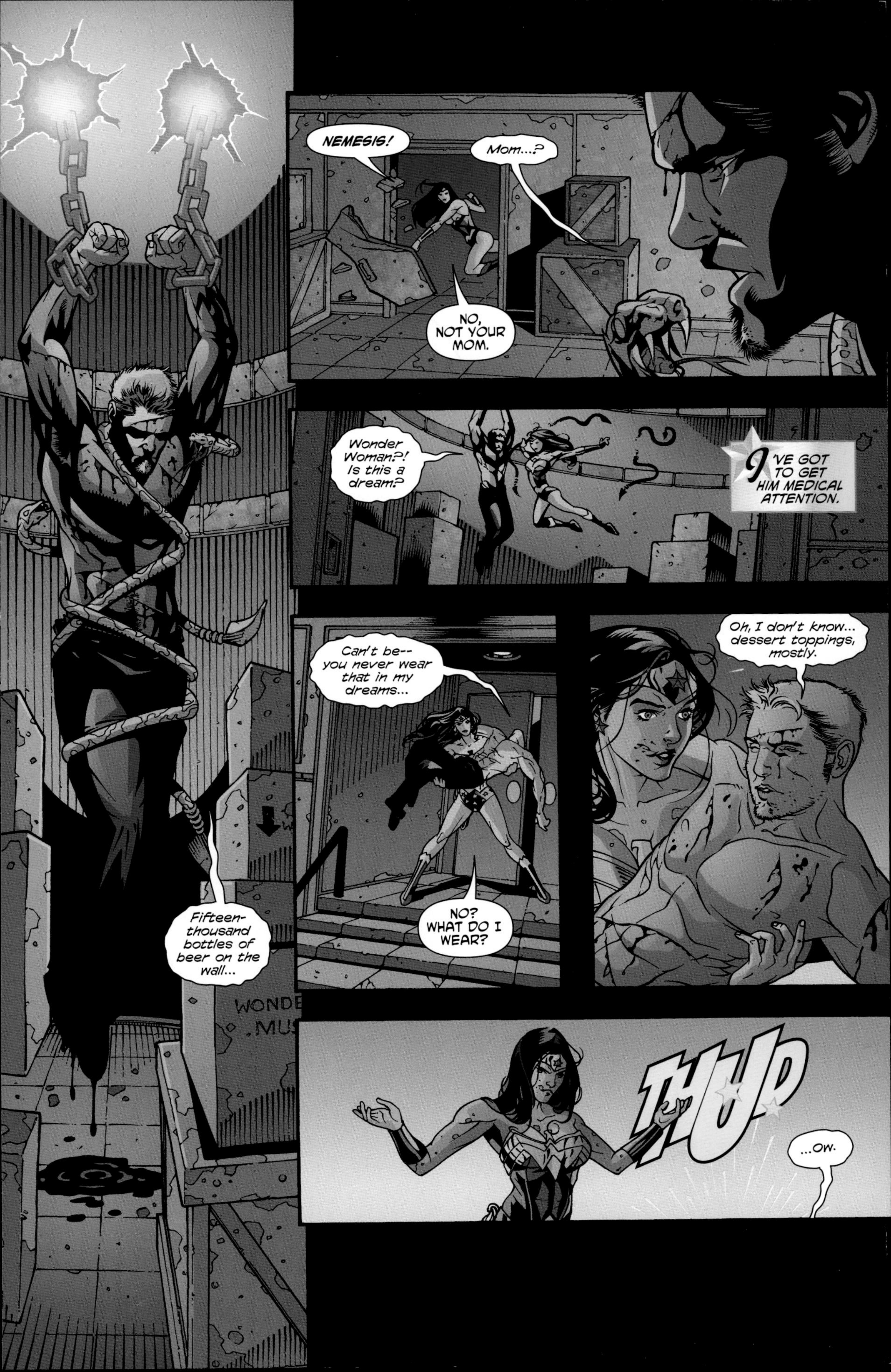
NEMESIS!
Mom...?
NO, NOT YOUR MOM.
Wonder Woman?! Is this a dream?
I'VE GOT TO GET HIM MEDICAL ATTENTION.
Can't be-- you never wear that in my dreams...
NO? WHAT DO I WEAR?
Oh, I don't know... dessert toppings, mostly.
Fifteen-thousand bottles of beer on the wall...
WONDE
MUS
THUD
...OW.

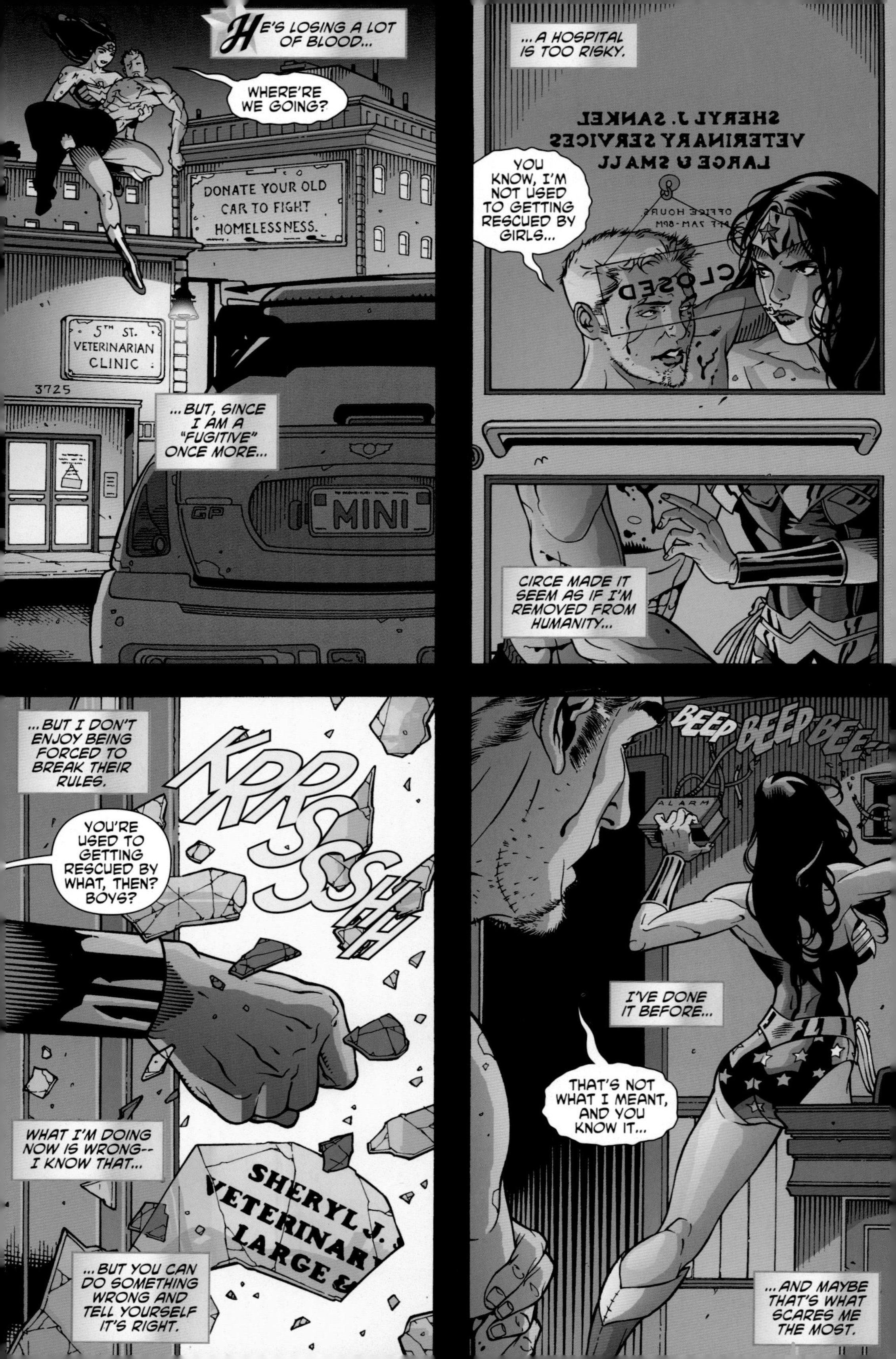
HE'S LOSING A LOT OF BLOOD...
WHERE'RE WE GOING?
DONATE YOUR OLD CAR TO FIGHT HOMELESSNESS.
5TH ST. VETERINARIAN CLINIC
3725
...BUT, SINCE I AM A "FUGITIVE" ONCE MORE...
MINI
...A HOSPITAL IS TOO RISKY.
SHERYL J. SANKEL
VETERINARY SERVICES
LARGE & SMALL
YOU KNOW, I'M NOT USED TO GETTING RESCUED BY GIRLS...
CLOSED
CIRCE MADE IT SEEM AS IF I'M REMOVED FROM HUMANITY...
...BUT I DON'T ENJOY BEING FORCED TO BREAK THEIR RULES.
KRRASSSHH
YOU'RE USED TO GETTING RESCUED BY WHAT, THEN? BOYS?
WHAT I'M DOING NOW IS WRONG-- I KNOW THAT...
SHERYL J. VETERINARY LARGE &
...BUT YOU CAN DO SOMETHING WRONG AND TELL YOURSELF IT'S RIGHT.
BEEP BEEP BEE--
ALARM
I'VE DONE IT BEFORE...
THAT'S NOT WHAT I MEANT, AND YOU KNOW IT...
...AND MAYBE THAT'S WHAT SCARES ME THE MOST.

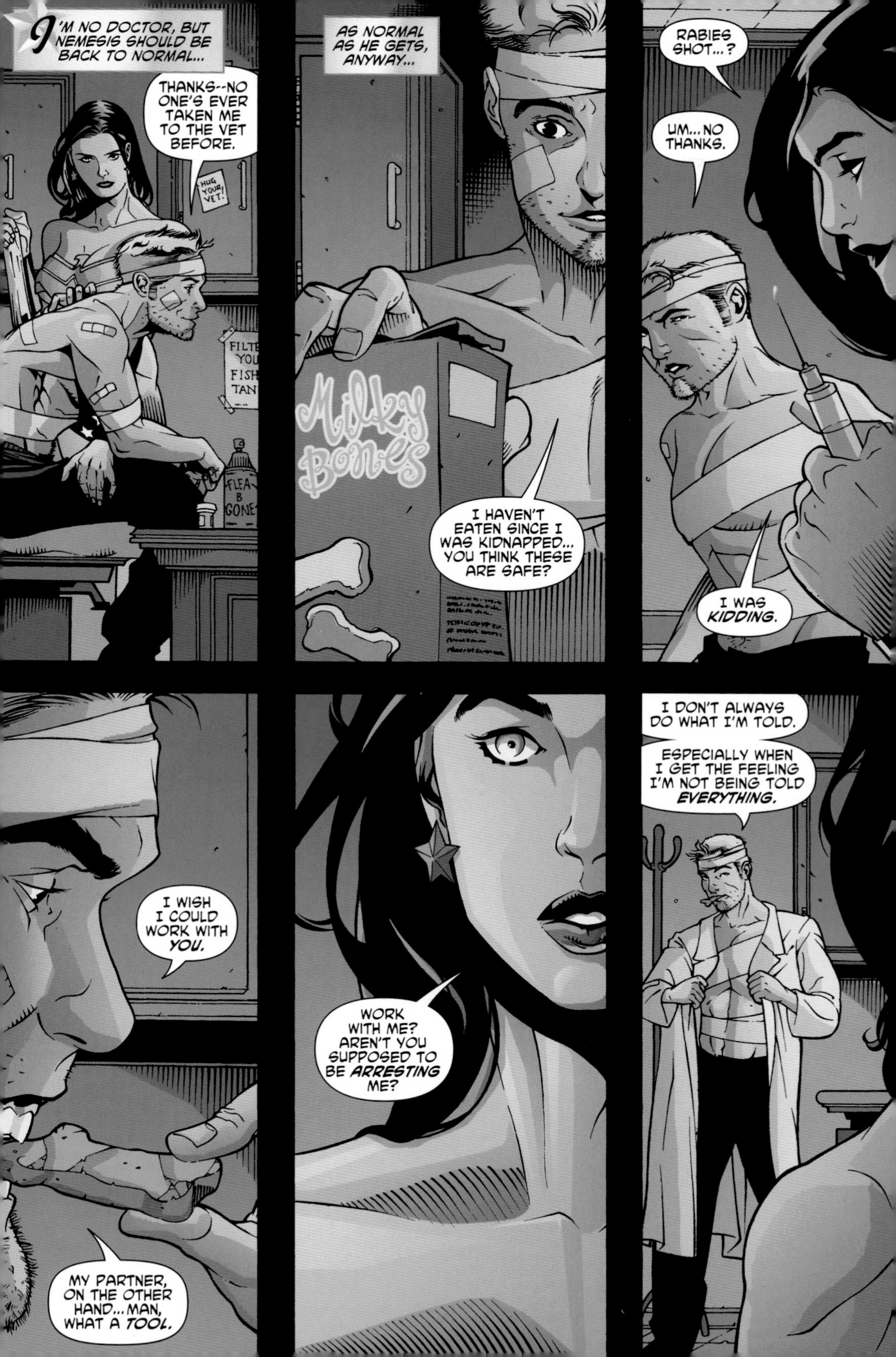
I'M NO DOCTOR, BUT NEMESIS SHOULD BE BACK TO NORMAL...
THANKS--NO ONE'S EVER TAKEN ME TO THE VET BEFORE.
HUG YOUR VET.
FILTE YOU FISH TAN
FLEA B GONE
AS NORMAL AS HE GETS, ANYWAY...
Milky Bones
I HAVEN'T EATEN SINCE I WAS KIDNAPPED... YOU THINK THESE ARE SAFE?
RABIES SHOT...?
UM...NO THANKS.
I WAS KIDDING.
I WISH I COULD WORK WITH YOU.
MY PARTNER, ON THE OTHER HAND...MAN, WHAT A TOOL.
WORK WITH ME? AREN'T YOU SUPPOSED TO BE ARRESTING ME?
I DON'T ALWAYS DO WHAT I'M TOLD.
ESPECIALLY WHEN I GET THE FEELING I'M NOT BEING TOLD EVERYTHING.

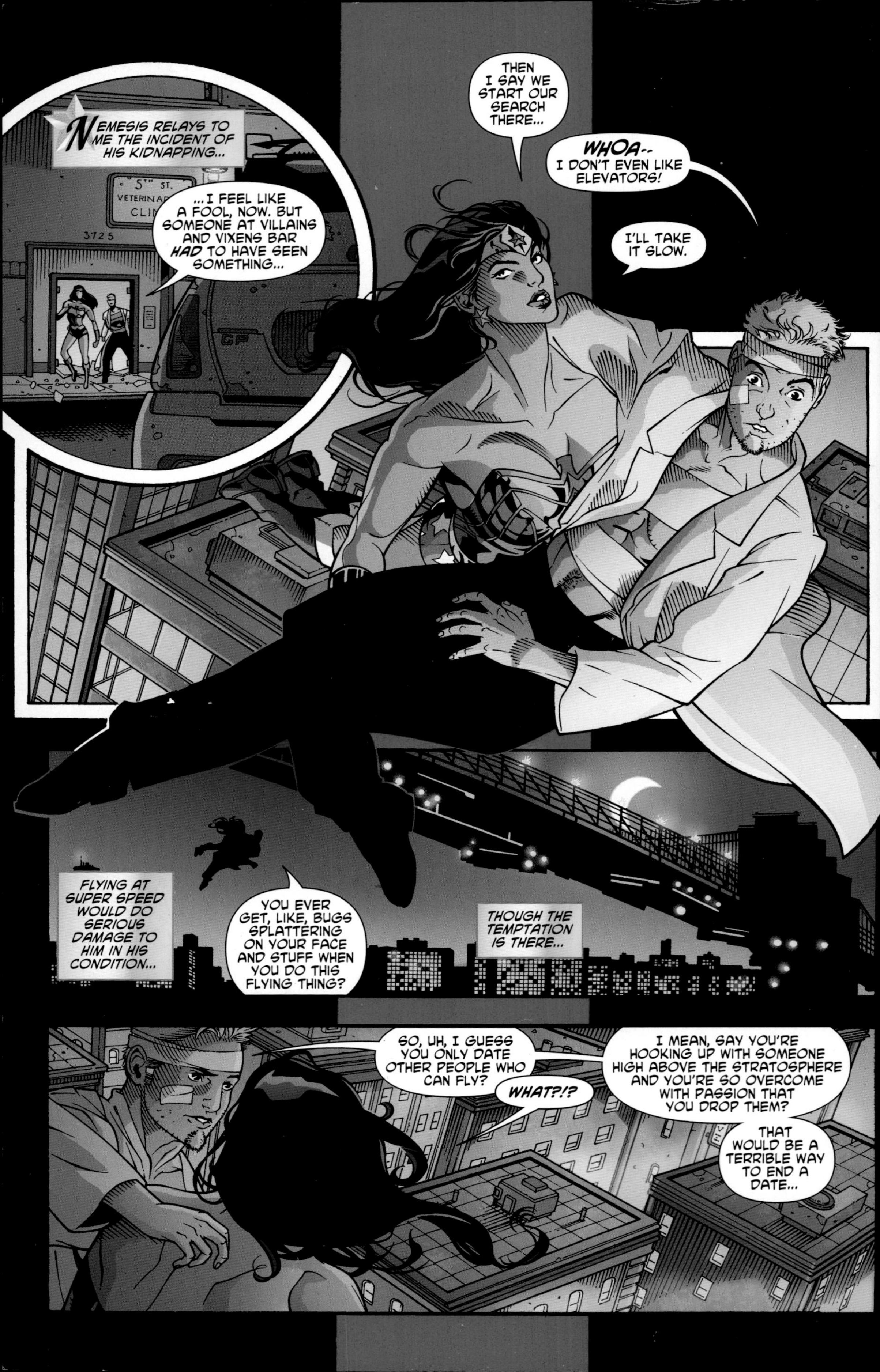
NEMESIS RELAYS TO ME THE INCIDENT OF HIS KIDNAPPING...
5TH ST. VETERINAR CLIN
3725
...I FEEL LIKE A FOOL, NOW. BUT SOMEONE AT VILLAINS AND VIXENS BAR HAD TO HAVE SEEN SOMETHING...
THEN I SAY WE START OUR SEARCH THERE...
WHOA-- I DON'T EVEN LIKE ELEVATORS!
I'LL TAKE IT SLOW.
FLYING AT SUPER SPEED WOULD DO SERIOUS DAMAGE TO HIM IN HIS CONDITION...
YOU EVER GET, LIKE, BUGS SPLATTERING ON YOUR FACE AND STUFF WHEN YOU DO THIS FLYING THING?
THOUGH THE TEMPTATION IS THERE...
SO, UH, I GUESS YOU ONLY DATE OTHER PEOPLE WHO CAN FLY?
WHAT?!?
I MEAN, SAY YOU'RE HOOKING UP WITH SOMEONE HIGH ABOVE THE STRATOSPHERE AND YOU'RE SO OVERCOME WITH PASSION THAT YOU DROP THEM?
THAT WOULD BE A TERRIBLE WAY TO END A DATE...

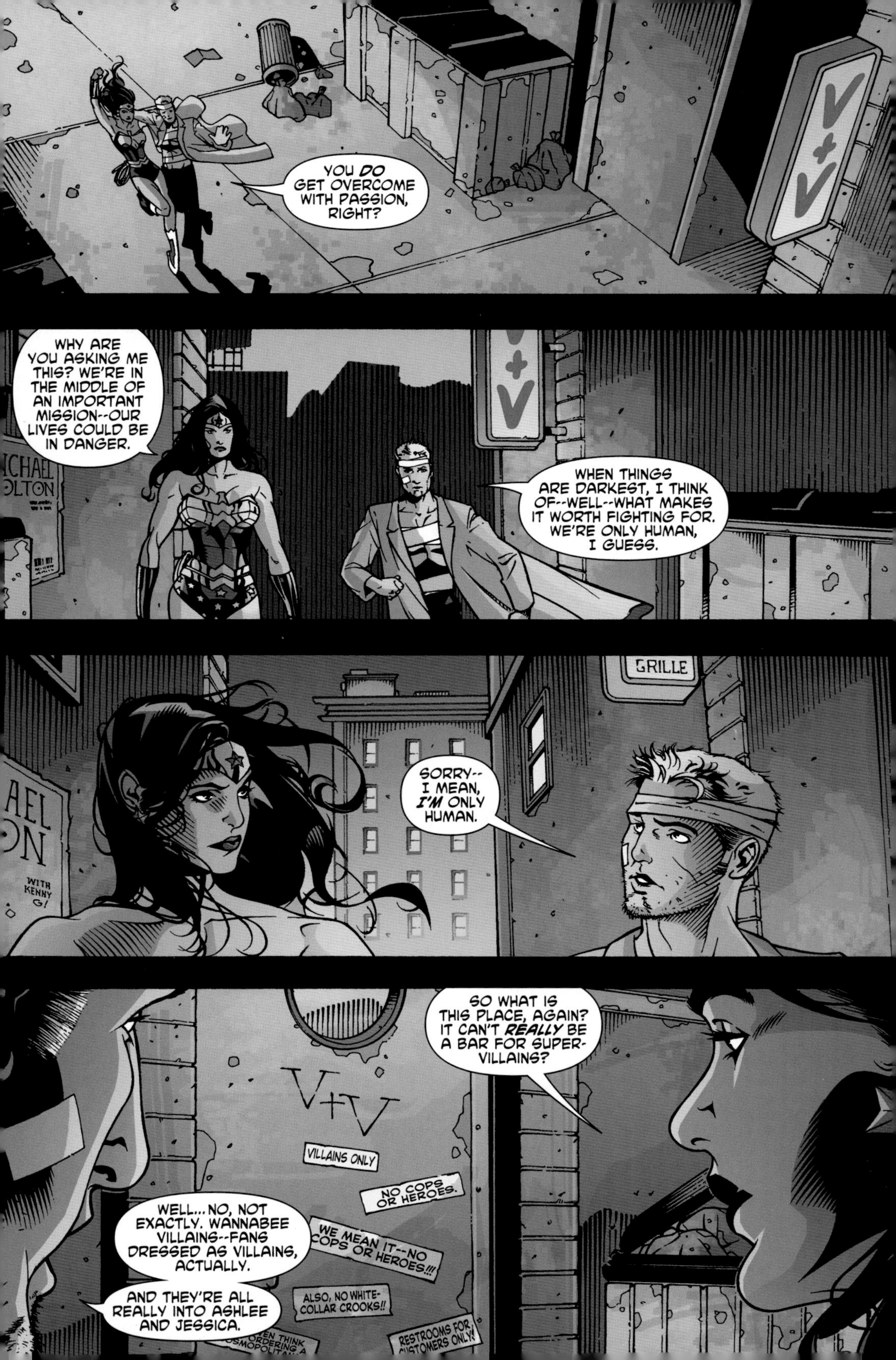

V+V
YOU *DO* GET OVERCOME WITH PASSION, RIGHT?
WHY ARE YOU ASKING ME THIS? WE'RE IN THE MIDDLE OF AN IMPORTANT MISSION--OUR LIVES COULD BE IN DANGER.
V+V
WHEN THINGS ARE DARKEST, I THINK OF--WELL--WHAT MAKES IT WORTH FIGHTING FOR. WE'RE ONLY HUMAN, I GUESS.
GRILLE
WITH KENNY G!
SORRY-- I MEAN, *I'M* ONLY HUMAN.
SO WHAT IS THIS PLACE, AGAIN? IT CAN'T *REALLY* BE A BAR FOR SUPER-VILLAINS?
V+V
VILLAINS ONLY
NO COPS OR HEROES.
WELL... NO, NOT EXACTLY. WANNABEE VILLAINS--FANS DRESSED AS VILLAINS, ACTUALLY.
WE MEAN IT--NO COPS OR HEROES!!!
AND THEY'RE ALL REALLY INTO ASHLEE AND JESSICA.
ALSO, NO WHITE-COLLAR CROOKS!!
RESTROOMS FOR CUSTOMERS ONLY!

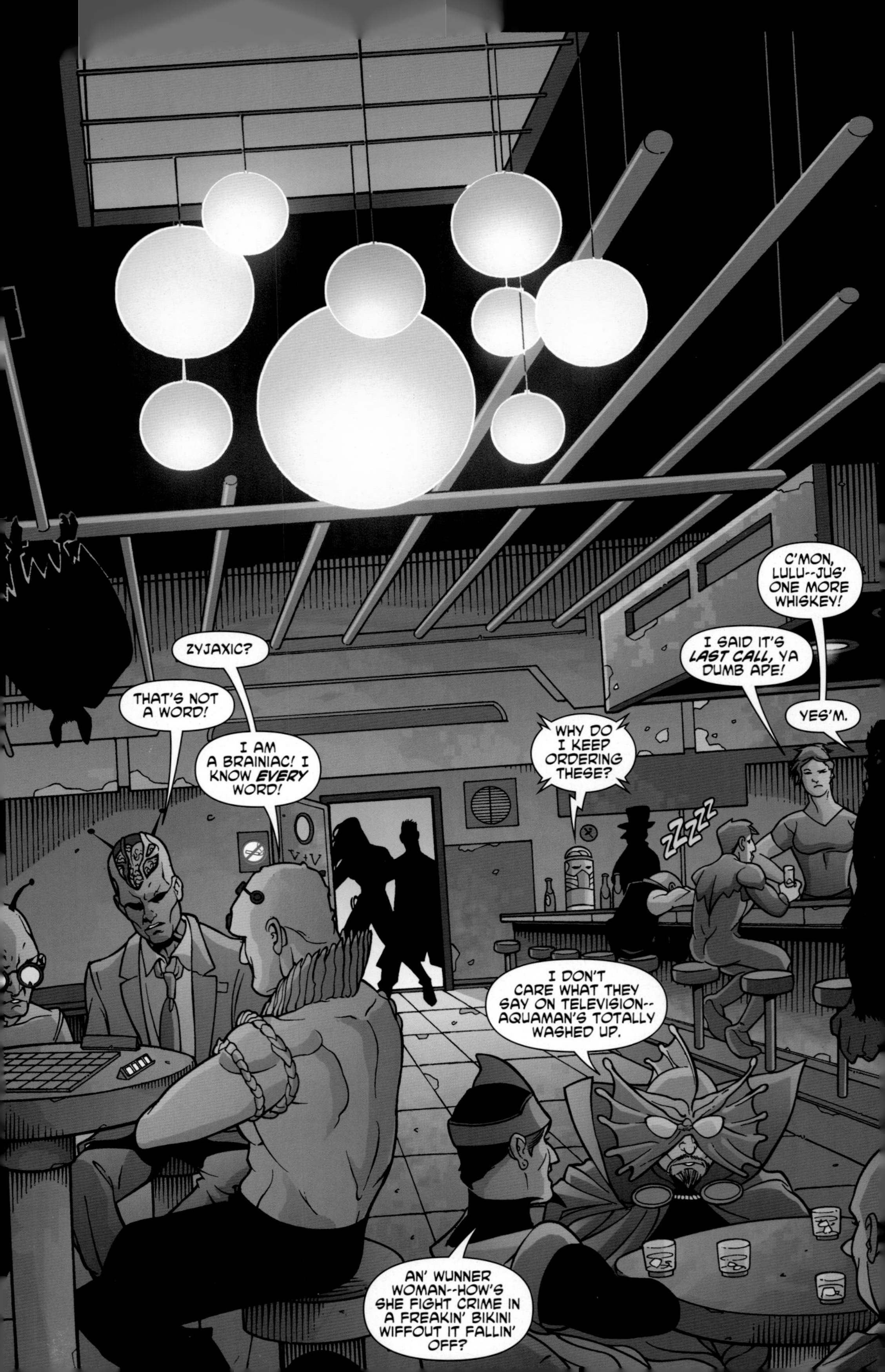
ZYJAXIC?
THAT'S NOT A WORD!
I AM A BRAINIAC! I KNOW *EVERY* WORD!
WHY DO I KEEP ORDERING THESE?
C'MON, LULU--JUS' ONE MORE WHISKEY!
I SAID IT'S *LAST CALL*, YA DUMB APE!
YES'M.
ZZZZZ
I DON'T CARE WHAT THEY SAY ON TELEVISION--AQUAMAN'S TOTALLY WASHED UP.
AN' WUNNER WOMAN--HOW'S SHE FIGHT CRIME IN A FREAKIN' BIKINI WIFFOUT IT FALLIN' OFF?

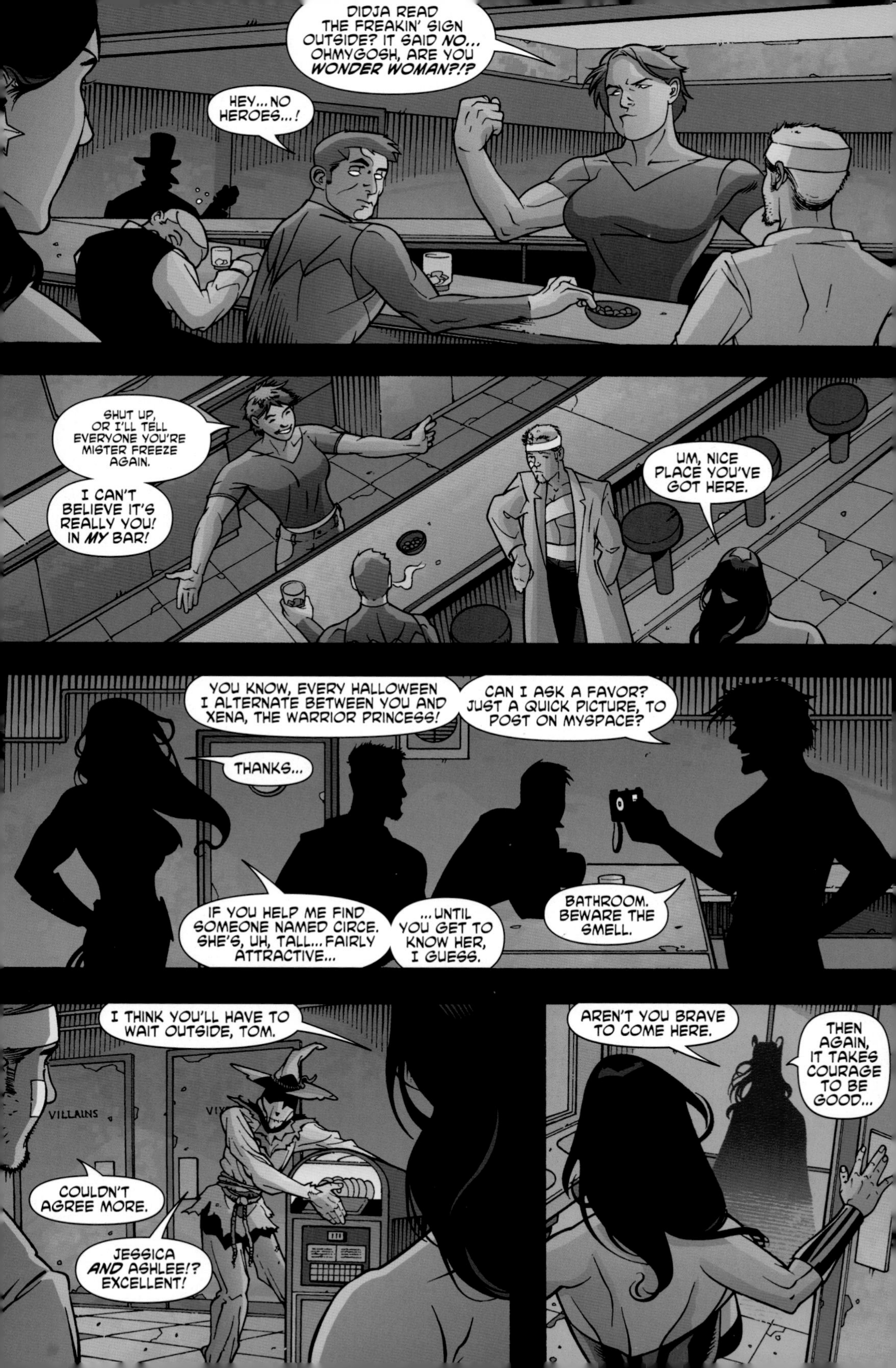
DIDJA READ THE FREAKIN' SIGN OUTSIDE? IT SAID NO... OHMYGOSH, ARE YOU WONDER WOMAN?!?
HEY... NO HEROES...!
SHUT UP, OR I'LL TELL EVERYONE YOU'RE MISTER FREEZE AGAIN.
I CAN'T BELIEVE IT'S REALLY YOU! IN MY BAR!
UM, NICE PLACE YOU'VE GOT HERE.
YOU KNOW, EVERY HALLOWEEN I ALTERNATE BETWEEN YOU AND XENA, THE WARRIOR PRINCESS!
THANKS...
CAN I ASK A FAVOR? JUST A QUICK PICTURE, TO POST ON MYSPACE?
IF YOU HELP ME FIND SOMEONE NAMED CIRCE. SHE'S, UH, TALL... FAIRLY ATTRACTIVE...
...UNTIL YOU GET TO KNOW HER, I GUESS.
BATHROOM. BEWARE THE SMELL.
I THINK YOU'LL HAVE TO WAIT OUTSIDE, TOM.
VILLAINS
COULDN'T AGREE MORE.
JESSICA AND ASHLEE!? EXCELLENT!
AREN'T YOU BRAVE TO COME HERE.
THEN AGAIN, IT TAKES COURAGE TO BE GOOD...

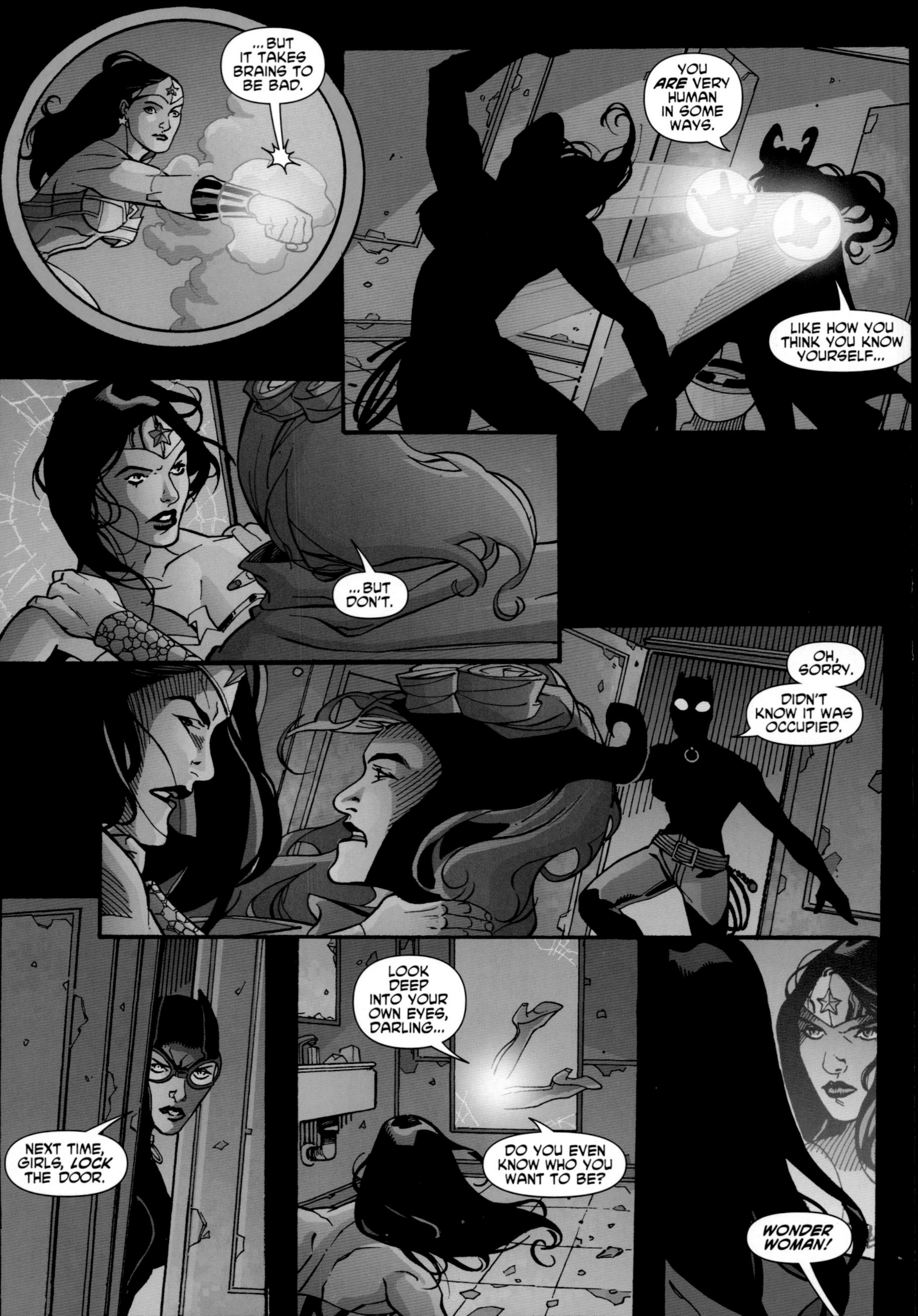
...BUT IT TAKES BRAINS TO BE BAD.
YOU *ARE* VERY HUMAN IN SOME WAYS.
LIKE HOW YOU THINK YOU KNOW YOURSELF...
...BUT DON'T.
OH, SORRY.
DIDN'T KNOW IT WAS OCCUPIED.
NEXT TIME, GIRLS, *LOCK* THE DOOR.
LOOK DEEP INTO YOUR OWN EYES, DARLING...
DO YOU EVEN KNOW WHO YOU WANT TO BE?
WONDER WOMAN!

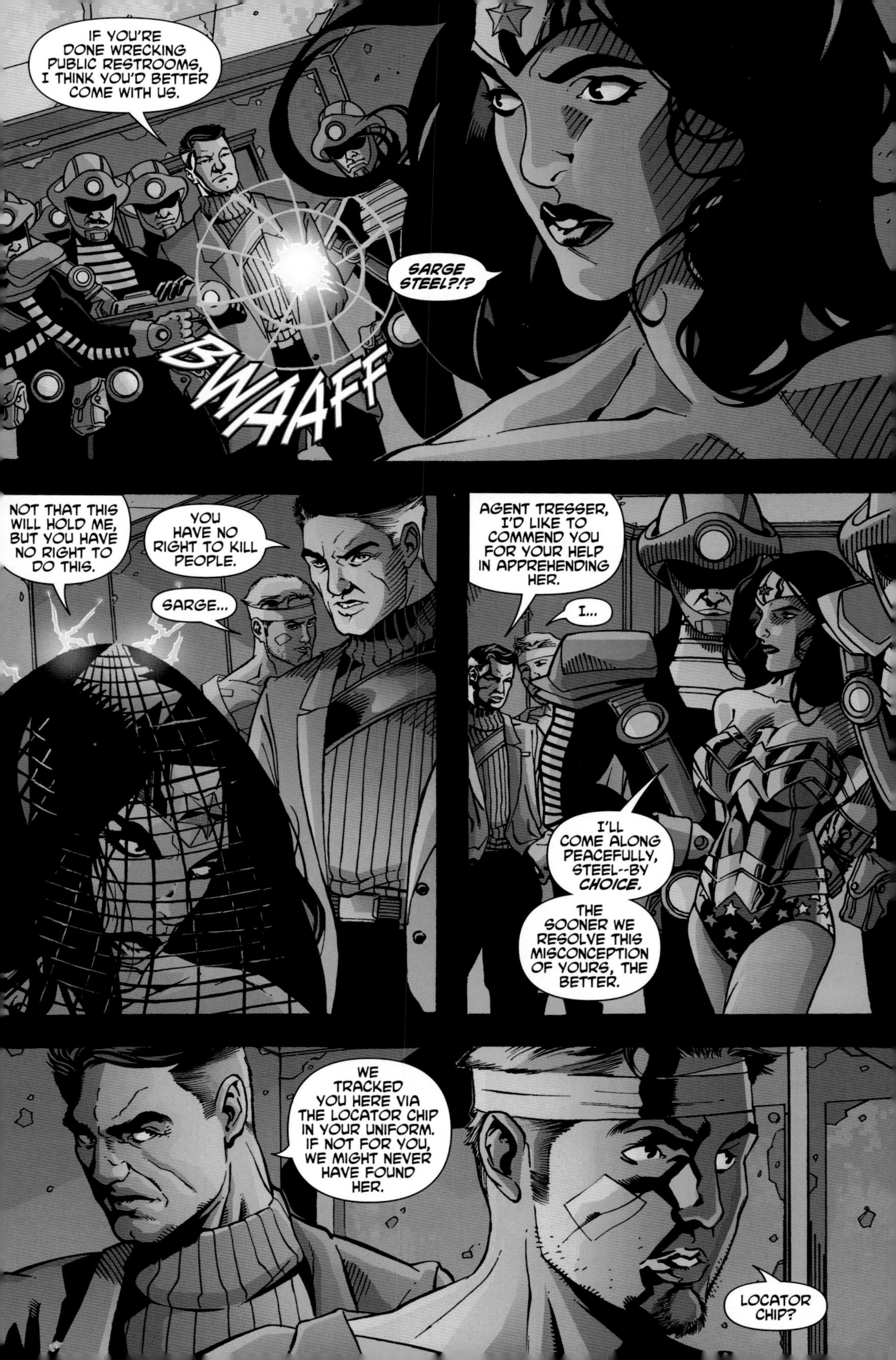
IF YOU'RE DONE WRECKING PUBLIC RESTROOMS, I THINK YOU'D BETTER COME WITH US.
SARGE STEEL?!?
BWAAFF
NOT THAT THIS WILL HOLD ME, BUT YOU HAVE NO RIGHT TO DO THIS.
YOU HAVE NO RIGHT TO KILL PEOPLE.
SARGE...
AGENT TRESSER, I'D LIKE TO COMMEND YOU FOR YOUR HELP IN APPREHENDING HER.
I...
I'LL COME ALONG PEACEFULLY, STEEL--BY *CHOICE.*
THE SOONER WE RESOLVE THIS MISCONCEPTION OF YOURS, THE BETTER.
WE TRACKED YOU HERE VIA THE LOCATOR CHIP IN YOUR UNIFORM. IF NOT FOR YOU, WE MIGHT NEVER HAVE FOUND HER.
LOCATOR CHIP?

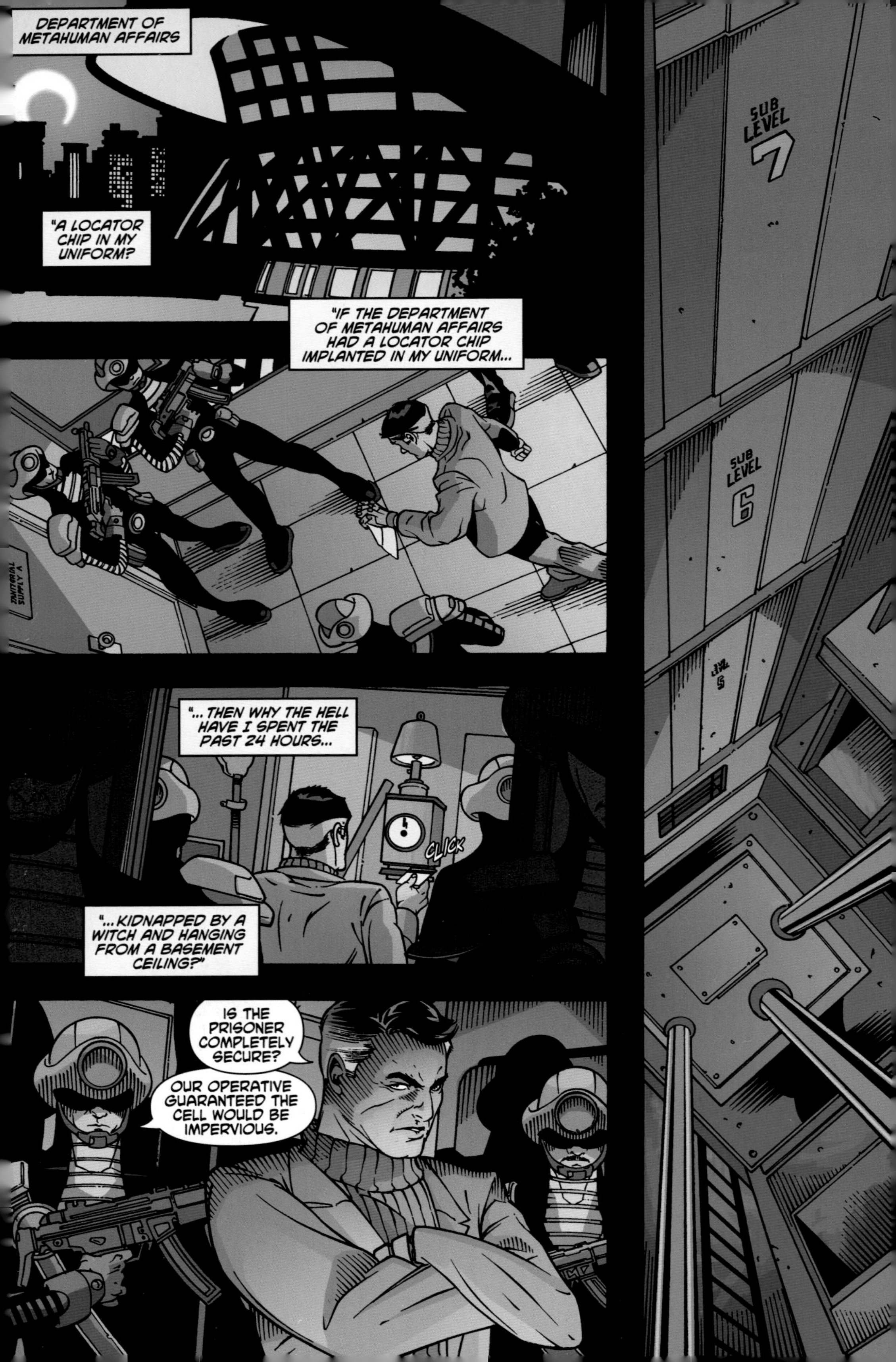
DEPARTMENT OF METAHUMAN AFFAIRS
"A LOCATOR CHIP IN MY UNIFORM?
"IF THE DEPARTMENT OF METAHUMAN AFFAIRS HAD A LOCATOR CHIP IMPLANTED IN MY UNIFORM...
"...THEN WHY THE HELL HAVE I SPENT THE PAST 24 HOURS...
CLICK
"...KIDNAPPED BY A WITCH AND HANGING FROM A BASEMENT CEILING?"
IS THE PRISONER COMPLETELY SECURE?
OUR OPERATIVE GUARANTEED THE CELL WOULD BE IMPERVIOUS.
SUB LEVEL 7
SUB LEVEL 6

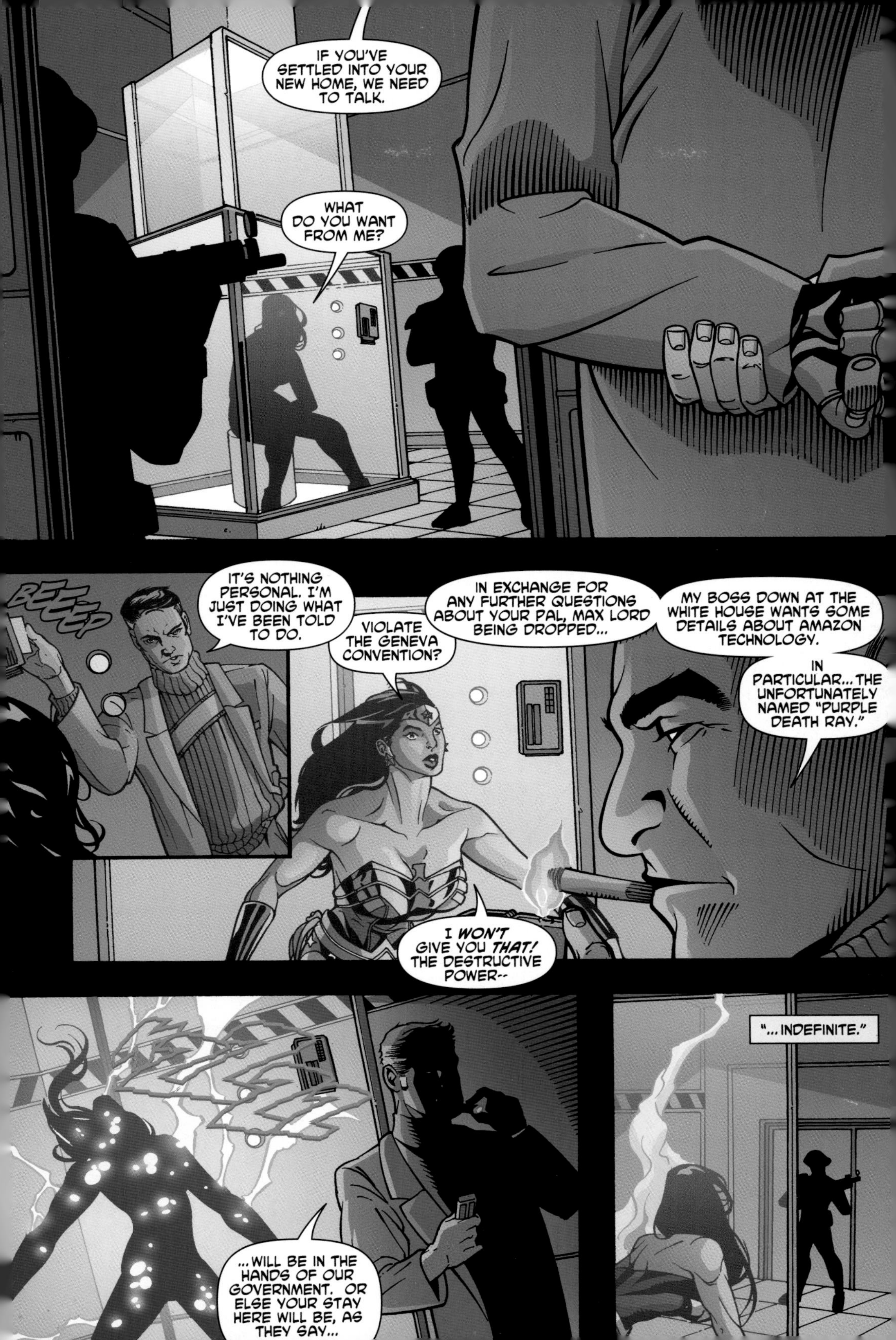
IF YOU'VE SETTLED INTO YOUR NEW HOME, WE NEED TO TALK.
WHAT DO YOU WANT FROM ME?
BEEEEP
IT'S NOTHING PERSONAL. I'M JUST DOING WHAT I'VE BEEN TOLD TO DO.
VIOLATE THE GENEVA CONVENTION?
IN EXCHANGE FOR ANY FURTHER QUESTIONS ABOUT YOUR PAL, MAX LORD BEING DROPPED...
MY BOSS DOWN AT THE WHITE HOUSE WANTS SOME DETAILS ABOUT AMAZON TECHNOLOGY.
IN PARTICULAR... THE UNFORTUNATELY NAMED "PURPLE DEATH RAY."
I *WON'T* GIVE YOU *THAT!* THE DESTRUCTIVE POWER--
...WILL BE IN THE HANDS OF OUR GOVERNMENT. OR ELSE YOUR STAY HERE WILL BE, AS THEY SAY...
"...INDEFINITE."

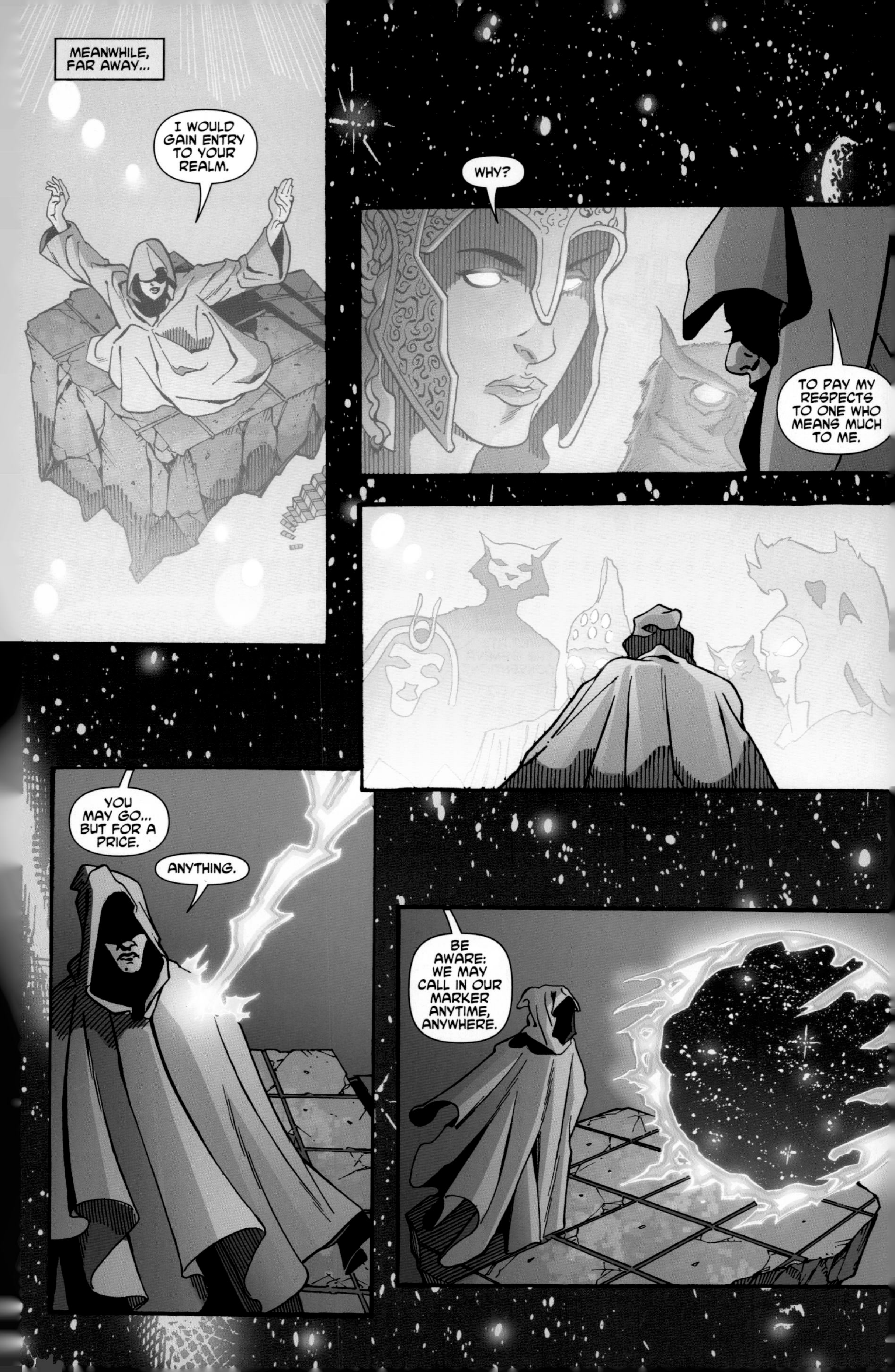
MEANWHILE, FAR AWAY...
I WOULD GAIN ENTRY TO YOUR REALM.
WHY?
TO PAY MY RESPECTS TO ONE WHO MEANS MUCH TO ME.
YOU MAY GO... BUT FOR A PRICE.
ANYTHING.
BE AWARE: WE MAY CALL IN OUR MARKER ANYTIME, ANYWHERE.

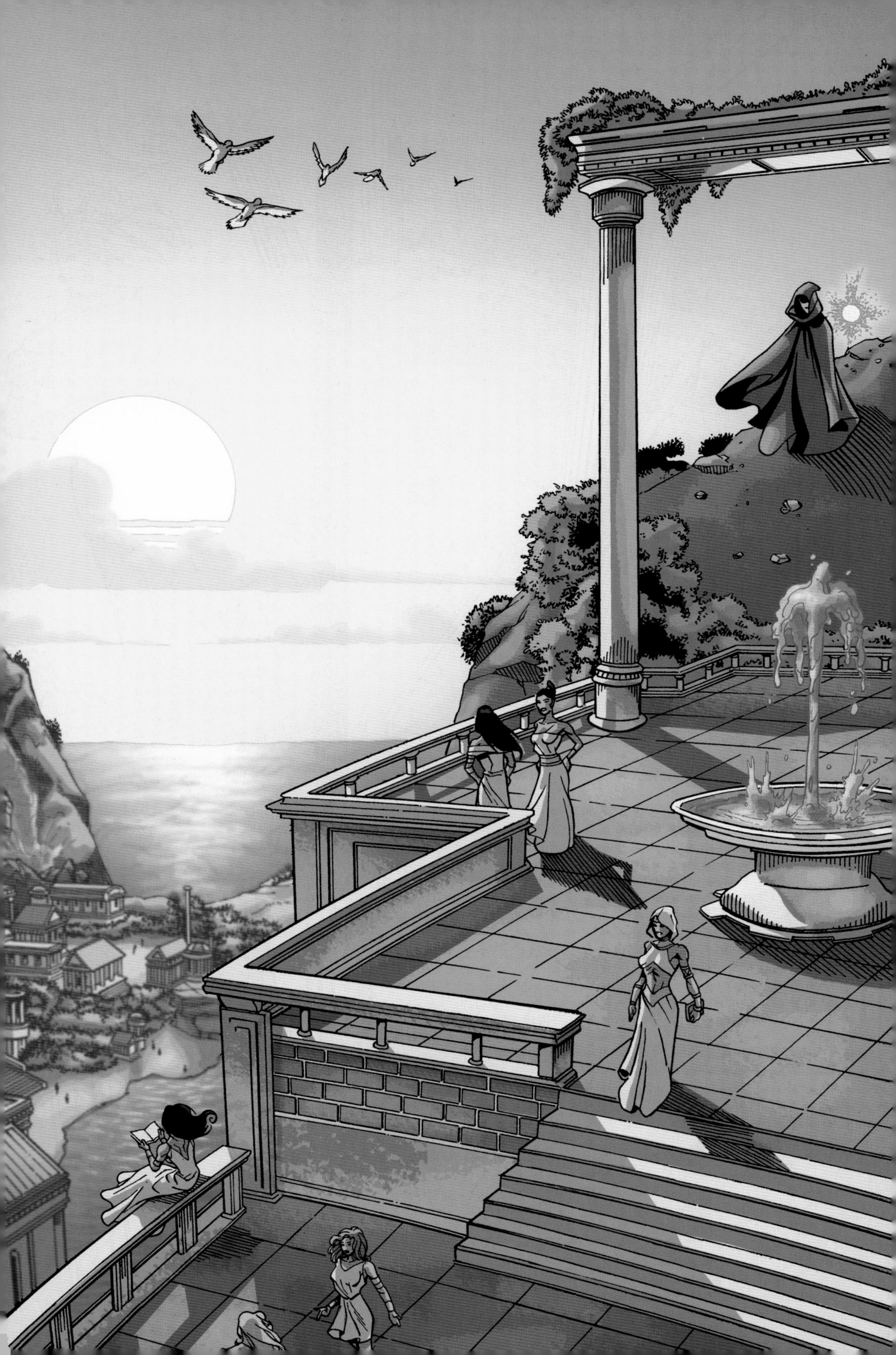

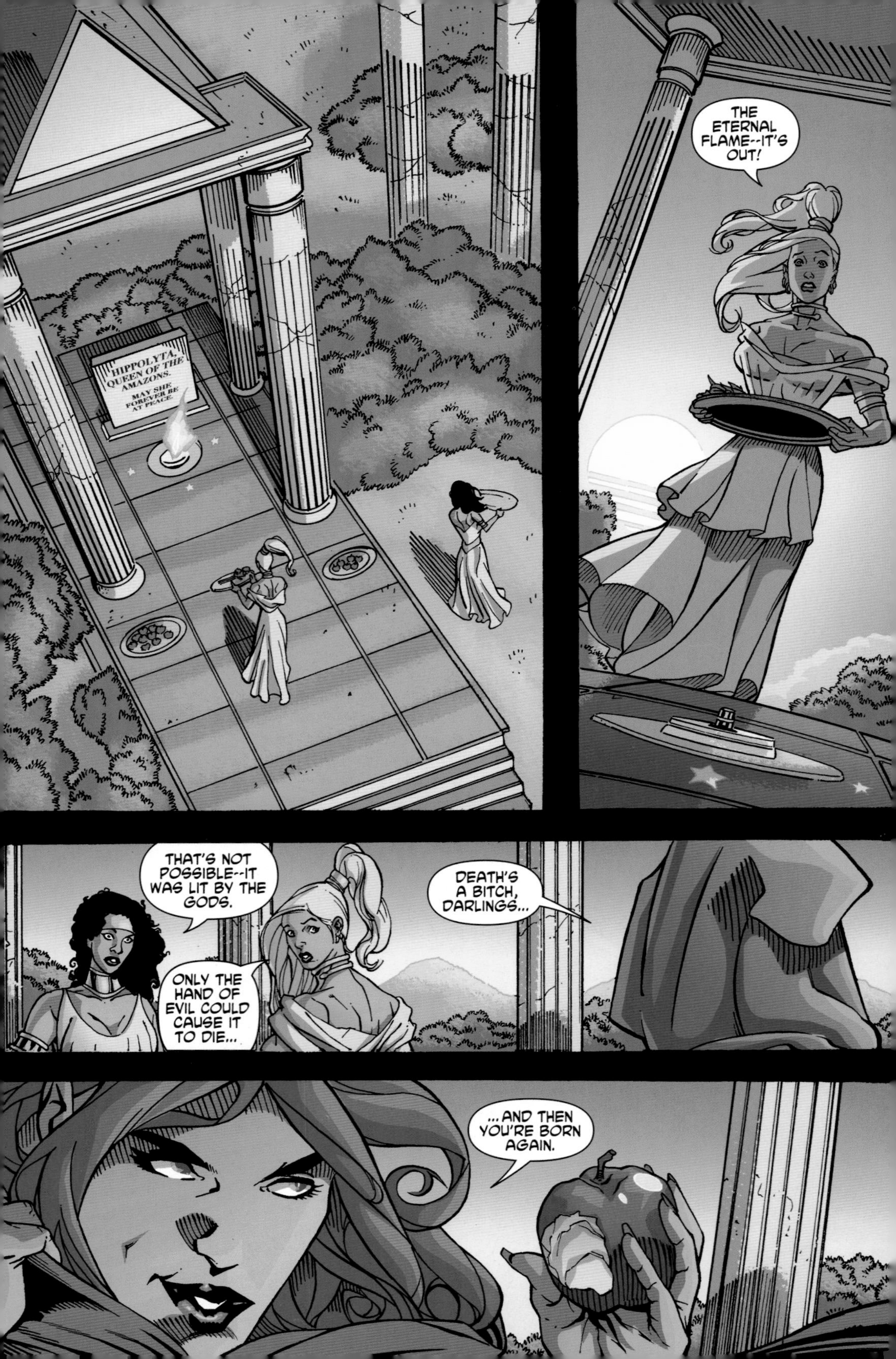
HIPPOLYTA, QUEEN OF THE AMAZONS.
MAY SHE FOREVER BE AT PEACE.
THE ETERNAL FLAME--IT'S OUT!
THAT'S NOT POSSIBLE--IT WAS LIT BY THE GODS.
ONLY THE HAND OF EVIL COULD CAUSE IT TO DIE...
DEATH'S A BITCH, DARLINGS...
...AND THEN YOU'RE BORN AGAIN.

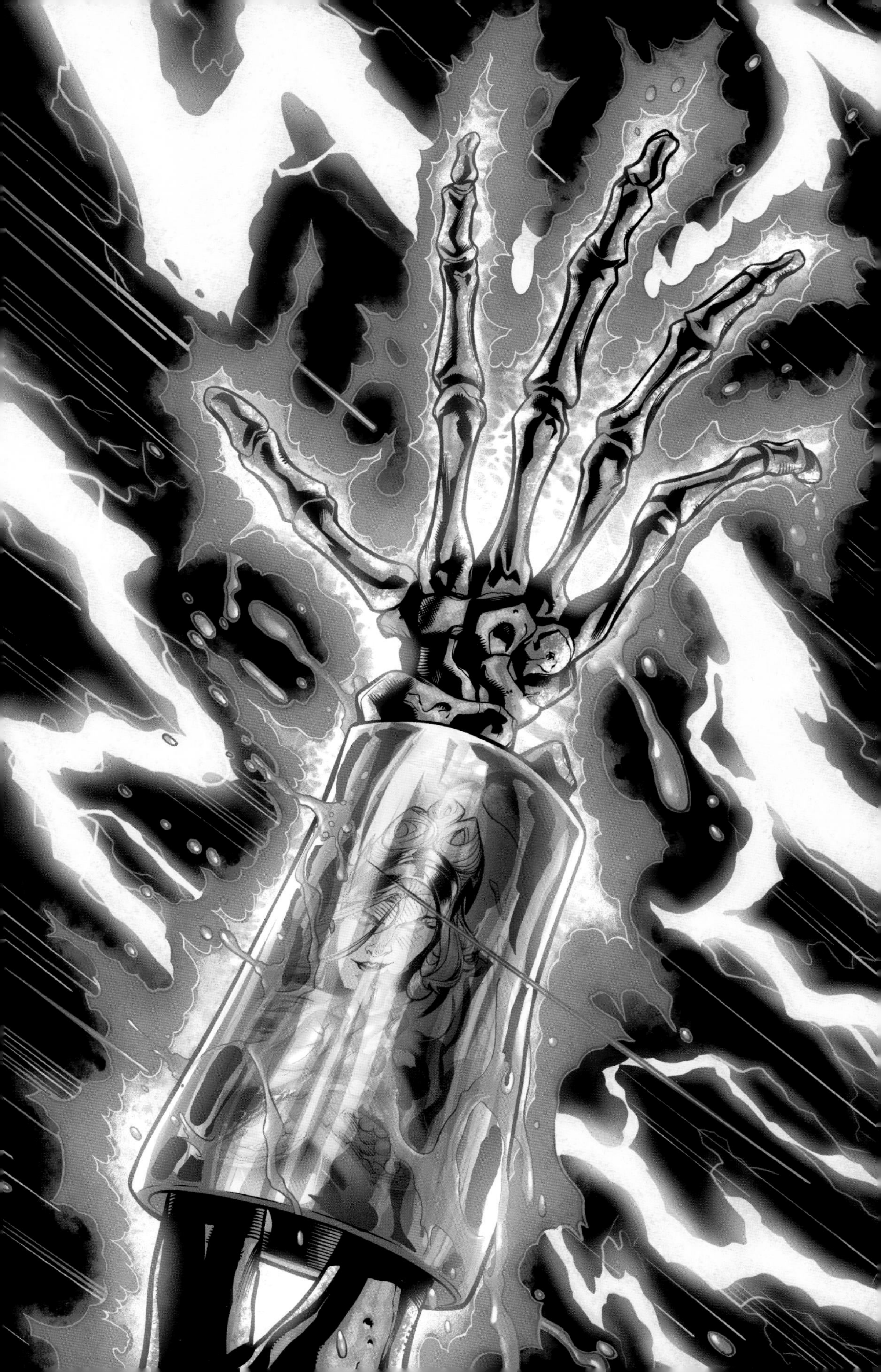

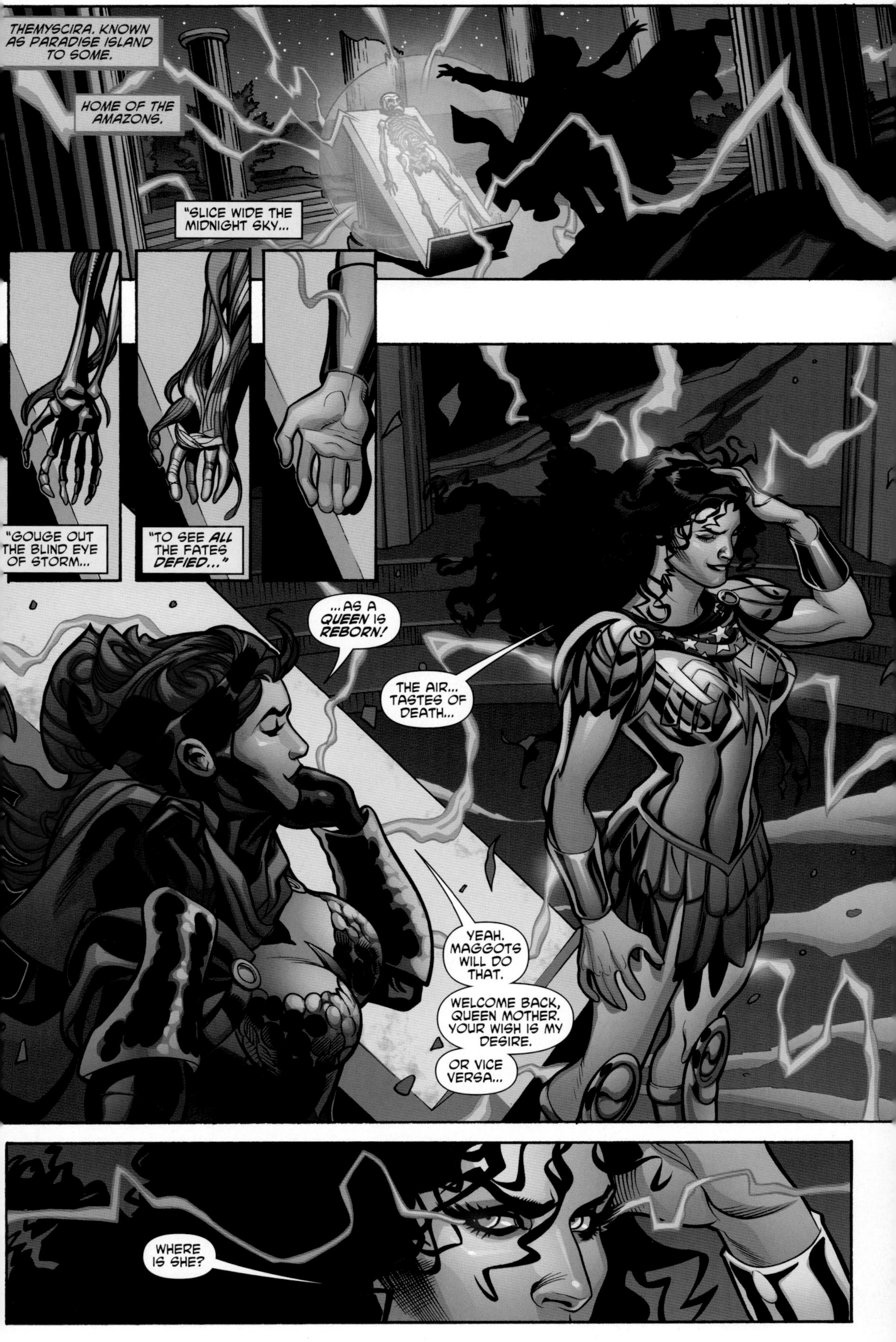

THEMYSCIRA. KNOWN AS PARADISE ISLAND TO SOME.
HOME OF THE AMAZONS.
"SLICE WIDE THE MIDNIGHT SKY...
"GOUGE OUT THE BLIND EYE OF STORM...
"TO SEE ALL THE FATES DEFIED..."
...AS A QUEEN IS REBORN!
THE AIR... TASTES OF DEATH...
YEAH. MAGGOTS WILL DO THAT.
WELCOME BACK, QUEEN MOTHER. YOUR WISH IS MY DESIRE.
OR VICE VERSA...
WHERE IS SHE?

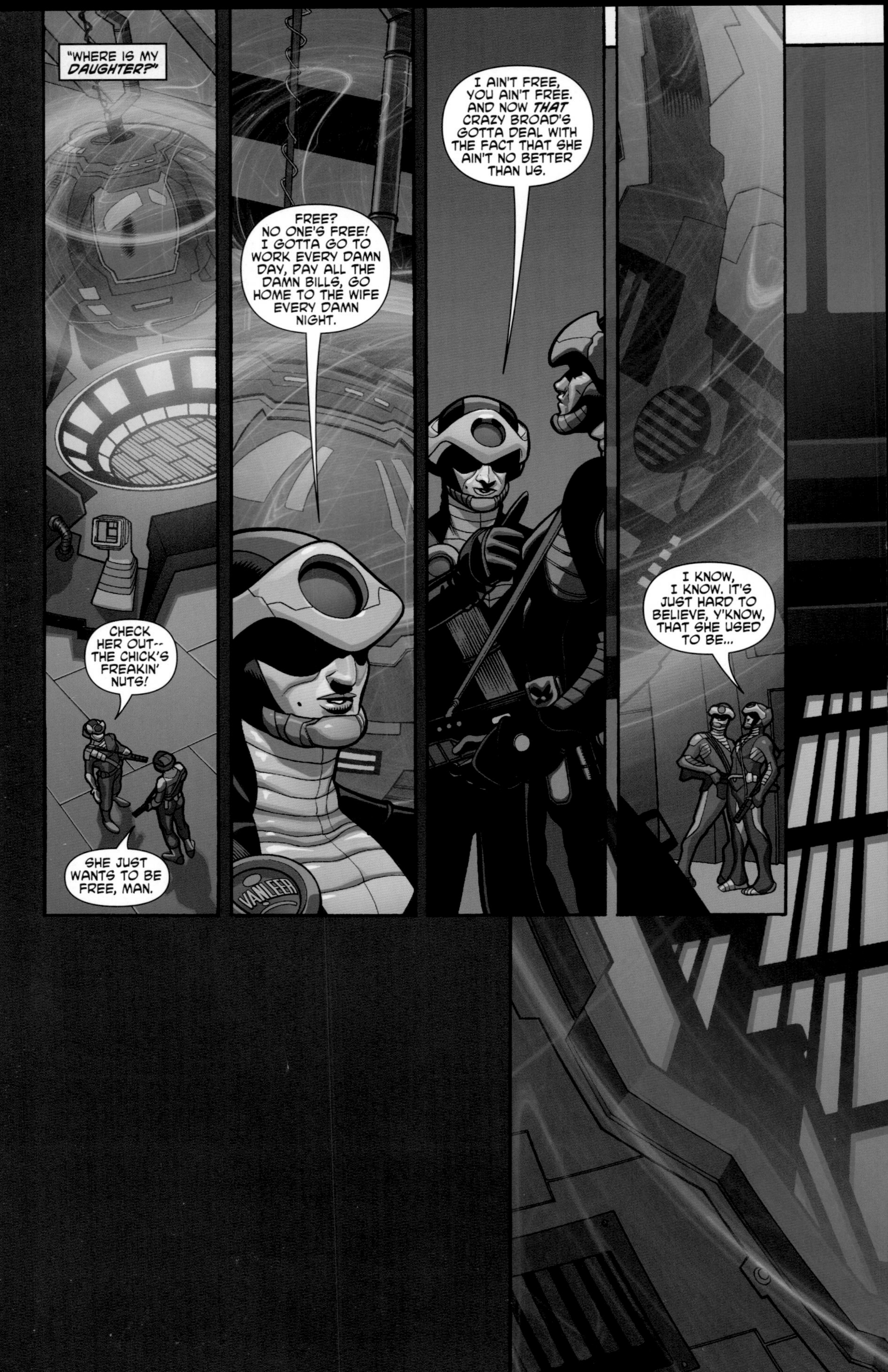
"WHERE IS MY DAUGHTER?"
CHECK HER OUT-- THE CHICK'S FREAKIN' NUTS!
SHE JUST WANTS TO BE FREE, MAN.
FREE? NO ONE'S FREE! I GOTTA GO TO WORK EVERY DAMN DAY, PAY ALL THE DAMN BILLS, GO HOME TO THE WIFE EVERY DAMN NIGHT.
VANLEER
I AIN'T FREE, YOU AIN'T FREE. AND NOW THAT CRAZY BROAD'S GOTTA DEAL WITH THE FACT THAT SHE AIN'T NO BETTER THAN US.
I KNOW, I KNOW. IT'S JUST HARD TO BELIEVE, Y'KNOW, THAT SHE USED TO BE...

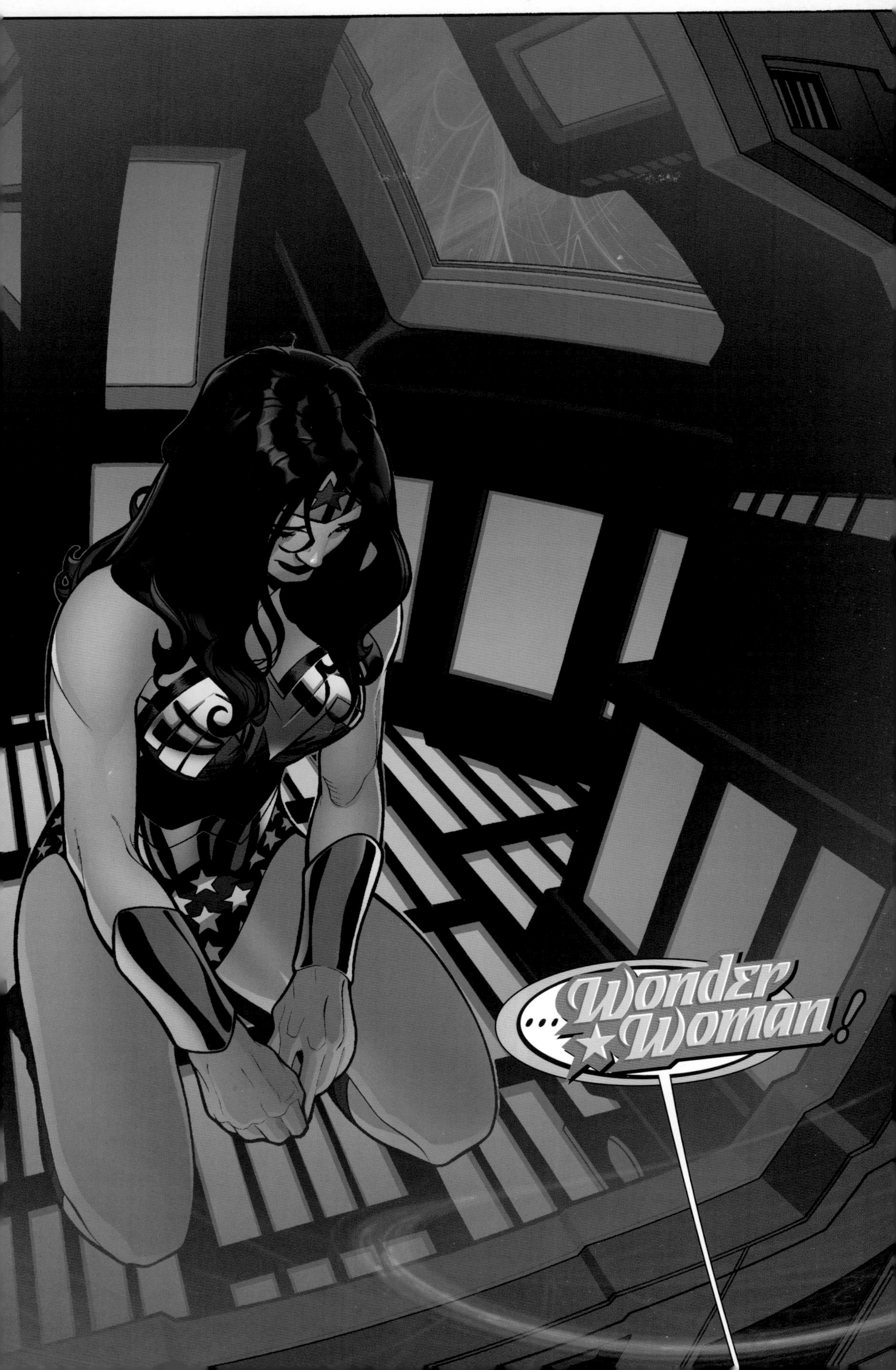
...Wonder Woman!

BY THE GODS!

QUEEN MOTHER, YOU'RE ALIVE!

IT'S A BLESSING...

BUT HOW?

MY DAUGHTER!

IS IN GRAVE DANGER. YOU *ALL* ARE.

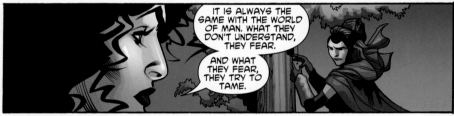

WHY WOULD YOU DO THIS FOR US?

BECAUSE THE ENEMY OF MY ENEMY IS MY FRIEND.

MY QUEEN, YOU NEED TO SEE THIS.

IT IS ALWAYS THE SAME WITH THE WORLD OF MAN. WHAT THEY DON'T UNDERSTAND, THEY FEAR.

AND WHAT THEY FEAR, THEY TRY TO TAME.

TO THEM, MY DAUGHTER IS THE ENEMY...

AND ENEMIES MUST BE CRUSHED.

IF IT IS WAR THAT THEY WANT...

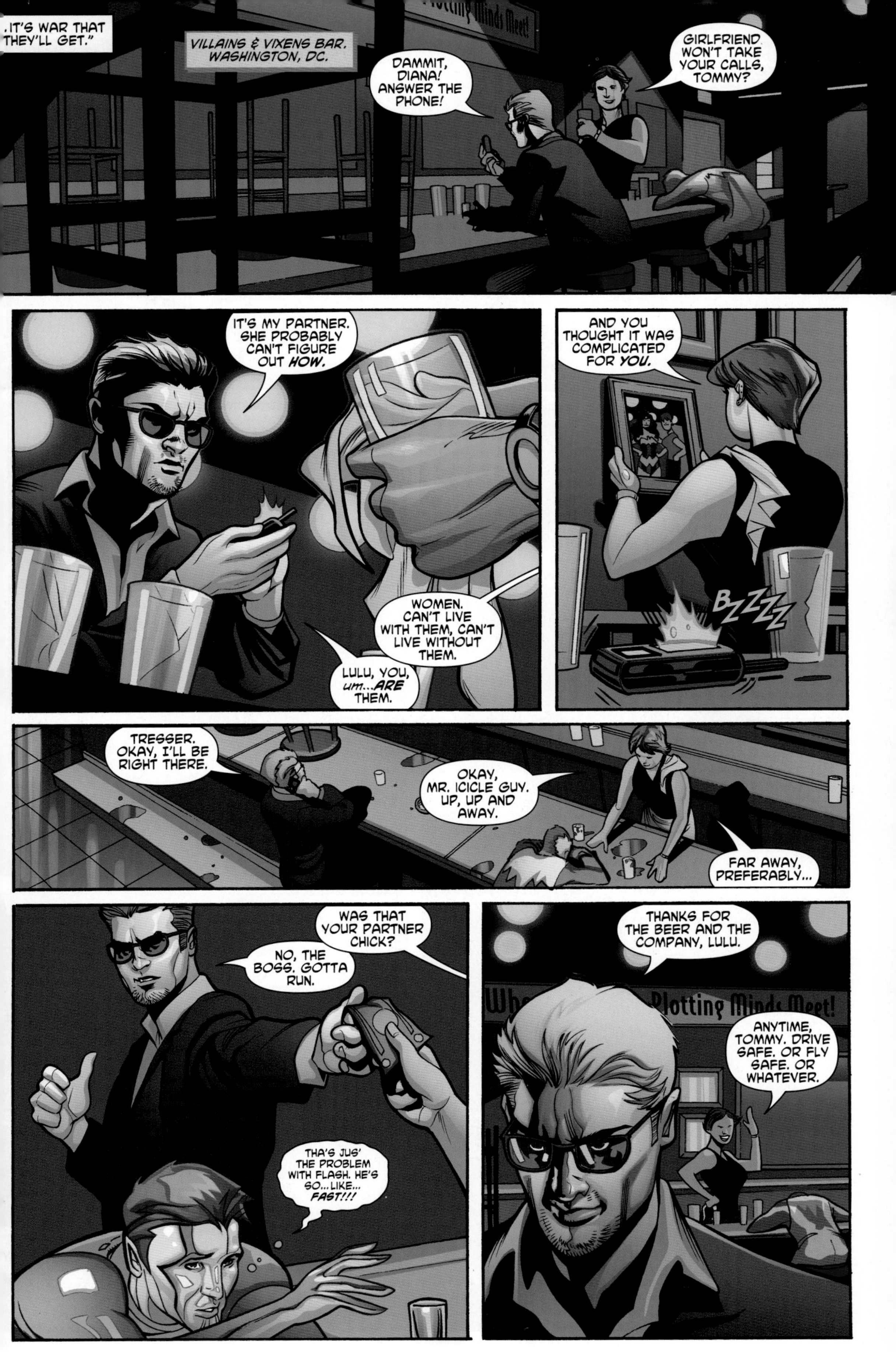

...IT'S WAR THAT THEY'LL GET."
VILLAINS & VIXENS BAR. WASHINGTON, DC.
Plotting Minds Meet!
DAMMIT, DIANA! ANSWER THE PHONE!
GIRLFRIEND WON'T TAKE YOUR CALLS, TOMMY?
IT'S MY PARTNER. SHE PROBABLY CAN'T FIGURE OUT HOW.
AND YOU THOUGHT IT WAS COMPLICATED FOR YOU.
WOMEN. CAN'T LIVE WITH THEM, CAN'T LIVE WITHOUT THEM.
LULU, YOU, um...ARE THEM.
BZZZZ
TRESSER. OKAY, I'LL BE RIGHT THERE.
OKAY, MR. ICICLE GUY. UP, UP AND AWAY.
FAR AWAY, PREFERABLY...
WAS THAT YOUR PARTNER CHICK?
NO, THE BOSS. GOTTA RUN.
THA'S JUS' THE PROBLEM WITH FLASH. HE'S SO...LIKE... FAST!!!
THANKS FOR THE BEER AND THE COMPANY, LULU.
Plotting Minds Meet!
ANYTIME, TOMMY. DRIVE SAFE. OR FLY SAFE. OR WHATEVER.

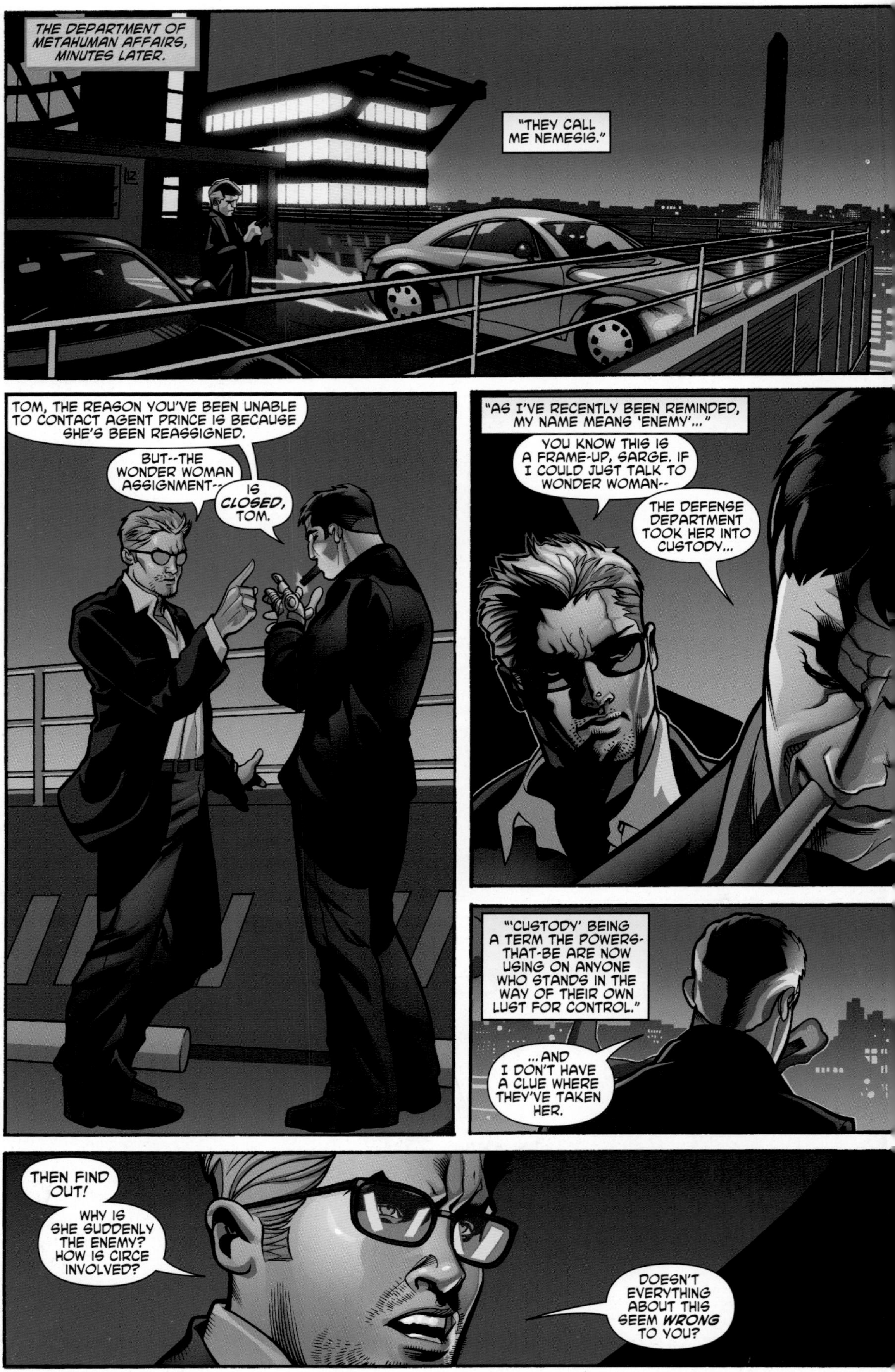
THE DEPARTMENT OF METAHUMAN AFFAIRS, MINUTES LATER.
"THEY CALL ME NEMESIS."
TOM, THE REASON YOU'VE BEEN UNABLE TO CONTACT AGENT PRINCE IS BECAUSE SHE'S BEEN REASSIGNED.
BUT--THE WONDER WOMAN ASSIGNMENT--
IS *CLOSED,* TOM.
"AS I'VE RECENTLY BEEN REMINDED, MY NAME MEANS 'ENEMY'..."
YOU KNOW THIS IS A FRAME-UP, SARGE. IF I COULD JUST TALK TO WONDER WOMAN--
THE DEFENSE DEPARTMENT TOOK HER INTO CUSTODY...
"'CUSTODY' BEING A TERM THE POWERS-THAT-BE ARE NOW USING ON ANYONE WHO STANDS IN THE WAY OF THEIR OWN LUST FOR CONTROL."
...AND I DON'T HAVE A CLUE WHERE THEY'VE TAKEN HER.
THEN FIND OUT!
WHY IS SHE SUDDENLY THE ENEMY? HOW IS CIRCE INVOLVED?
DOESN'T EVERYTHING ABOUT THIS SEEM *WRONG* TO YOU?

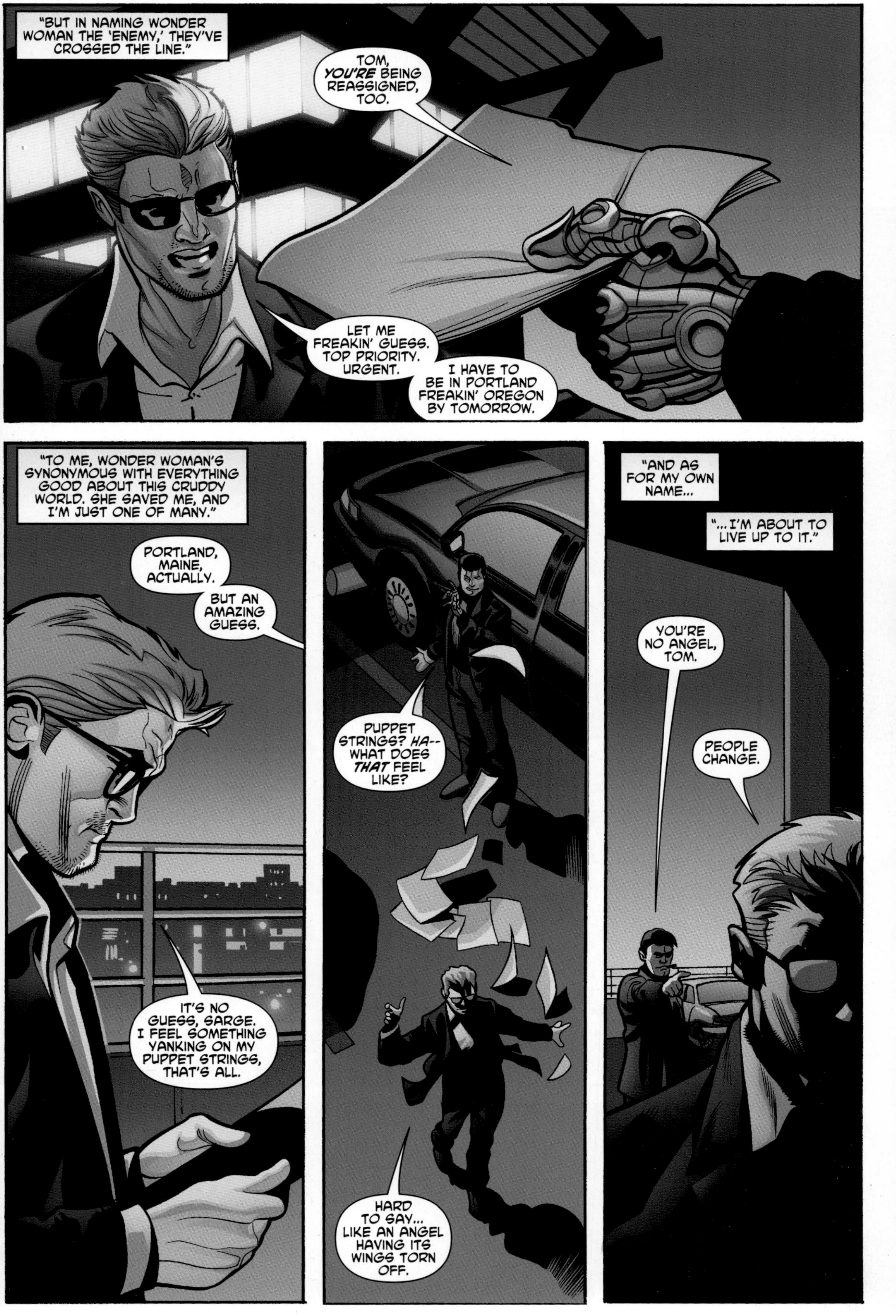
"BUT IN NAMING WONDER WOMAN THE 'ENEMY,' THEY'VE CROSSED THE LINE."
TOM, *YOU'RE* BEING REASSIGNED, TOO.
LET ME FREAKIN' GUESS. TOP PRIORITY. URGENT.
I HAVE TO BE IN PORTLAND FREAKIN' OREGON BY TOMORROW.
"TO ME, WONDER WOMAN'S SYNONYMOUS WITH EVERYTHING GOOD ABOUT THIS CRUDDY WORLD. SHE SAVED ME, AND I'M JUST ONE OF MANY."
PORTLAND, MAINE, ACTUALLY.
BUT AN AMAZING GUESS.
IT'S NO GUESS, SARGE. I FEEL SOMETHING YANKING ON MY PUPPET STRINGS, THAT'S ALL.
PUPPET STRINGS? *HA--* WHAT DOES *THAT* FEEL LIKE?
HARD TO SAY... LIKE AN ANGEL HAVING ITS WINGS TORN OFF.
"AND AS FOR MY OWN NAME...
"...I'M ABOUT TO LIVE UP TO IT."
YOU'RE NO ANGEL, TOM.
PEOPLE CHANGE.

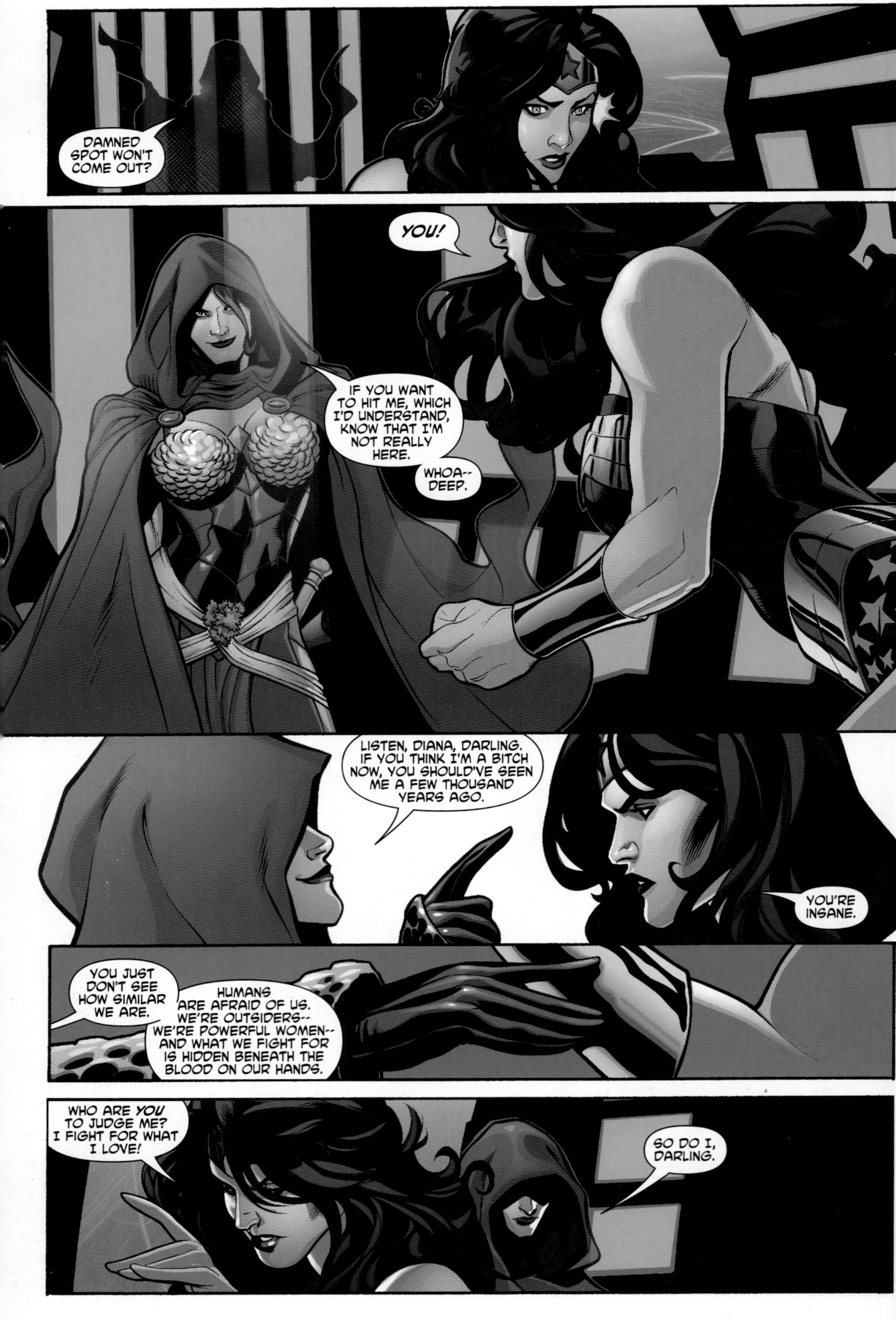
DAMNED SPOT WON'T COME OUT?
YOU!
IF YOU WANT TO HIT ME, WHICH I'D UNDERSTAND, KNOW THAT I'M NOT REALLY HERE.
WHOA-- DEEP.
LISTEN, DIANA, DARLING. IF YOU THINK I'M A BITCH NOW, YOU SHOULD'VE SEEN ME A FEW THOUSAND YEARS AGO.
YOU'RE INSANE.
YOU JUST DON'T SEE HOW SIMILAR WE ARE.
HUMANS ARE AFRAID OF US. WE'RE OUTSIDERS-- WE'RE POWERFUL WOMEN-- AND WHAT WE FIGHT FOR IS HIDDEN BENEATH THE BLOOD ON OUR HANDS.
WHO ARE *YOU* TO JUDGE ME? I FIGHT FOR WHAT I LOVE!
SO DO I, DARLING.

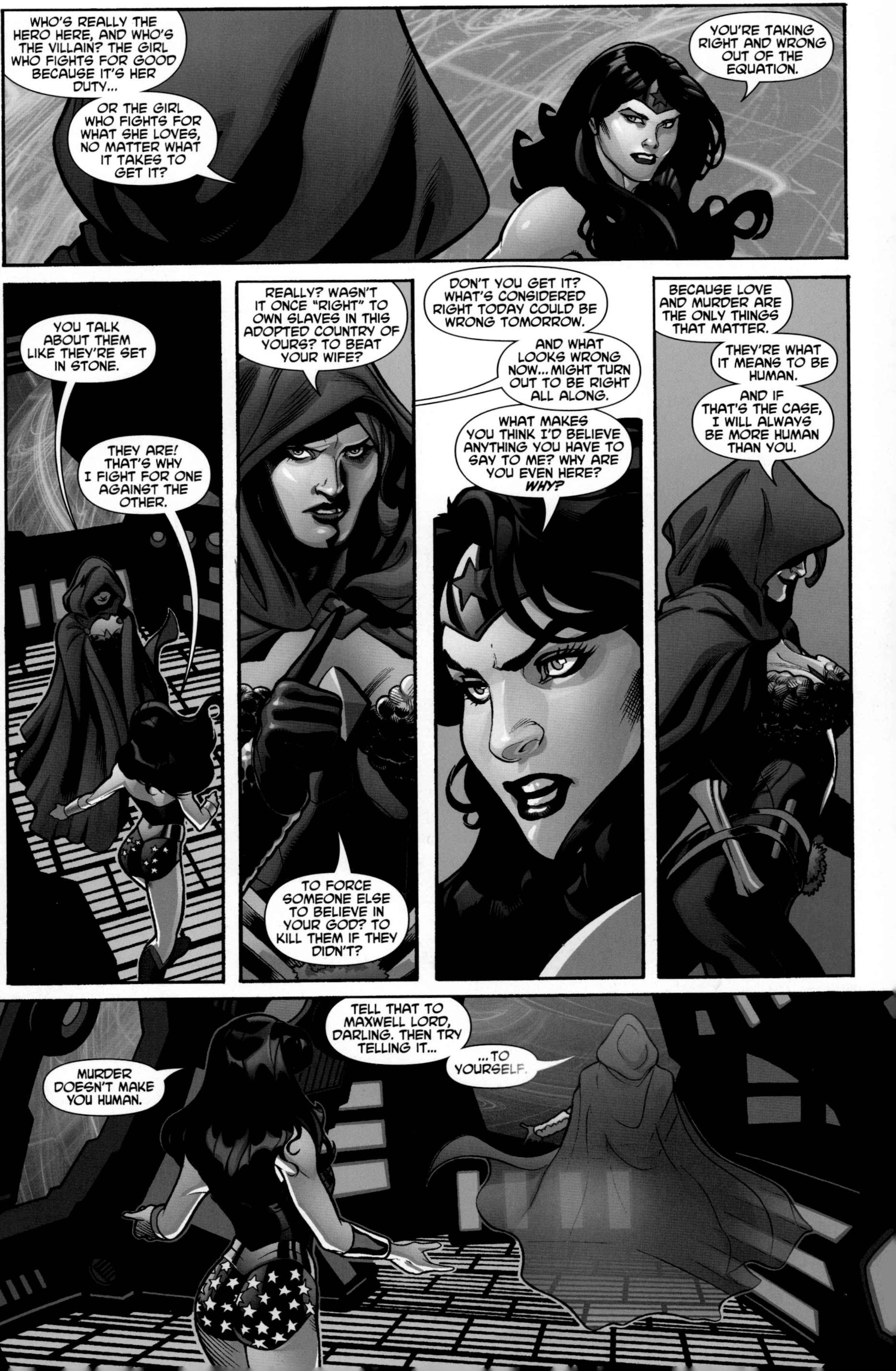
WHO'S REALLY THE HERO HERE, AND WHO'S THE VILLAIN? THE GIRL WHO FIGHTS FOR GOOD BECAUSE IT'S HER DUTY...
OR THE GIRL WHO FIGHTS FOR WHAT SHE LOVES, NO MATTER WHAT IT TAKES TO GET IT?
YOU'RE TAKING RIGHT AND WRONG OUT OF THE EQUATION.
YOU TALK ABOUT THEM LIKE THEY'RE SET IN STONE.
THEY ARE! THAT'S WHY I FIGHT FOR ONE AGAINST THE OTHER.
REALLY? WASN'T IT ONCE "RIGHT" TO OWN SLAVES IN THIS ADOPTED COUNTRY OF YOURS? TO BEAT YOUR WIFE?
TO FORCE SOMEONE ELSE TO BELIEVE IN YOUR GOD? TO KILL THEM IF THEY DIDN'T?
DON'T YOU GET IT? WHAT'S CONSIDERED RIGHT TODAY COULD BE WRONG TOMORROW.
AND WHAT LOOKS WRONG NOW... MIGHT TURN OUT TO BE RIGHT ALL ALONG.
WHAT MAKES YOU THINK I'D BELIEVE ANYTHING YOU HAVE TO SAY TO ME? WHY ARE YOU EVEN HERE? *WHY?*
BECAUSE LOVE AND MURDER ARE THE ONLY THINGS THAT MATTER.
THEY'RE WHAT IT MEANS TO BE HUMAN.
AND IF THAT'S THE CASE, I WILL ALWAYS BE MORE HUMAN THAN YOU.
MURDER DOESN'T MAKE YOU HUMAN.
TELL THAT TO MAXWELL LORD, DARLING. THEN TRY TELLING IT...
...TO YOURSELF.

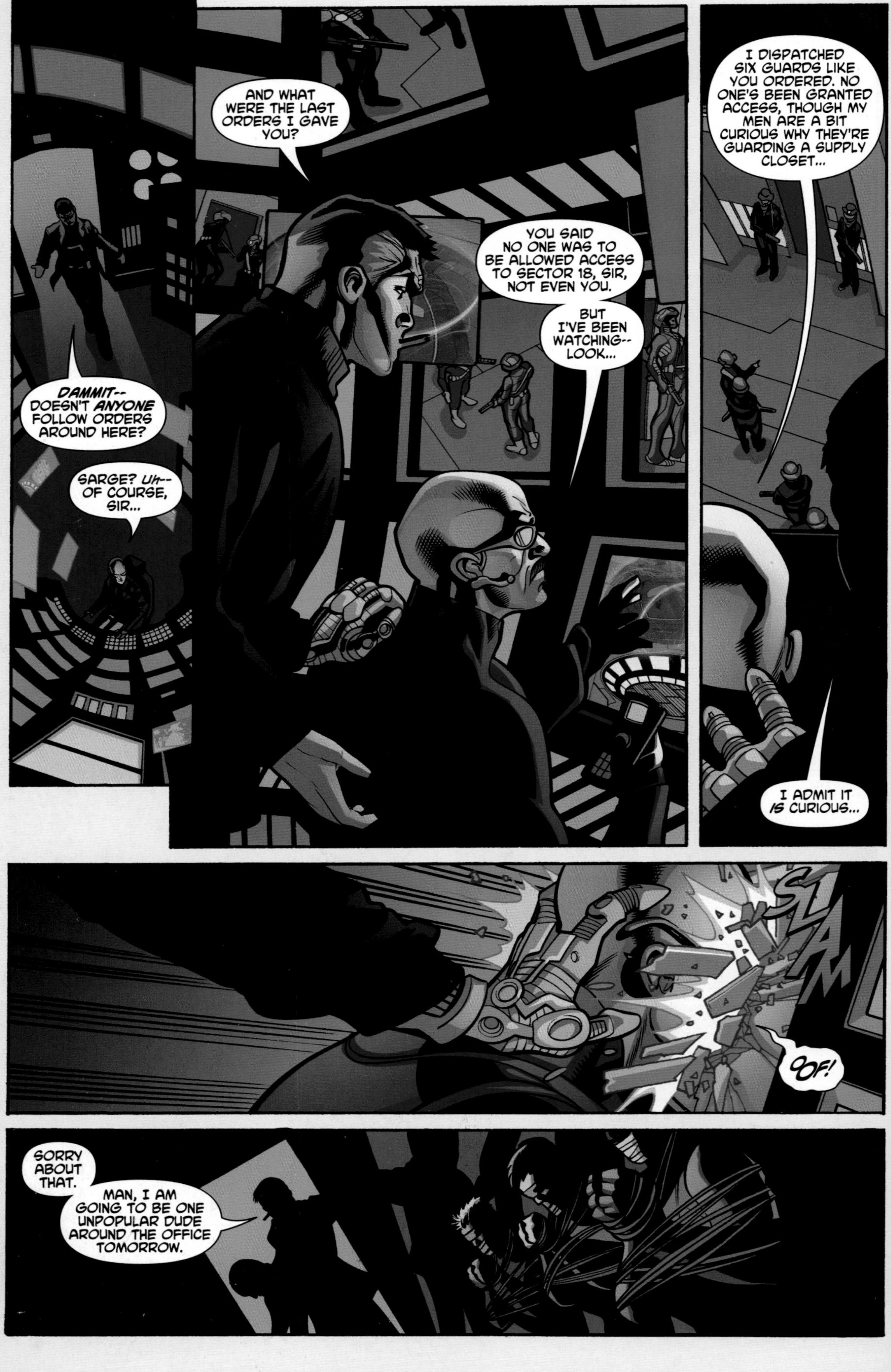
AND WHAT WERE THE LAST ORDERS I GAVE YOU?
YOU SAID NO ONE WAS TO BE ALLOWED ACCESS TO SECTOR 18, SIR, NOT EVEN YOU.
BUT I'VE BEEN WATCHING-- LOOK...
DAMMIT-- DOESN'T ANYONE FOLLOW ORDERS AROUND HERE?
SARGE? UH-- OF COURSE, SIR...
I DISPATCHED SIX GUARDS LIKE YOU ORDERED. NO ONE'S BEEN GRANTED ACCESS, THOUGH MY MEN ARE A BIT CURIOUS WHY THEY'RE GUARDING A SUPPLY CLOSET...
I ADMIT IT IS CURIOUS...
SLAM
OOF!
SORRY ABOUT THAT.
MAN, I AM GOING TO BE ONE UNPOPULAR DUDE AROUND THE OFFICE TOMORROW.

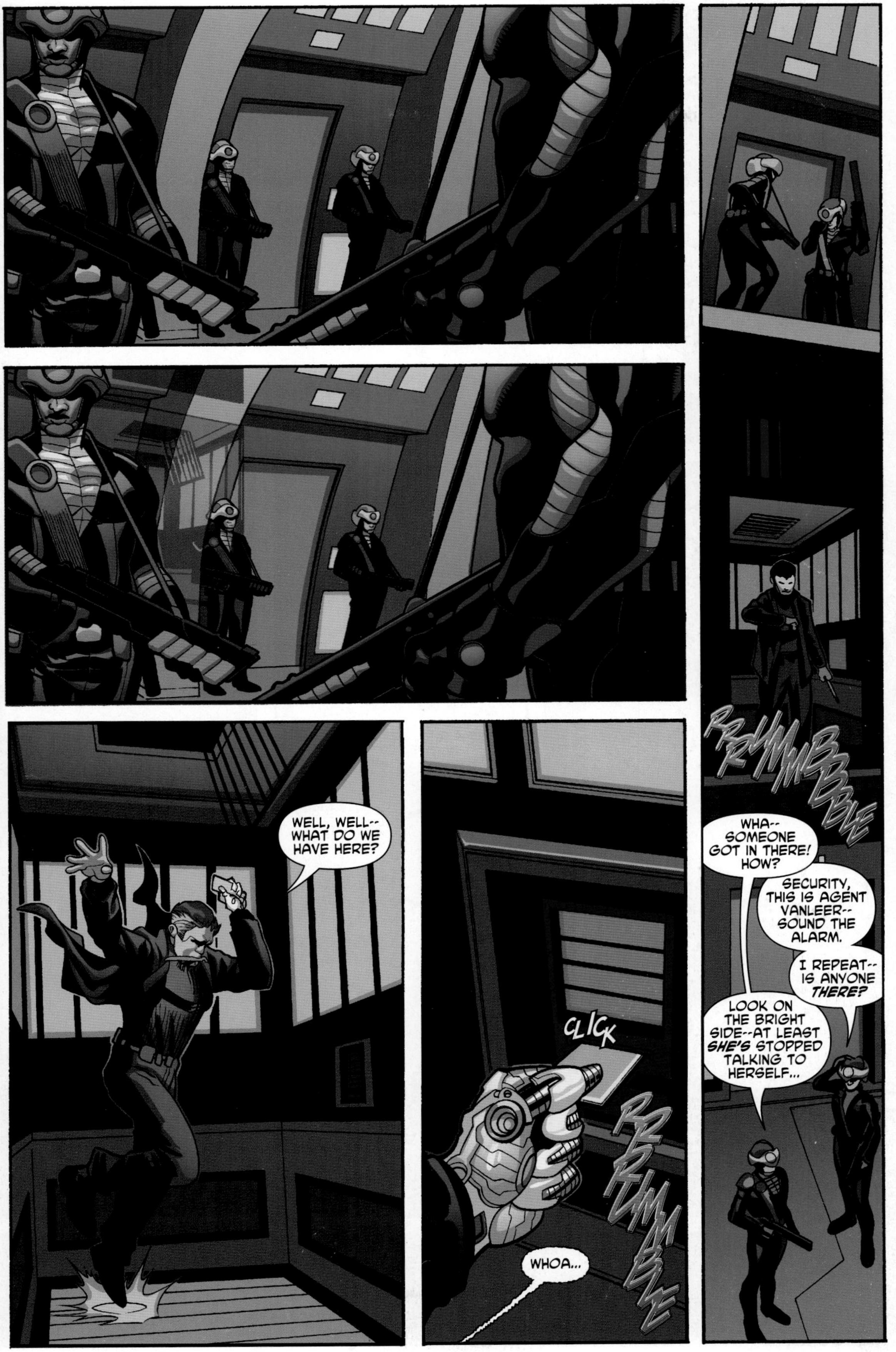
WELL, WELL--
WHAT DO WE
HAVE HERE?
CLICK
RRRUMMBBLE
WHOA...
RRRUMMBBLE
WHA--
SOMEONE
GOT IN THERE!
HOW?
SECURITY,
THIS IS AGENT
VANLEER--
SOUND THE
ALARM.
I REPEAT--
IS ANYONE
THERE?
LOOK ON
THE BRIGHT
SIDE--AT LEAST
SHE'S STOPPED
TALKING TO
HERSELF...

SARGE? WHERE DID YOU--ER...

NO ONE'S ALLOWED ACCESS HERE, SIR, NOT EVEN YOU. I'M SORRY, BUT YOU SAID SO YOURSELF, SIR.

THAT'S PRETTY DUMB, GENTLEMEN. IF I HAVE THE AUTHORITY TO ORDER YOU TO DENY ME ACCESS, I ALSO HAVE THE AUTHORITY TO DENY MY PREVIOUS ORDER TO DENY ME ACCESS.

UM...COULD YOU REPEAT THAT, SIR?

WELL, DO YOU REALLY THINK I WOULD ISSUE SUCH AN IDIOTIC ORDER?

WELL, NO, SIR--BUT YOU TOLD US IN PERSON--

THWONK

STEEL? WHAT DO YOU WANT FROM ME NOW?

CLICK

AAROOOGA

THE ALARMS! CRAP!

YOU'D BETTER BE PREPARED TO KILL ME, BECAUSE I WON'T TELL YOU ANYTHING WHILE THERE'S STILL BREATH LEFT IN MY BODY!

I'D BACK OFF IF I WERE YOU...

GO TO HELL!

NO, I MEAN IT. BACK OFF, WONDER WOMAN.

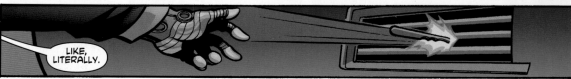

LIKE, LITERALLY.

AAAROOGA

BOOM

I HAVE NOTHING TO SAY TO YOU.

WELL, THEN...

KLIK

...HOW ABOUT ME?

I HAVE NOTHING TO SAY TO YOU, EITHER. THE LAST TIME I SAW YOU I WAS BEING CAPTURED, AND SARGE WAS PATTING YOU ON THE BACK FOR DOING A GOOD JOB.

I HAVE NO REASON TO TRUST YOU, AGENT TRESSER.

I'M HURT. IT WASN'T EXACTLY A CAKE-WALK GETTING IN HERE.

BOUND TO COST ME MY JOB. BEST DENTAL PLAN I'VE EVER HAD.

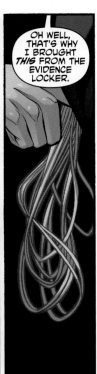

OH WELL, THAT'S WHY I BROUGHT THIS FROM THE EVIDENCE LOCKER.

IT'S A MAGIC LASSO, RIGHT? I'M COMPELLED TO TELL YOU THE TRUTH. SO GO ON--ASK IF YOU CAN TRUST ME.

THAT'S EXACTLY WHAT I'LL DO...

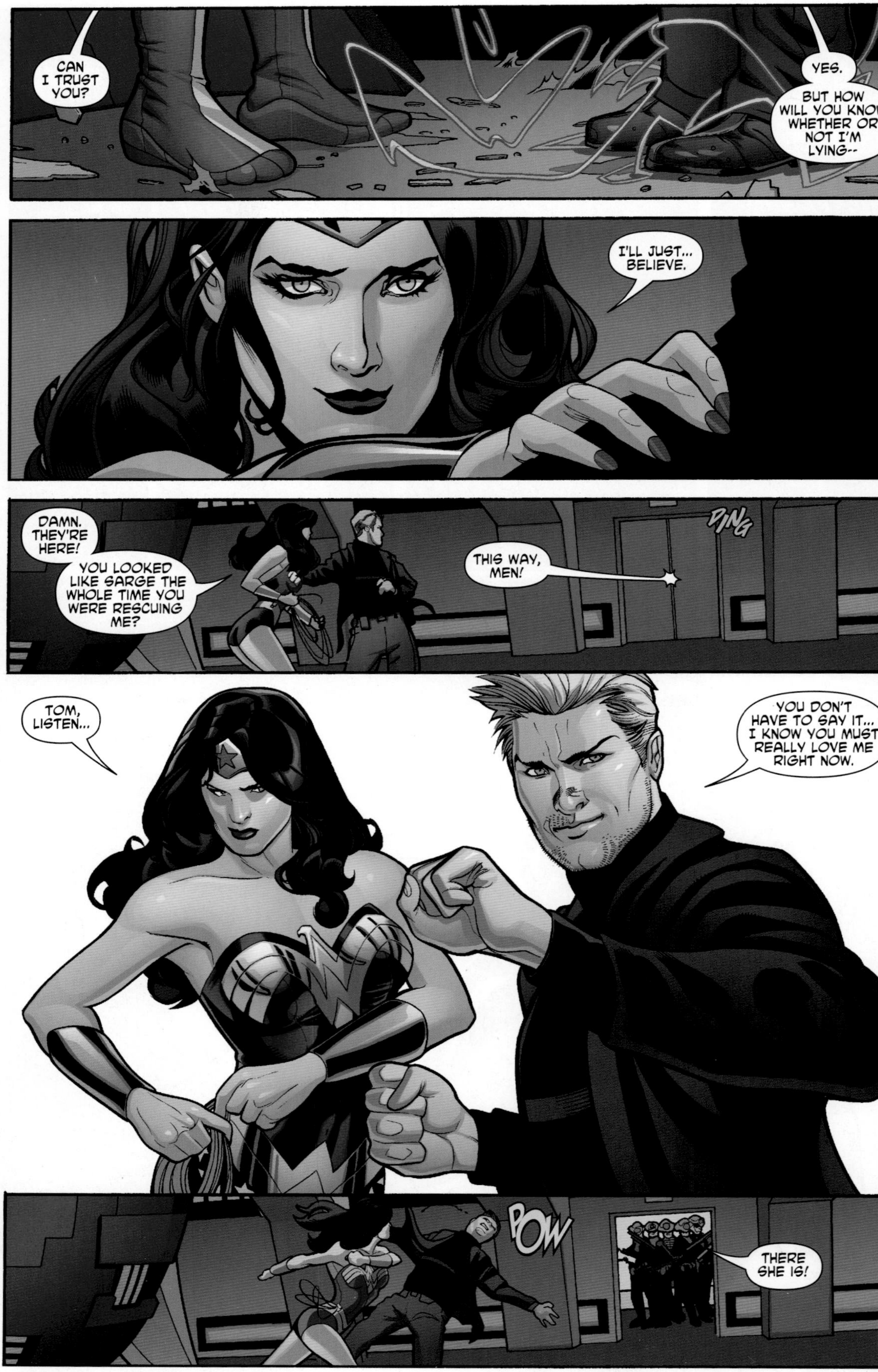
CAN I TRUST YOU?
YES.
BUT HOW WILL YOU KNOW WHETHER OR NOT I'M LYING--
I'LL JUST... BELIEVE.
DING
DAMN. THEY'RE HERE!
YOU LOOKED LIKE SARGE THE WHOLE TIME YOU WERE RESCUING ME?
THIS WAY, MEN!
TOM, LISTEN...
YOU DON'T HAVE TO SAY IT... I KNOW YOU MUST REALLY LOVE ME RIGHT NOW.
POW
THERE SHE IS!

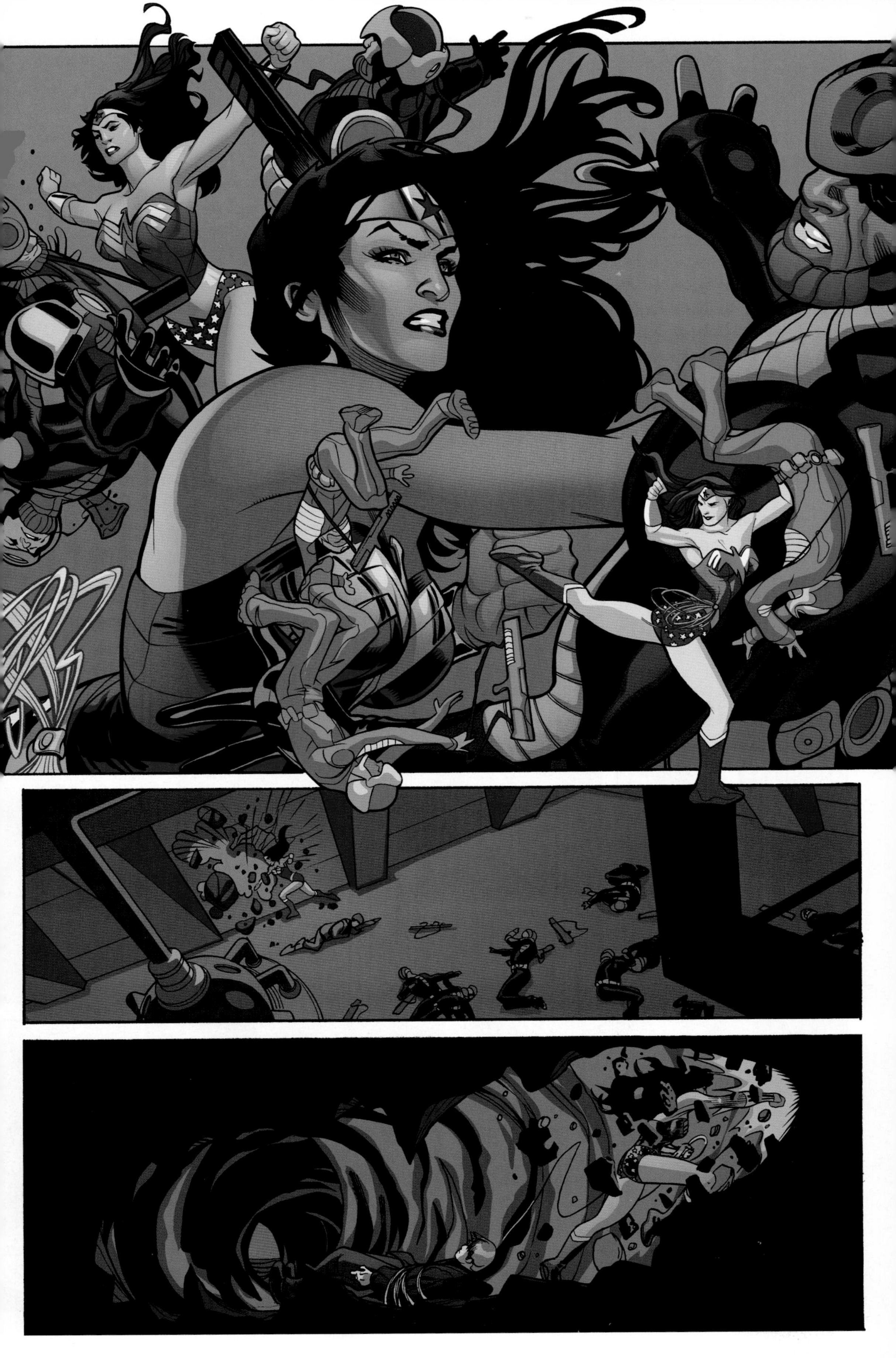

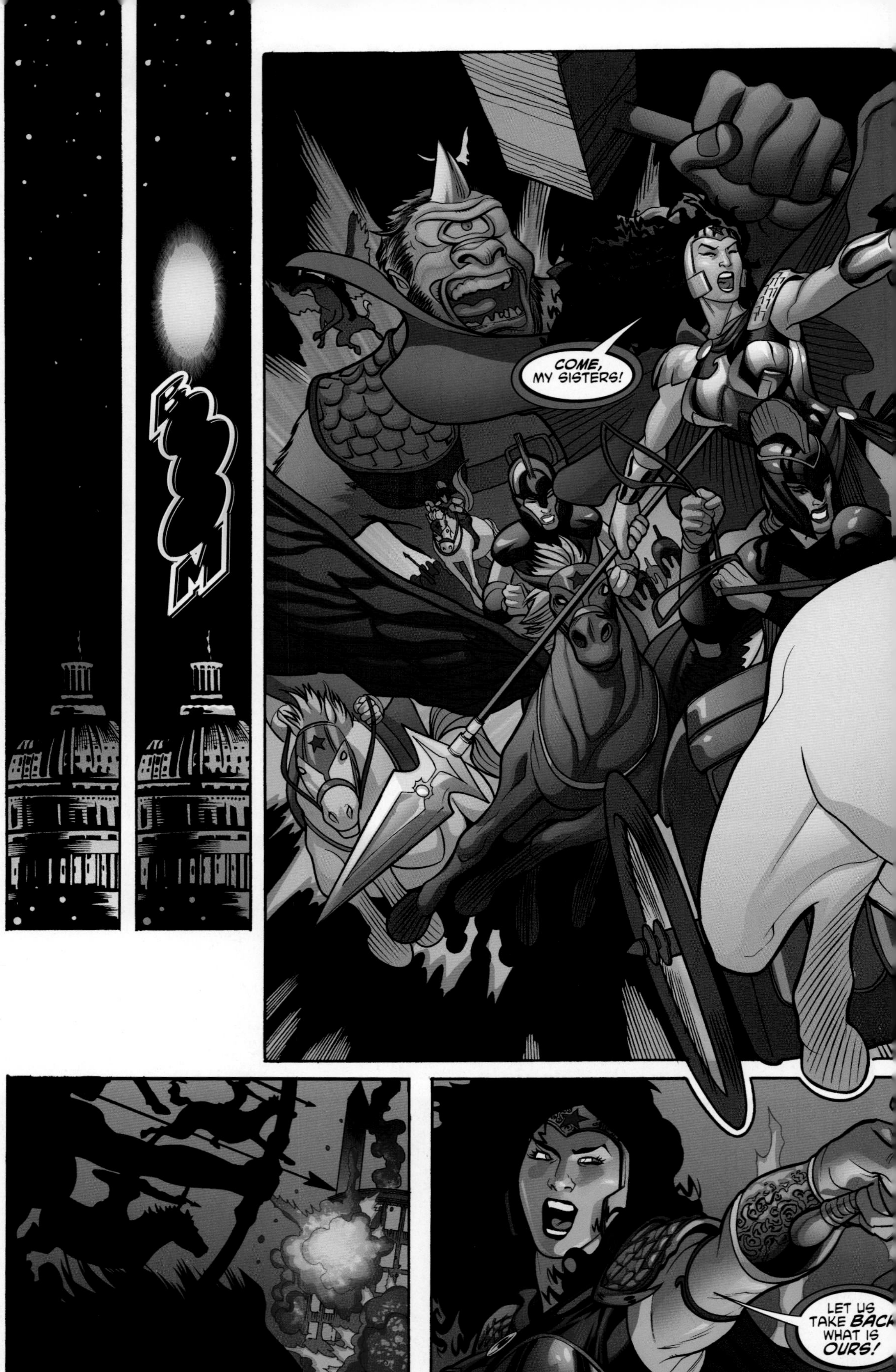
COME, MY SISTERS!
LET US TAKE BACK WHAT IS OURS!

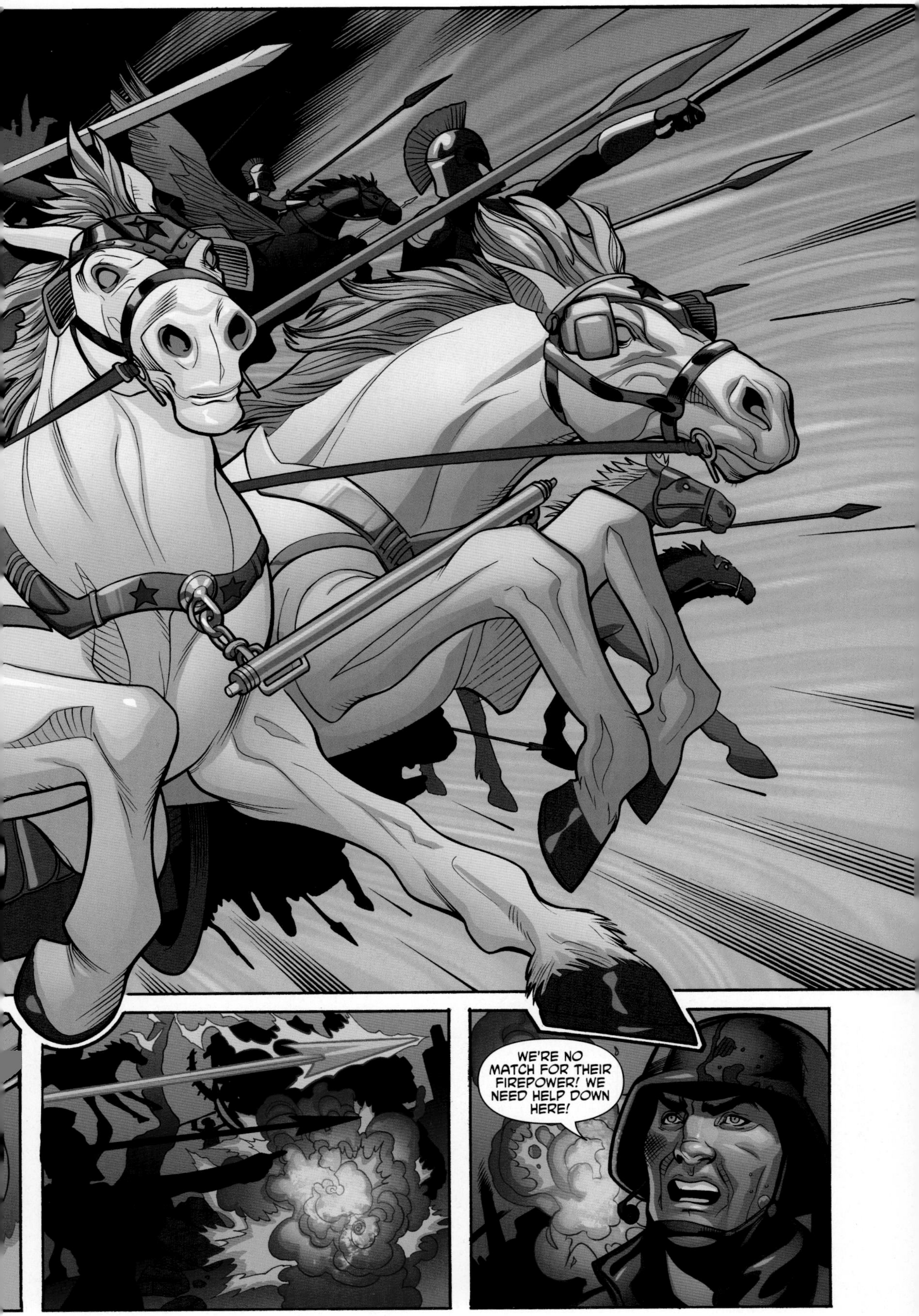
WE'RE NO MATCH FOR THEIR FIREPOWER! WE NEED HELP DOWN HERE!

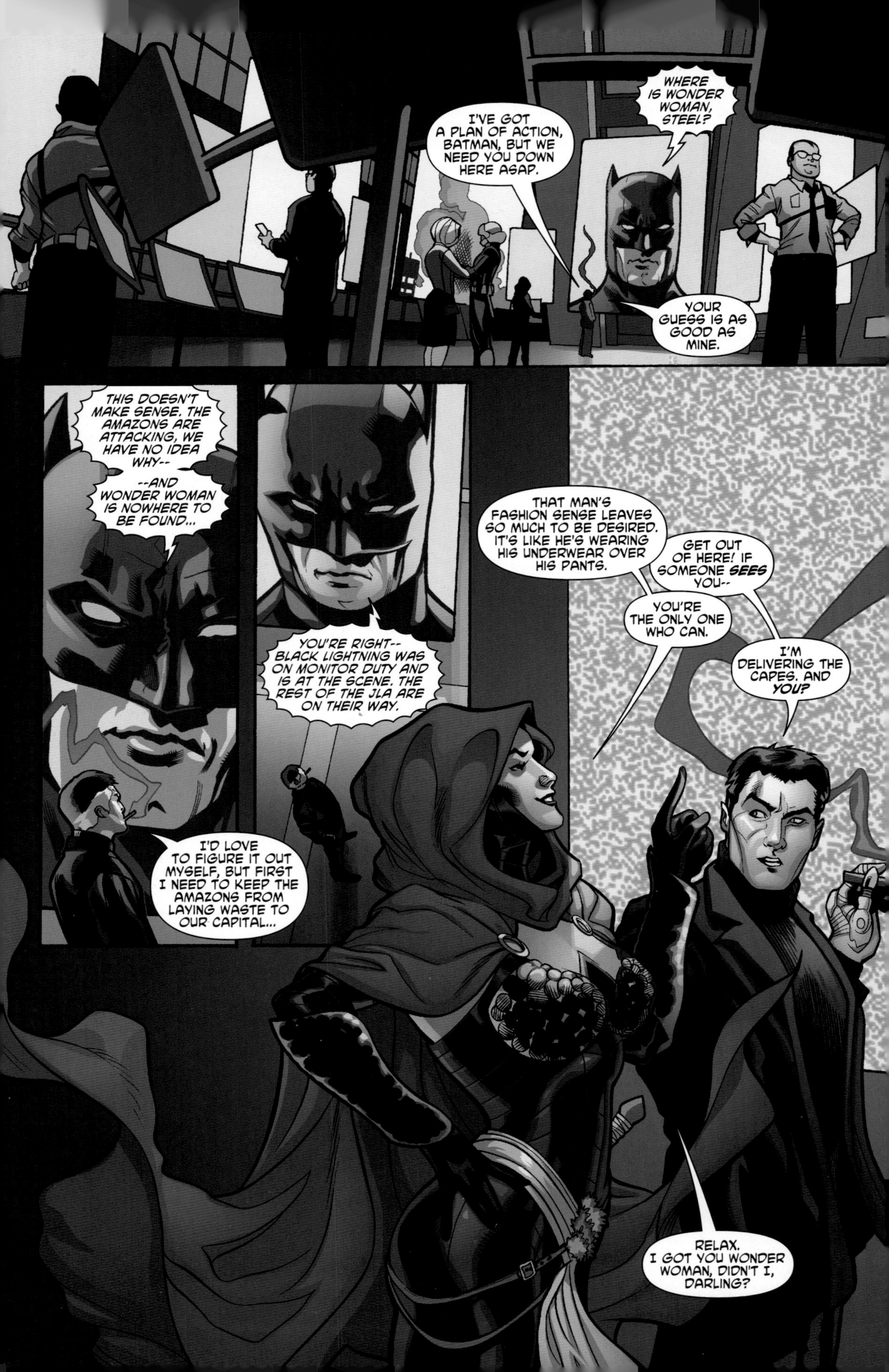
I'VE GOT A PLAN OF ACTION, BATMAN, BUT WE NEED YOU DOWN HERE ASAP.
WHERE IS WONDER WOMAN, STEEL?
YOUR GUESS IS AS GOOD AS MINE.
THIS DOESN'T MAKE SENSE. THE AMAZONS ARE ATTACKING, WE HAVE NO IDEA WHY--
--AND WONDER WOMAN IS NOWHERE TO BE FOUND...
YOU'RE RIGHT-- BLACK LIGHTNING WAS ON MONITOR DUTY AND IS AT THE SCENE. THE REST OF THE JLA ARE ON THEIR WAY.
I'D LOVE TO FIGURE IT OUT MYSELF, BUT FIRST I NEED TO KEEP THE AMAZONS FROM LAYING WASTE TO OUR CAPITAL...
THAT MAN'S FASHION SENSE LEAVES SO MUCH TO BE DESIRED. IT'S LIKE HE'S WEARING HIS UNDERWEAR OVER HIS PANTS.
GET OUT OF HERE! IF SOMEONE SEES YOU--
YOU'RE THE ONLY ONE WHO CAN.
I'M DELIVERING THE CAPES. AND YOU?
RELAX. I GOT YOU WONDER WOMAN, DIDN'T I, DARLING?

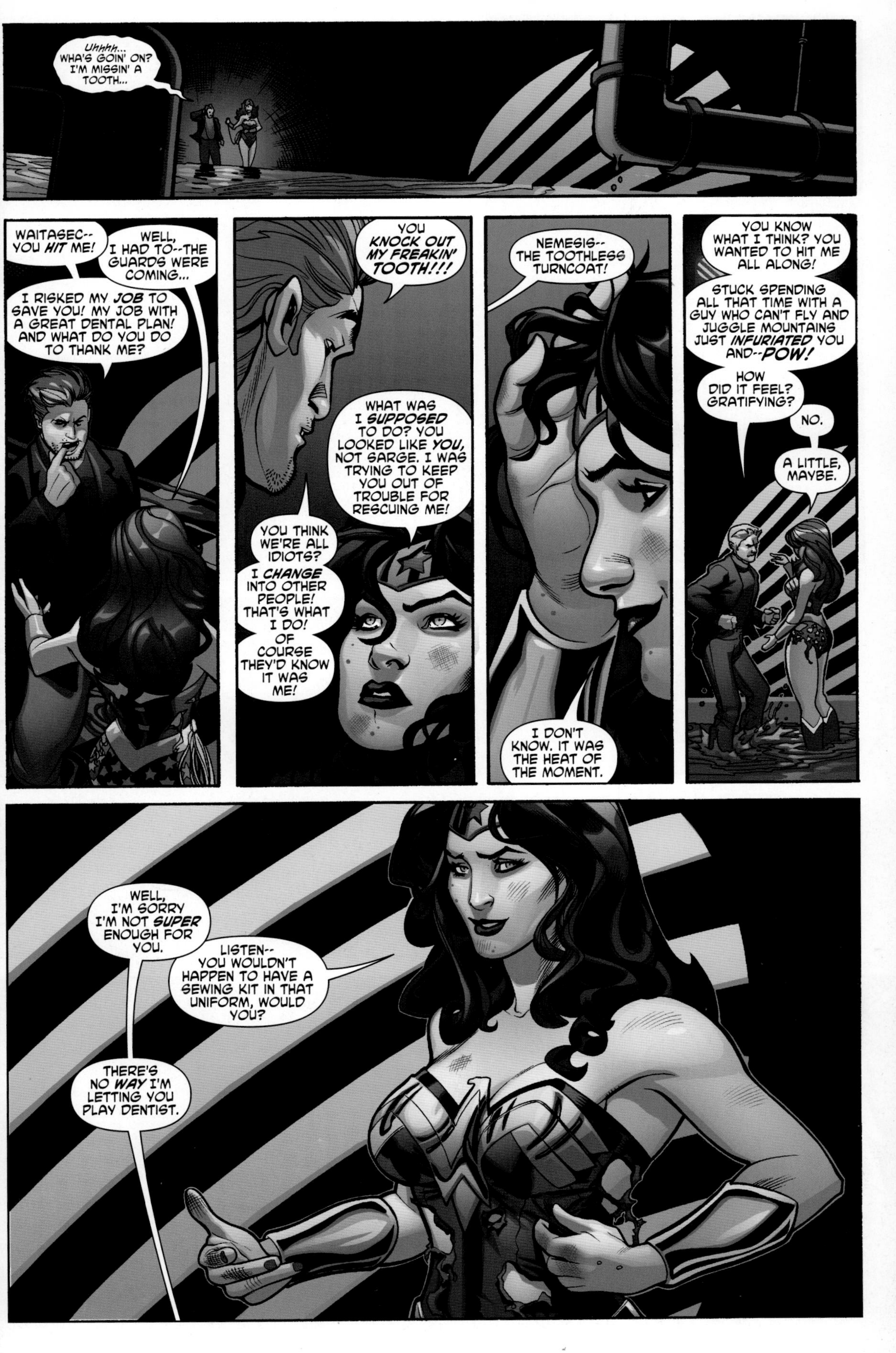
Uhhhh... WHA'S GOIN' ON? I'M MISSIN' A TOOTH...
WAITASEC-- YOU HIT ME!
WELL, I HAD TO--THE GUARDS WERE COMING...
I RISKED MY JOB TO SAVE YOU! MY JOB WITH A GREAT DENTAL PLAN! AND WHAT DO YOU DO TO THANK ME?
YOU KNOCK OUT MY FREAKIN' TOOTH!!!
WHAT WAS I SUPPOSED TO DO? YOU LOOKED LIKE YOU, NOT SARGE. I WAS TRYING TO KEEP YOU OUT OF TROUBLE FOR RESCUING ME!
YOU THINK WE'RE ALL IDIOTS? I CHANGE INTO OTHER PEOPLE! THAT'S WHAT I DO! OF COURSE THEY'D KNOW IT WAS ME!
NEMESIS-- THE TOOTHLESS TURNCOAT!
I DON'T KNOW. IT WAS THE HEAT OF THE MOMENT.
YOU KNOW WHAT I THINK? YOU WANTED TO HIT ME ALL ALONG!
STUCK SPENDING ALL THAT TIME WITH A GUY WHO CAN'T FLY AND JUGGLE MOUNTAINS JUST INFURIATED YOU AND--POW!
HOW DID IT FEEL? GRATIFYING?
NO.
A LITTLE, MAYBE.
WELL, I'M SORRY I'M NOT SUPER ENOUGH FOR YOU.
LISTEN-- YOU WOULDN'T HAPPEN TO HAVE A SEWING KIT IN THAT UNIFORM, WOULD YOU?
THERE'S NO WAY I'M LETTING YOU PLAY DENTIST.

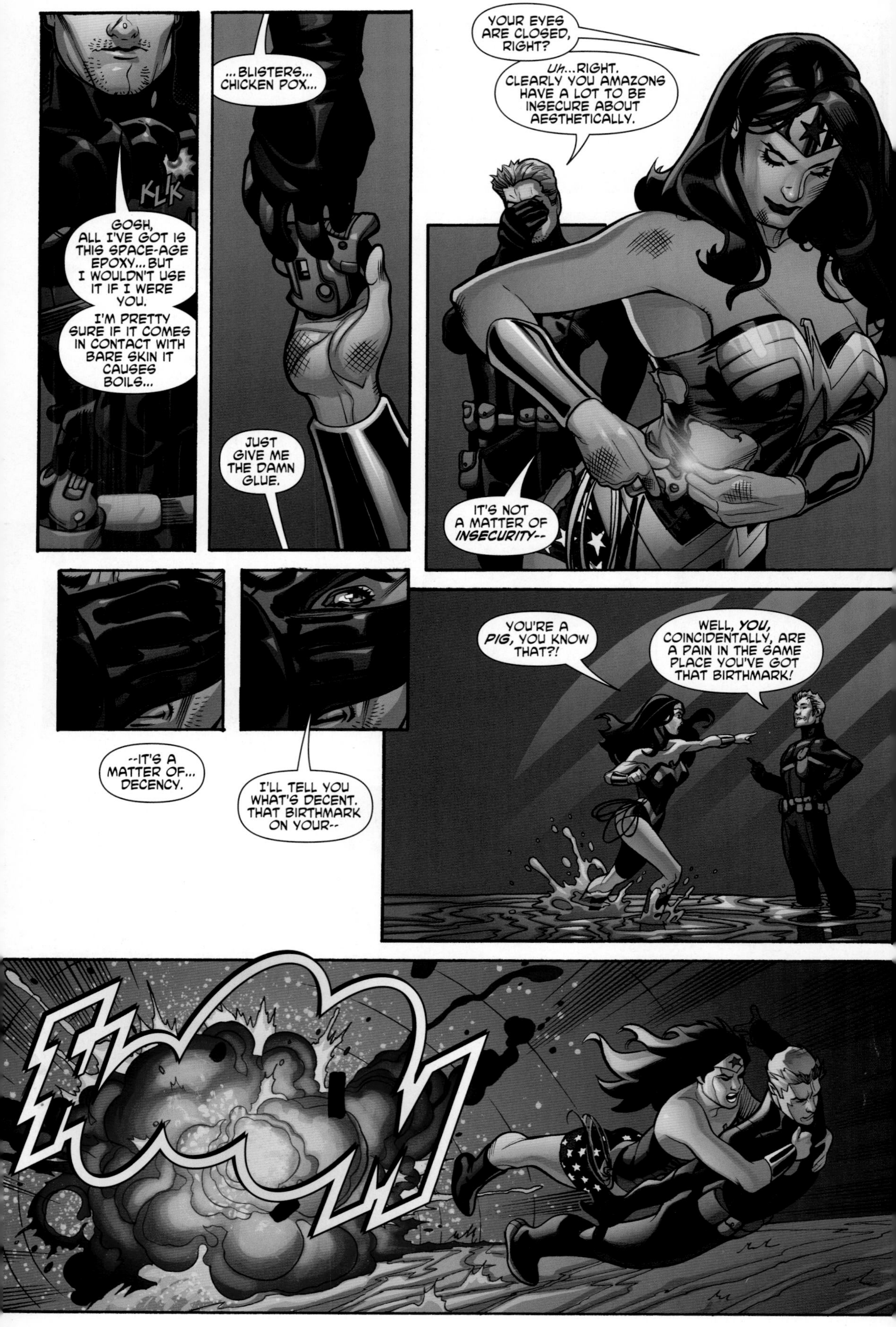
KLIK
GOSH, ALL I'VE GOT IS THIS SPACE-AGE EPOXY...BUT I WOULDN'T USE IT IF I WERE YOU.
I'M PRETTY SURE IF IT COMES IN CONTACT WITH BARE SKIN IT CAUSES BOILS...
...BLISTERS... CHICKEN POX...
JUST GIVE ME THE DAMN GLUE.
YOUR EYES ARE CLOSED, RIGHT?
UH...RIGHT. CLEARLY YOU AMAZONS HAVE A LOT TO BE INSECURE ABOUT AESTHETICALLY.
IT'S NOT A MATTER OF *INSECURITY*--
--IT'S A MATTER OF... DECENCY.
I'LL TELL YOU WHAT'S DECENT. THAT BIRTHMARK ON YOUR--
YOU'RE A *PIG*, YOU KNOW THAT?!
WELL, *YOU*, COINCIDENTALLY, ARE A PAIN IN THE SAME PLACE YOU'VE GOT THAT BIRTHMARK!

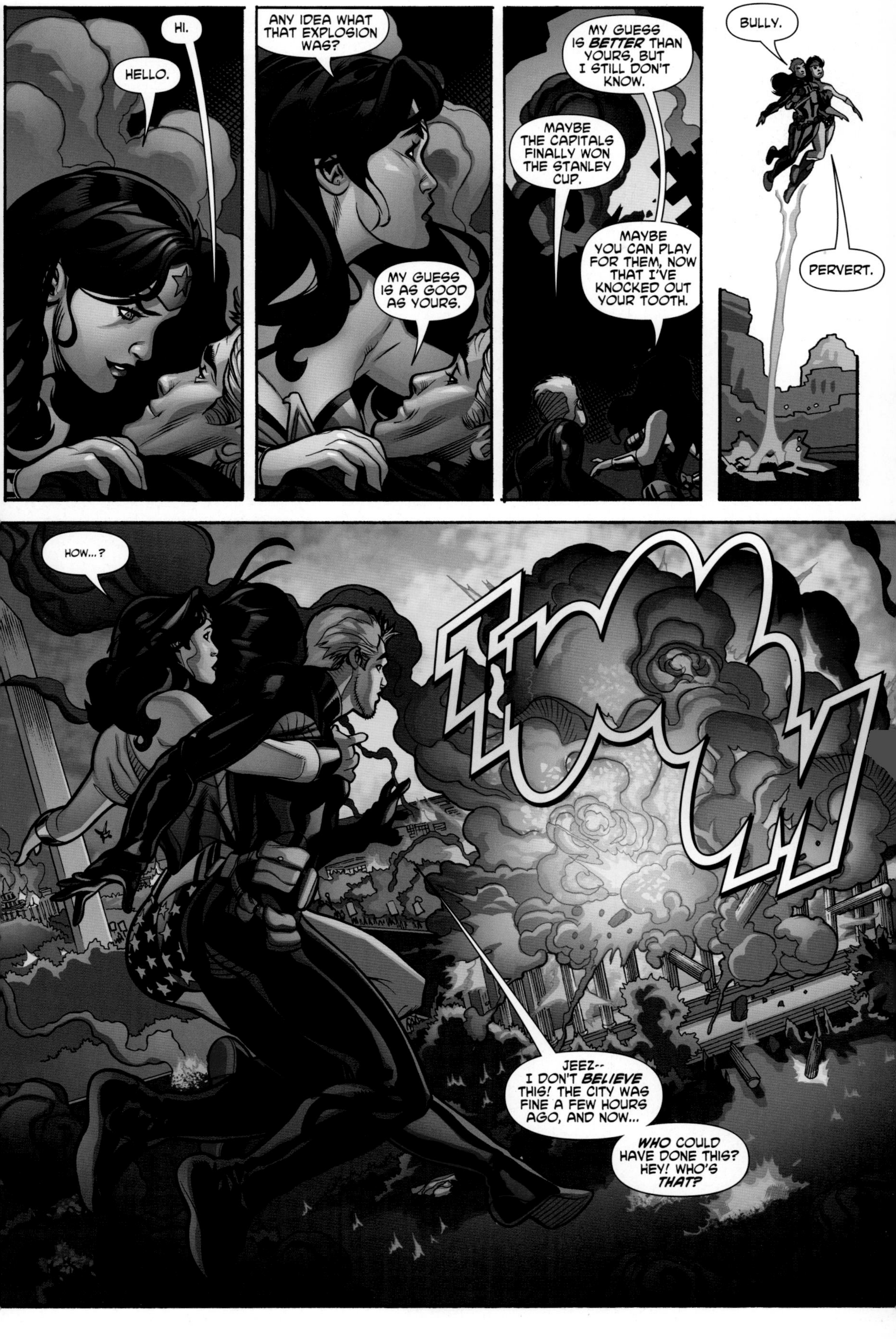
HI.
HELLO.
ANY IDEA WHAT THAT EXPLOSION WAS?
MY GUESS IS AS GOOD AS YOURS.
MY GUESS IS BETTER THAN YOURS, BUT I STILL DON'T KNOW.
MAYBE THE CAPITALS FINALLY WON THE STANLEY CUP.
MAYBE YOU CAN PLAY FOR THEM, NOW THAT I'VE KNOCKED OUT YOUR TOOTH.
BULLY.
PERVERT.
HOW...?
JEEZ-- I DON'T BELIEVE THIS! THE CITY WAS FINE A FEW HOURS AGO, AND NOW...
WHO COULD HAVE DONE THIS? HEY! WHO'S THAT?

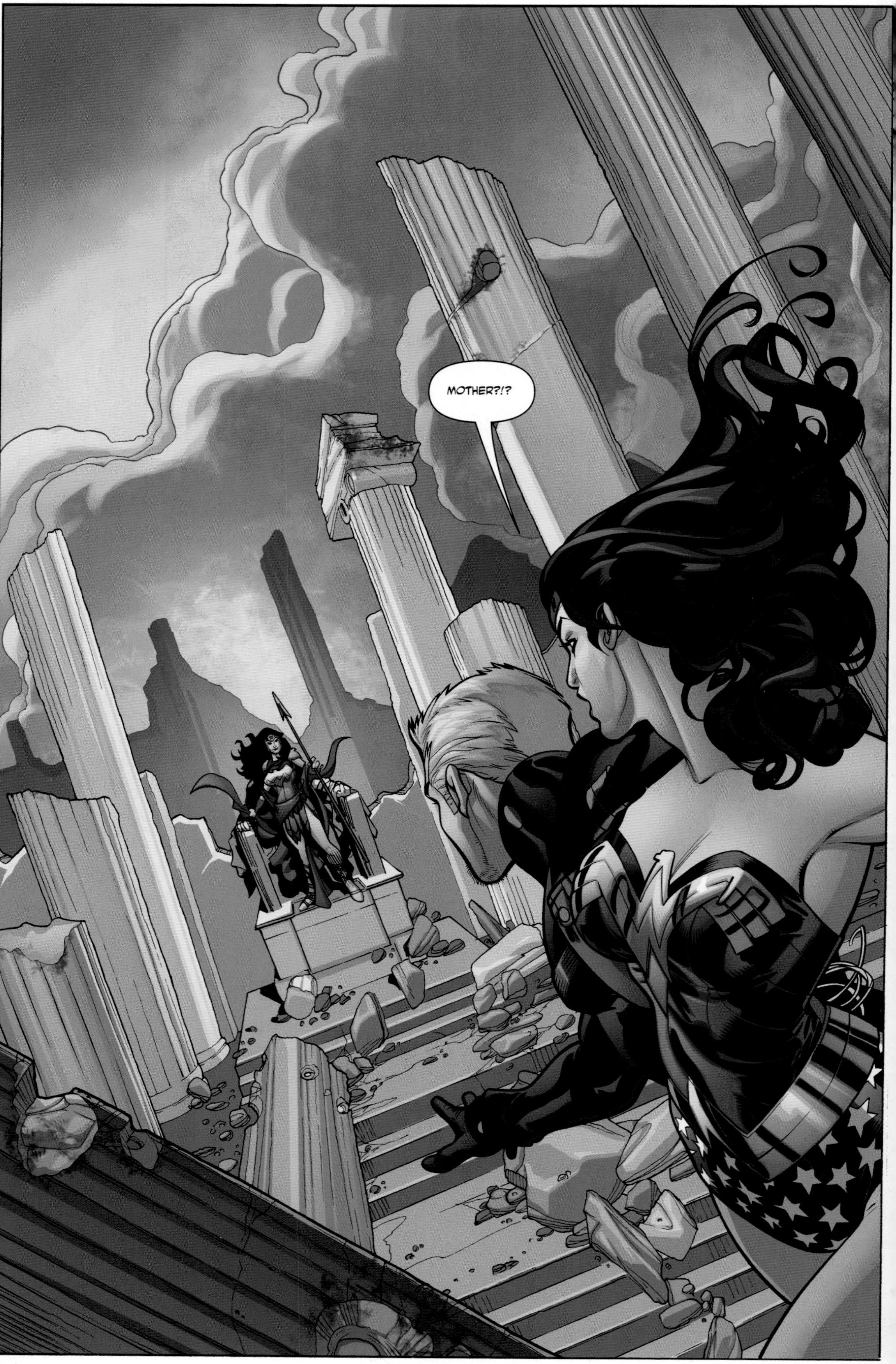
MOTHER?!?

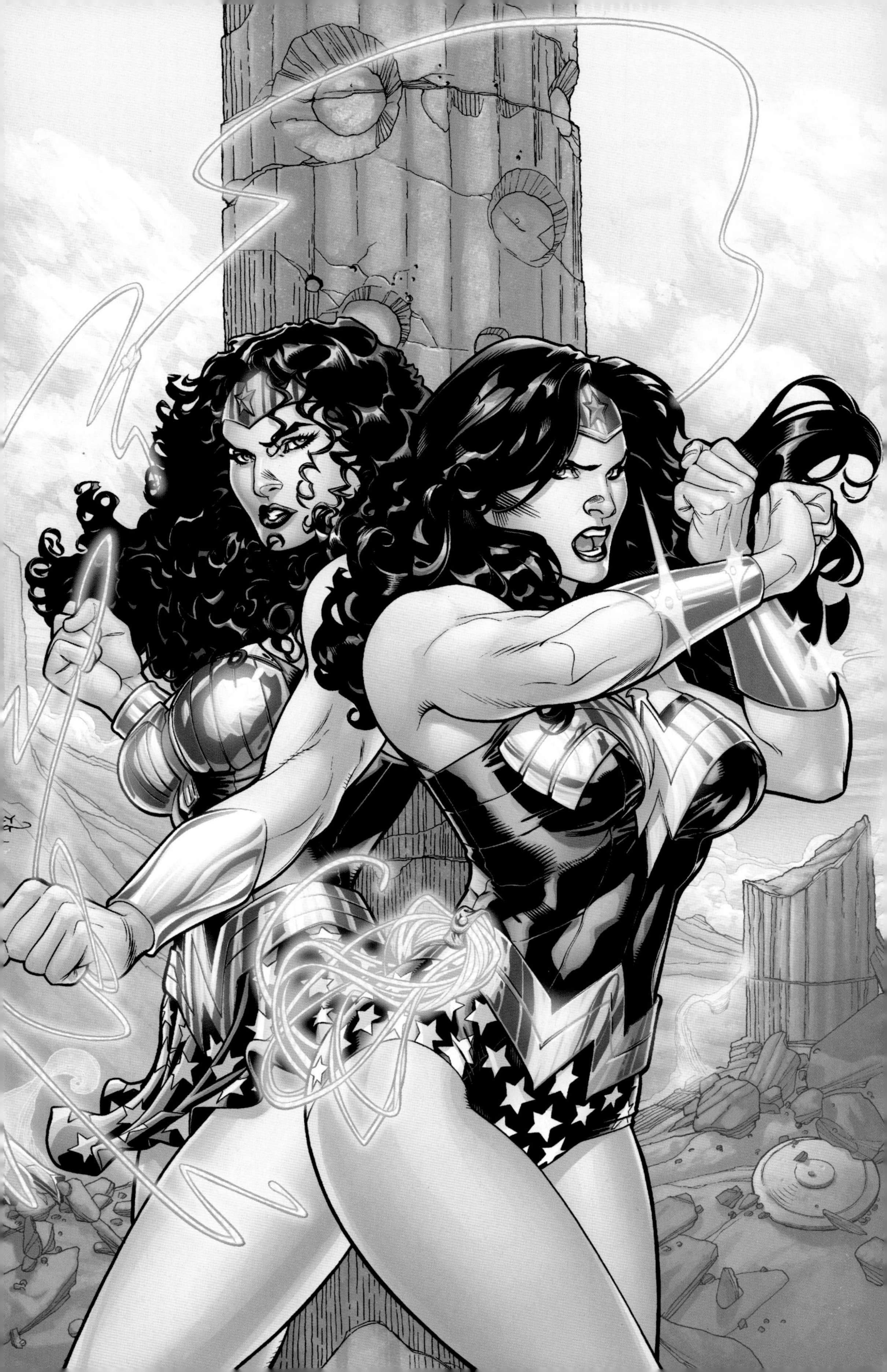

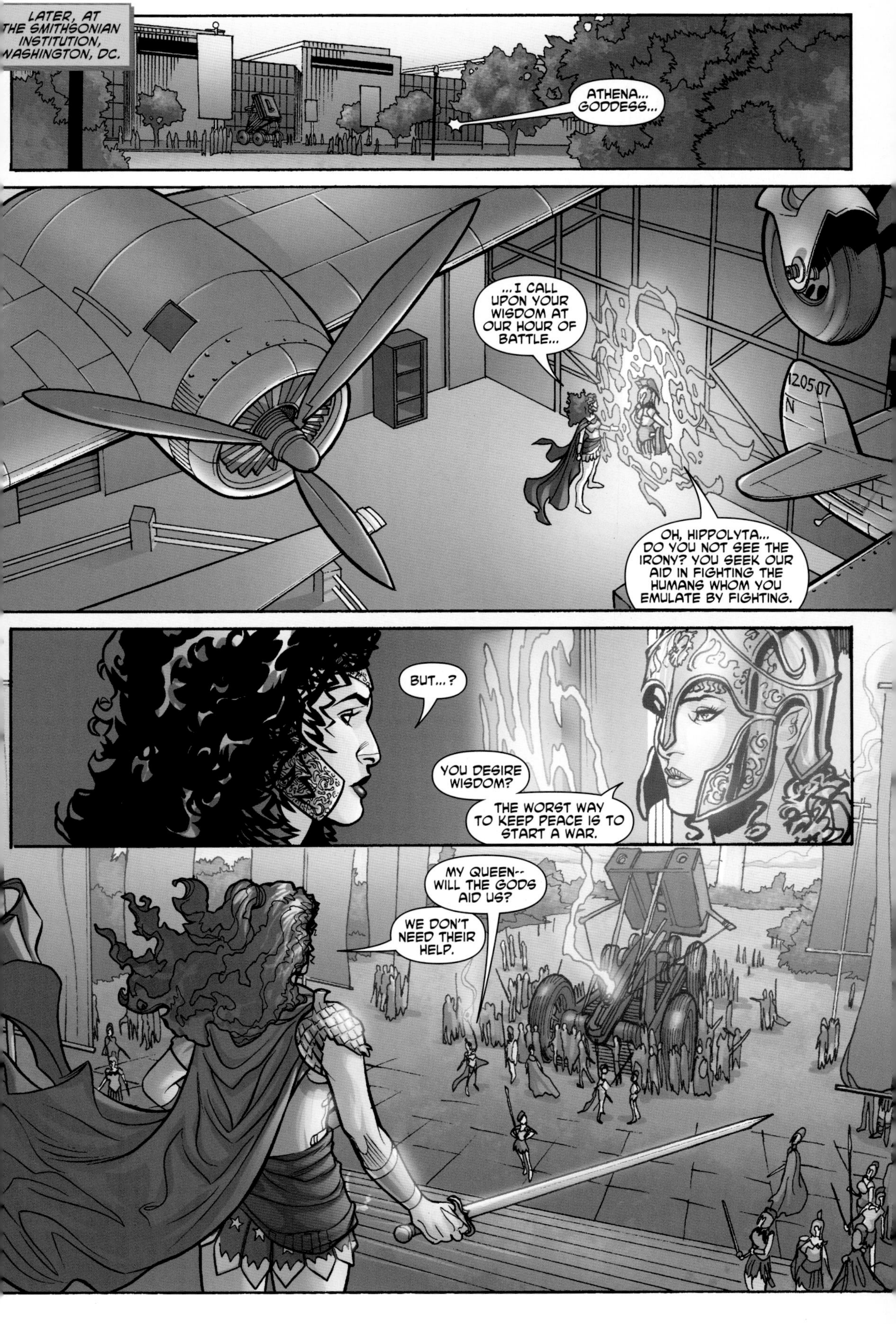
LATER, AT THE SMITHSONIAN INSTITUTION, WASHINGTON, DC.
ATHENA... GODDESS...
...I CALL UPON YOUR WISDOM AT OUR HOUR OF BATTLE...
OH, HIPPOLYTA... DO YOU NOT SEE THE IRONY? YOU SEEK OUR AID IN FIGHTING THE HUMANS WHOM YOU EMULATE BY FIGHTING.
BUT...?
YOU DESIRE WISDOM?
THE WORST WAY TO KEEP PEACE IS TO START A WAR.
MY QUEEN-- WILL THE GODS AID US?
WE DON'T NEED THEIR HELP.

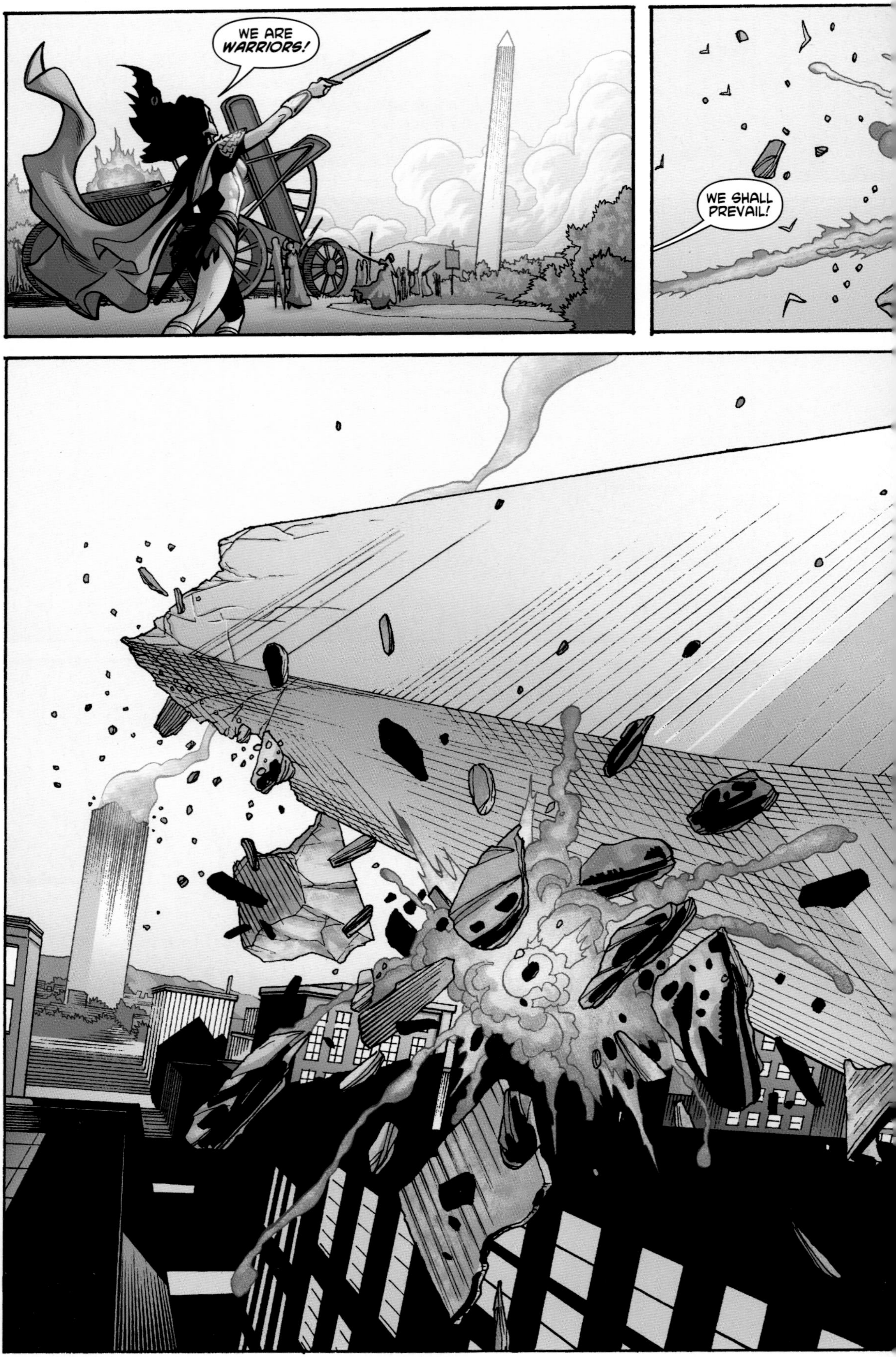
WE ARE WARRIORS!
WE SHALL PREVAIL!

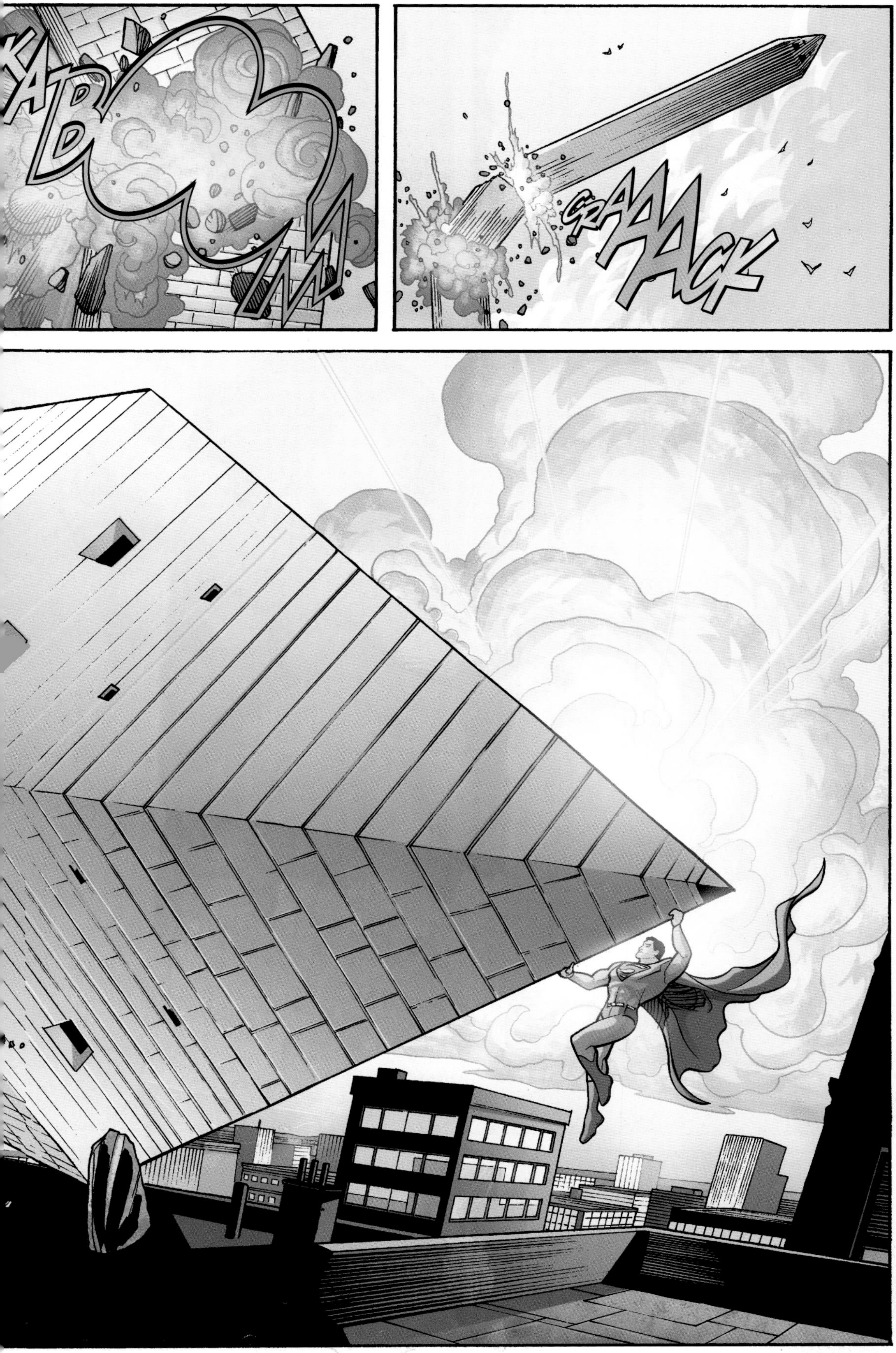
KABOOM
CRAAAACK

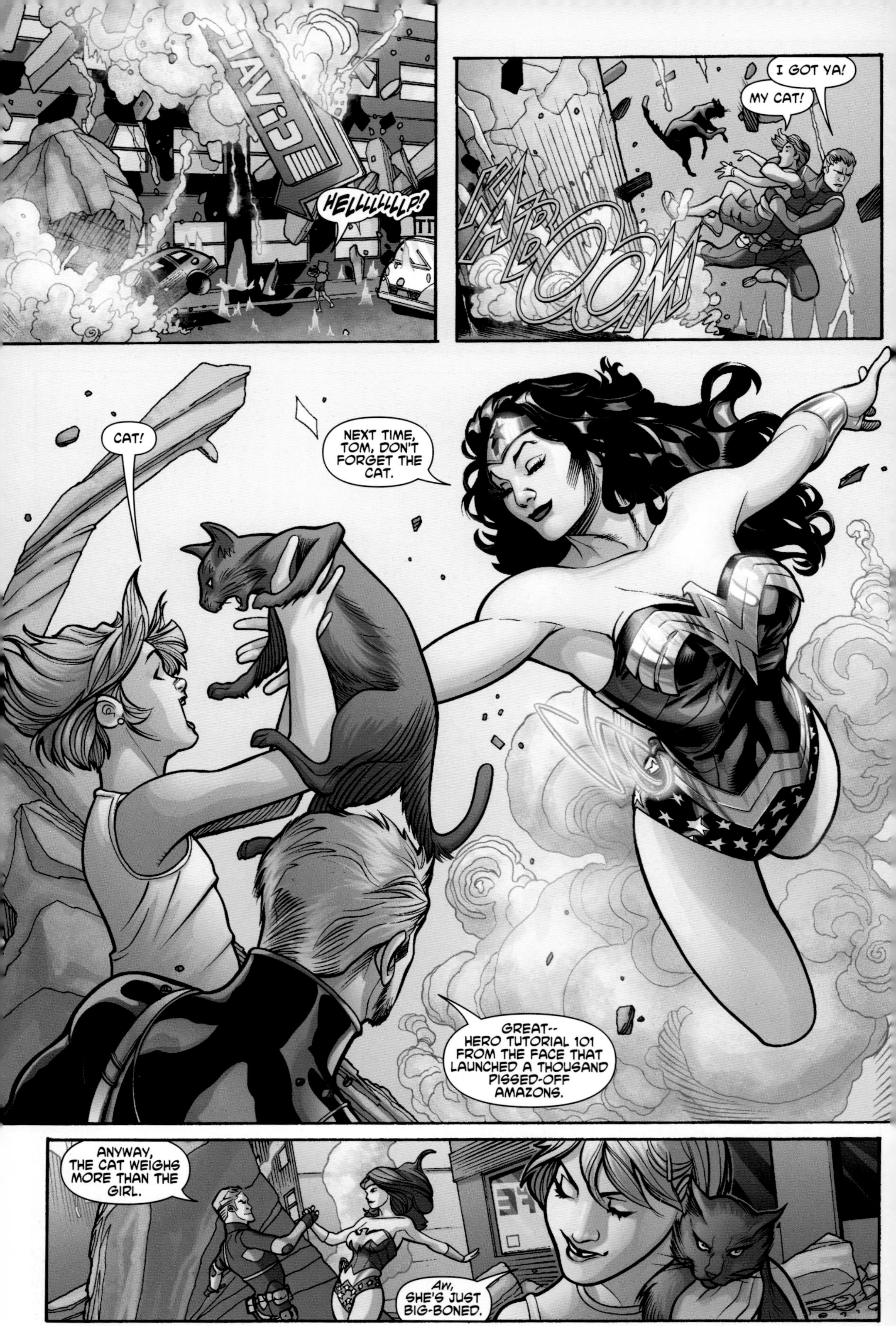
HELLLLLLLLP!
I GOT YA!
MY CAT!
KA-BOOOM
CAT!
NEXT TIME, TOM, DON'T FORGET THE CAT.
GREAT-- HERO TUTORIAL 101 FROM THE FACE THAT LAUNCHED A THOUSAND PISSED-OFF AMAZONS.
ANYWAY, THE CAT WEIGHS MORE THAN THE GIRL.
AW, SHE'S JUST BIG-BONED.

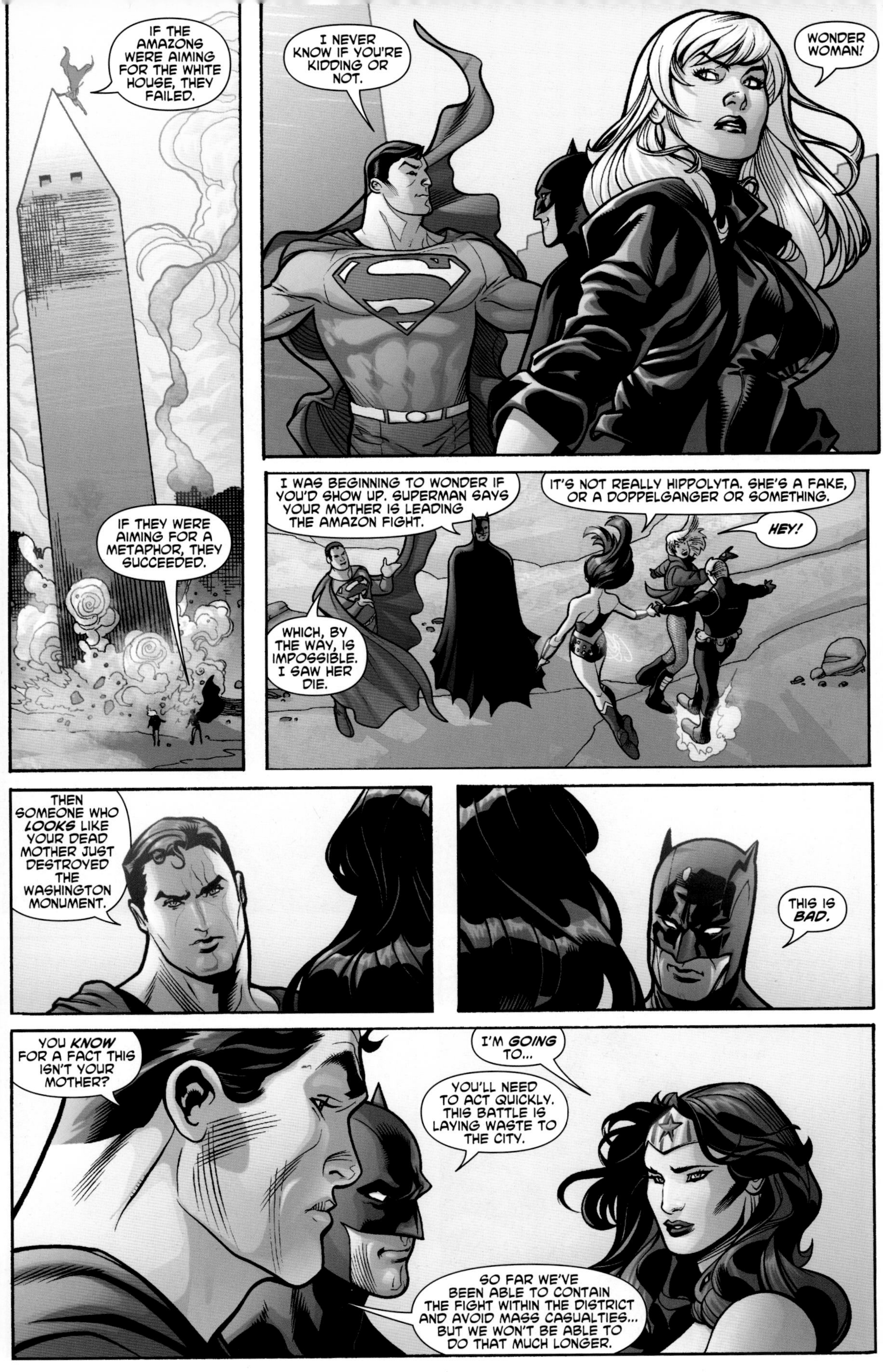
IF THE AMAZONS WERE AIMING FOR THE WHITE HOUSE, THEY FAILED.
IF THEY WERE AIMING FOR A METAPHOR, THEY SUCCEEDED.
I NEVER KNOW IF YOU'RE KIDDING OR NOT.
WONDER WOMAN!
I WAS BEGINNING TO WONDER IF YOU'D SHOW UP. SUPERMAN SAYS YOUR MOTHER IS LEADING THE AMAZON FIGHT.
IT'S NOT REALLY HIPPOLYTA. SHE'S A FAKE, OR A DOPPELGANGER OR SOMETHING.
HEY!
WHICH, BY THE WAY, IS IMPOSSIBLE. I SAW HER DIE.
THEN SOMEONE WHO LOOKS LIKE YOUR DEAD MOTHER JUST DESTROYED THE WASHINGTON MONUMENT.
THIS IS BAD.
YOU KNOW FOR A FACT THIS ISN'T YOUR MOTHER?
I'M GOING TO...
YOU'LL NEED TO ACT QUICKLY. THIS BATTLE IS LAYING WASTE TO THE CITY.
SO FAR WE'VE BEEN ABLE TO CONTAIN THE FIGHT WITHIN THE DISTRICT AND AVOID MASS CASUALTIES... BUT WE WON'T BE ABLE TO DO THAT MUCH LONGER.

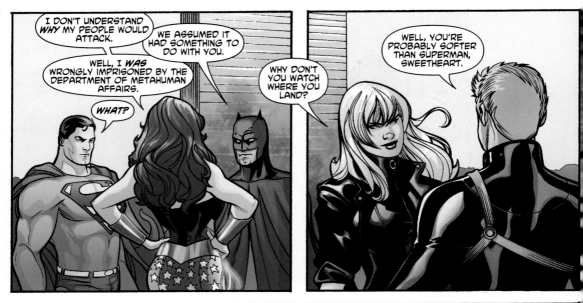

I DON'T UNDERSTAND *WHY* MY PEOPLE WOULD ATTACK.

WE ASSUMED IT HAD SOMETHING TO DO WITH YOU.

WELL, I *WAS* WRONGLY IMPRISONED BY THE DEPARTMENT OF METAHUMAN AFFAIRS.

WHAT?

WHY DON'T YOU WATCH WHERE YOU LAND?

WELL, YOU'RE PROBABLY SOFTER THAN SUPERMAN, SWEETHEART.

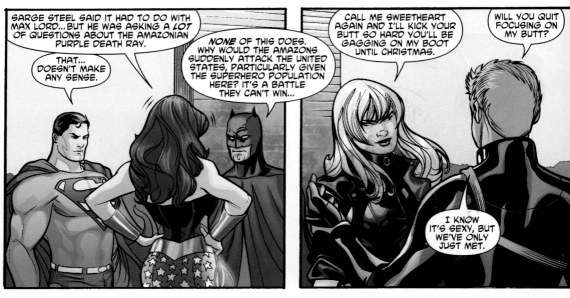

SARGE STEEL SAID IT HAD TO DO WITH MAX LORD... BUT HE WAS ASKING A *LOT* OF QUESTIONS ABOUT THE AMAZONIAN PURPLE DEATH RAY.

THAT... DOESN'T MAKE ANY SENSE.

NONE OF THIS DOES. WHY WOULD THE AMAZONS SUDDENLY ATTACK THE UNITED STATES, PARTICULARLY GIVEN THE SUPERHERO POPULATION HERE? IT'S A BATTLE THEY CAN'T WIN...

CALL ME SWEETHEART AGAIN AND I'LL KICK YOUR BUTT SO HARD YOU'LL BE GAGGING ON MY BOOT UNTIL CHRISTMAS.

WILL YOU QUIT FOCUSING ON MY BUTT?

I KNOW IT'S SEXY, BUT WE'VE ONLY JUST MET.

THE FIRST THING TO DO IS CONFRONT MY "MOTHER" AND GET TO THE BOTTOM OF THIS.

I'LL NEED TO TAKE NEMESIS ALONG FOR, *uh*... BACKUP.

HEY!

I THOUGHT YOU WORKED *ALONE!*

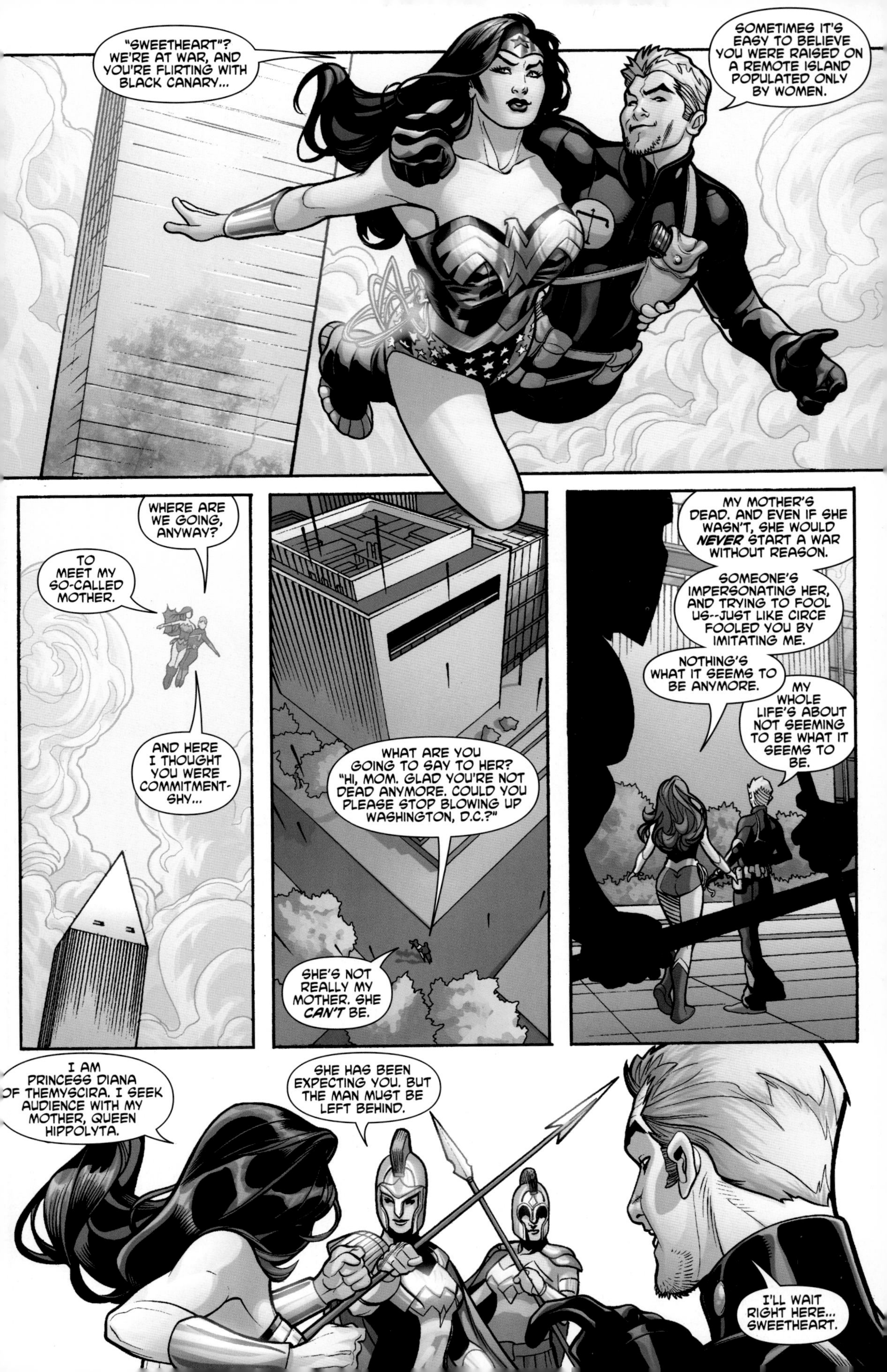
"SWEETHEART"? WE'RE AT WAR, AND YOU'RE FLIRTING WITH BLACK CANARY...
SOMETIMES IT'S EASY TO BELIEVE YOU WERE RAISED ON A REMOTE ISLAND POPULATED ONLY BY WOMEN.
WHERE ARE WE GOING, ANYWAY?
TO MEET MY SO-CALLED MOTHER.
AND HERE I THOUGHT YOU WERE COMMITMENT-SHY...
WHAT ARE YOU GOING TO SAY TO HER? "HI, MOM. GLAD YOU'RE NOT DEAD ANYMORE. COULD YOU PLEASE STOP BLOWING UP WASHINGTON, D.C.?"
SHE'S NOT REALLY MY MOTHER. SHE *CAN'T* BE.
MY MOTHER'S DEAD. AND EVEN IF SHE WASN'T, SHE WOULD ***NEVER*** START A WAR WITHOUT REASON.
SOMEONE'S IMPERSONATING HER, AND TRYING TO FOOL US--JUST LIKE CIRCE FOOLED YOU BY IMITATING ME.
NOTHING'S WHAT IT SEEMS TO BE ANYMORE.
MY WHOLE LIFE'S ABOUT NOT SEEMING TO BE WHAT IT SEEMS TO BE.
I AM PRINCESS DIANA OF THEMYSCIRA. I SEEK AUDIENCE WITH MY MOTHER, QUEEN HIPPOLYTA.
SHE HAS BEEN EXPECTING YOU. BUT THE MAN MUST BE LEFT BEHIND.
I'LL WAIT RIGHT HERE... SWEETHEART.

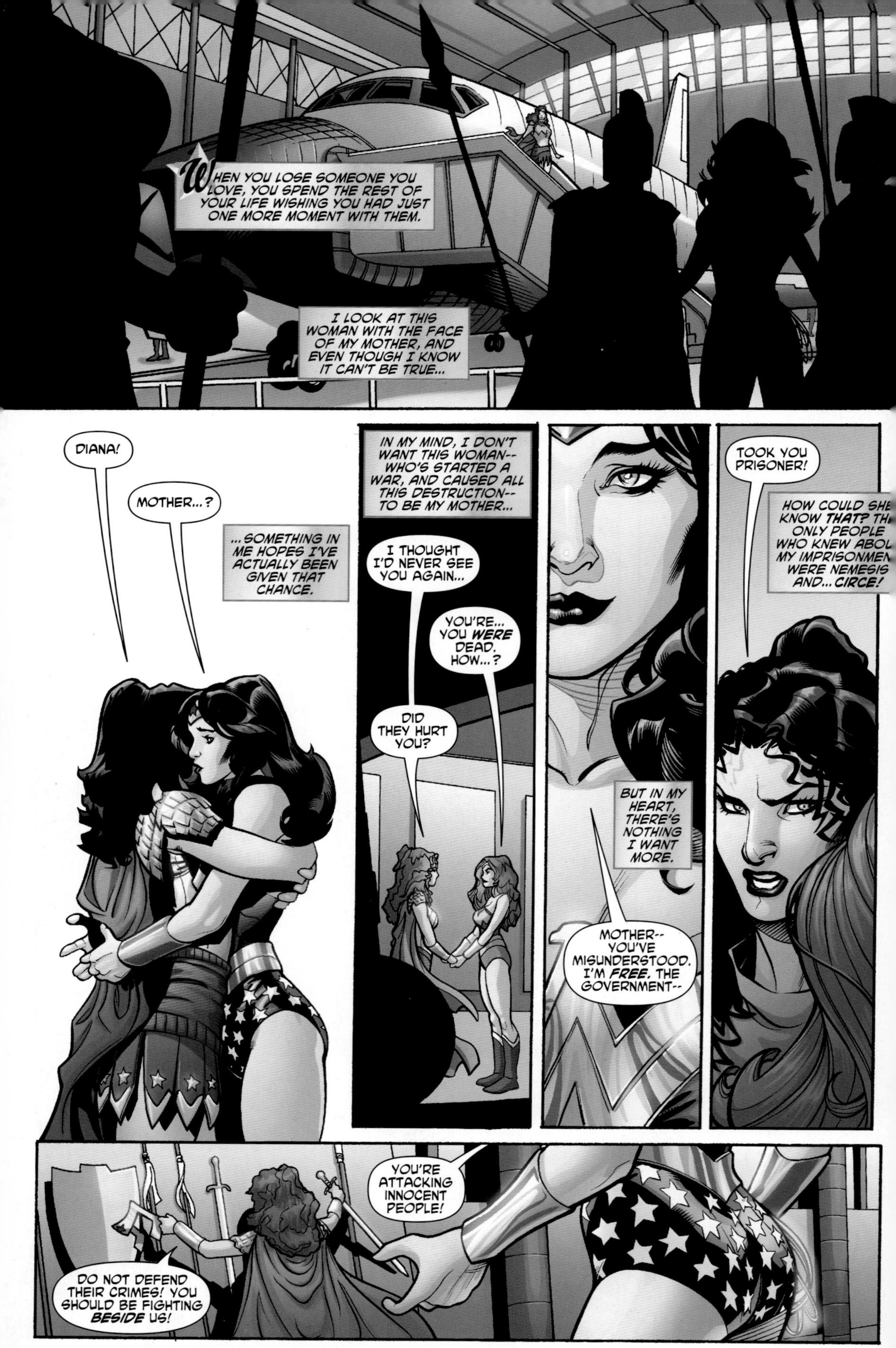
WHEN YOU LOSE SOMEONE YOU LOVE, YOU SPEND THE REST OF YOUR LIFE WISHING YOU HAD JUST ONE MORE MOMENT WITH THEM.
I LOOK AT THIS WOMAN WITH THE FACE OF MY MOTHER, AND EVEN THOUGH I KNOW IT CAN'T BE TRUE...
DIANA!
MOTHER...?
...SOMETHING IN ME HOPES I'VE ACTUALLY BEEN GIVEN THAT CHANCE.
IN MY MIND, I DON'T WANT THIS WOMAN--WHO'S STARTED A WAR, AND CAUSED ALL THIS DESTRUCTION--TO BE MY MOTHER...
I THOUGHT I'D NEVER SEE YOU AGAIN...
YOU'RE... YOU WERE DEAD. HOW...?
DID THEY HURT YOU?
BUT IN MY HEART, THERE'S NOTHING I WANT MORE.
MOTHER--YOU'VE MISUNDERSTOOD. I'M FREE. THE GOVERNMENT--
TOOK YOU PRISONER!
HOW COULD SHE KNOW THAT? THE ONLY PEOPLE WHO KNEW ABOUT MY IMPRISONMENT WERE NEMESIS AND... CIRCE!
YOU'RE ATTACKING INNOCENT PEOPLE!
DO NOT DEFEND THEIR CRIMES! YOU SHOULD BE FIGHTING BESIDE US!

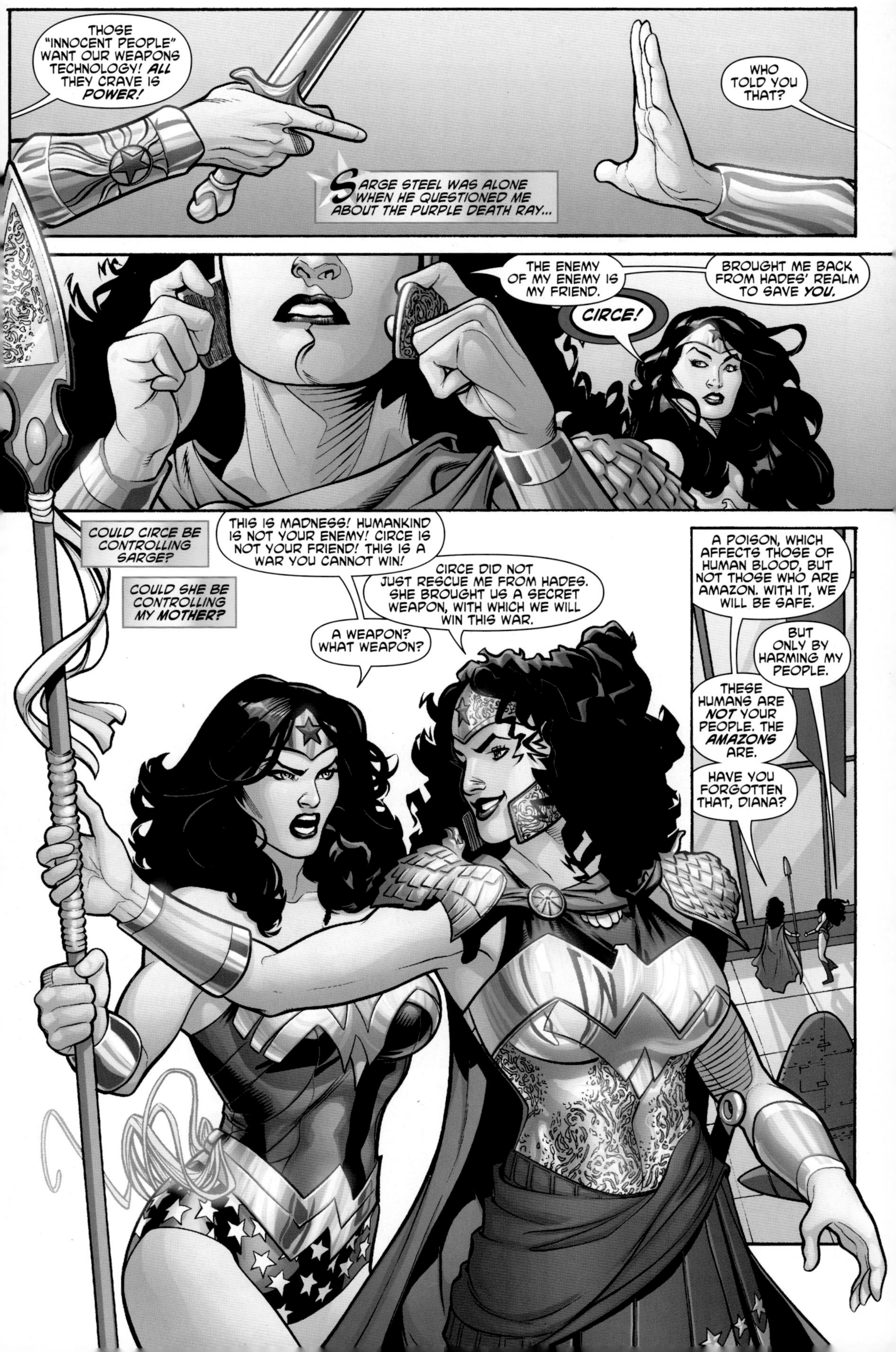
THOSE "INNOCENT PEOPLE" WANT OUR WEAPONS TECHNOLOGY! ALL THEY CRAVE IS POWER!
WHO TOLD YOU THAT?
SARGE STEEL WAS ALONE WHEN HE QUESTIONED ME ABOUT THE PURPLE DEATH RAY...
THE ENEMY OF MY ENEMY IS MY FRIEND.
BROUGHT ME BACK FROM HADES' REALM TO SAVE YOU.
CIRCE!
COULD CIRCE BE CONTROLLING SARGE?
COULD SHE BE CONTROLLING MY MOTHER?
THIS IS MADNESS! HUMANKIND IS NOT YOUR ENEMY! CIRCE IS NOT YOUR FRIEND! THIS IS A WAR YOU CANNOT WIN!
CIRCE DID NOT JUST RESCUE ME FROM HADES. SHE BROUGHT US A SECRET WEAPON, WITH WHICH WE WILL WIN THIS WAR.
A WEAPON? WHAT WEAPON?
A POISON, WHICH AFFECTS THOSE OF HUMAN BLOOD, BUT NOT THOSE WHO ARE AMAZON. WITH IT, WE WILL BE SAFE.
BUT ONLY BY HARMING MY PEOPLE.
THESE HUMANS ARE NOT YOUR PEOPLE. THE AMAZONS ARE.
HAVE YOU FORGOTTEN THAT, DIANA?

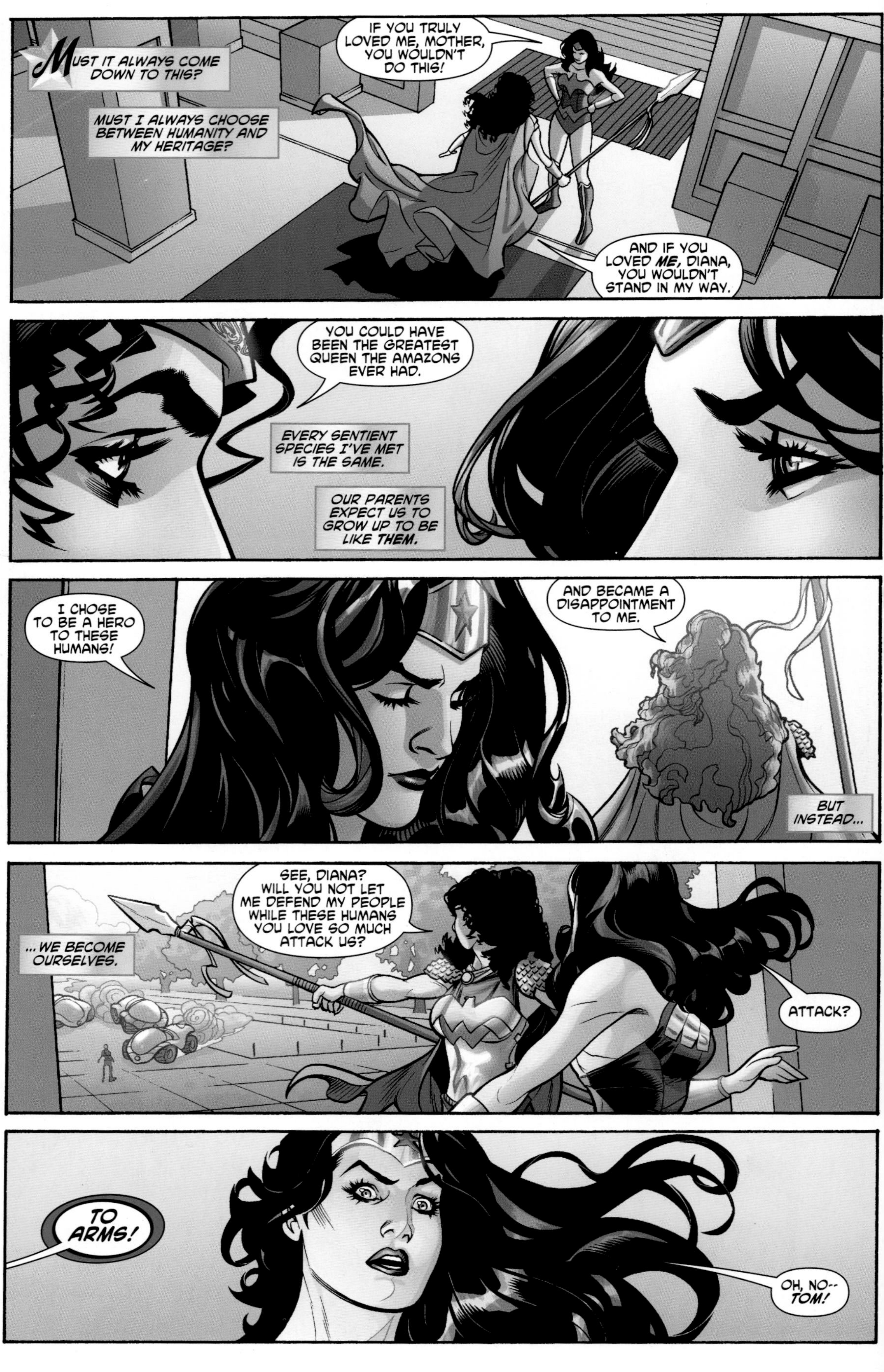

MUST IT ALWAYS COME DOWN TO THIS?
MUST I ALWAYS CHOOSE BETWEEN HUMANITY AND MY HERITAGE?
IF YOU TRULY LOVED ME, MOTHER, YOU WOULDN'T DO THIS!
AND IF YOU LOVED ME, DIANA, YOU WOULDN'T STAND IN MY WAY.
YOU COULD HAVE BEEN THE GREATEST QUEEN THE AMAZONS EVER HAD.
EVERY SENTIENT SPECIES I'VE MET IS THE SAME.
OUR PARENTS EXPECT US TO GROW UP TO BE LIKE THEM.
I CHOSE TO BE A HERO TO THESE HUMANS!
AND BECAME A DISAPPOINTMENT TO ME.
BUT INSTEAD...
...WE BECOME OURSELVES.
SEE, DIANA? WILL YOU NOT LET ME DEFEND MY PEOPLE WHILE THESE HUMANS YOU LOVE SO MUCH ATTACK US?
ATTACK?
TO ARMS!
OH, NO-- TOM!

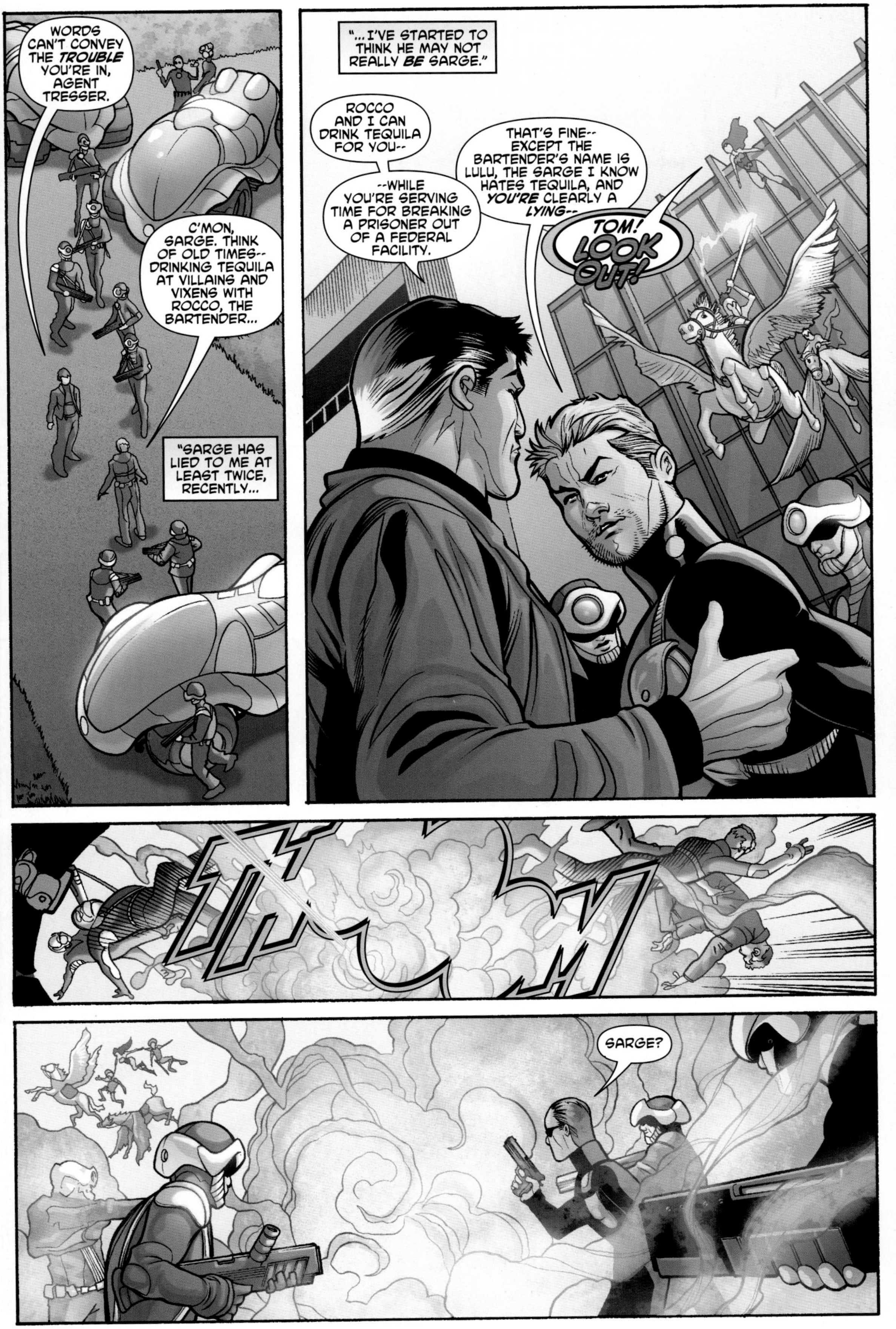
WORDS CAN'T CONVEY THE *TROUBLE* YOU'RE IN, AGENT TRESSER.
C'MON, SARGE. THINK OF OLD TIMES-- DRINKING TEQUILA AT VILLAINS AND VIXENS WITH ROCCO, THE BARTENDER...
"SARGE HAS LIED TO ME AT LEAST TWICE, RECENTLY...
"...I'VE STARTED TO THINK HE MAY NOT REALLY *BE* SARGE."
ROCCO AND I CAN DRINK TEQUILA FOR YOU--
--WHILE YOU'RE SERVING TIME FOR BREAKING A PRISONER OUT OF A FEDERAL FACILITY.
THAT'S FINE-- EXCEPT THE BARTENDER'S NAME IS LULU, THE SARGE I KNOW HATES TEQUILA, AND *YOU'RE* CLEARLY A *LYING*--
TOM! LOOK OUT!
SARGE?

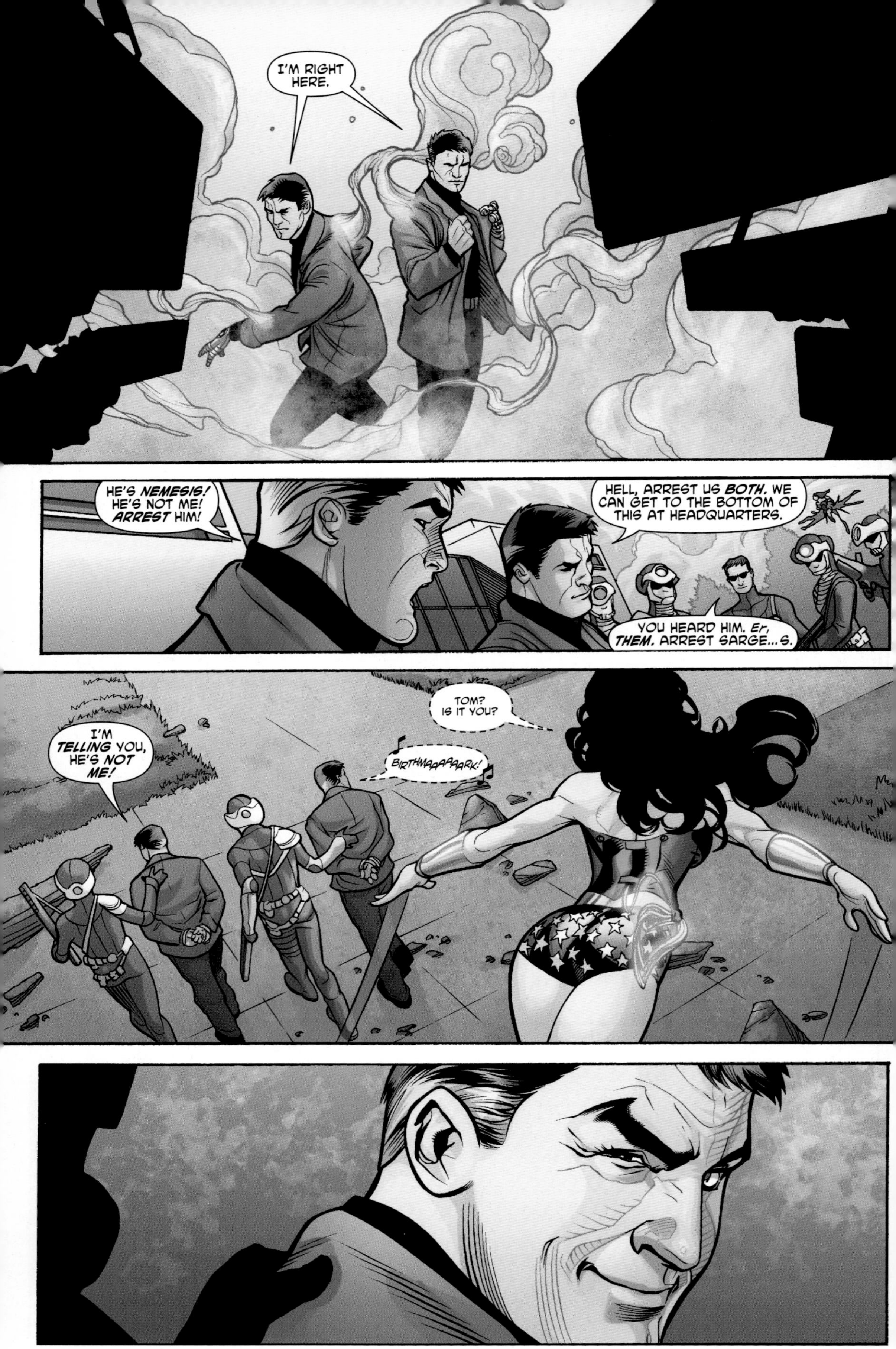
I'M RIGHT HERE.
HE'S NEMESIS! HE'S NOT ME! ARREST HIM!
HELL, ARREST US BOTH. WE CAN GET TO THE BOTTOM OF THIS AT HEADQUARTERS.
YOU HEARD HIM. Er, THEM. ARREST SARGE...S.
TOM? IS IT YOU?
I'M TELLING YOU, HE'S NOT ME!
BIRTHWAAAAAAARK!

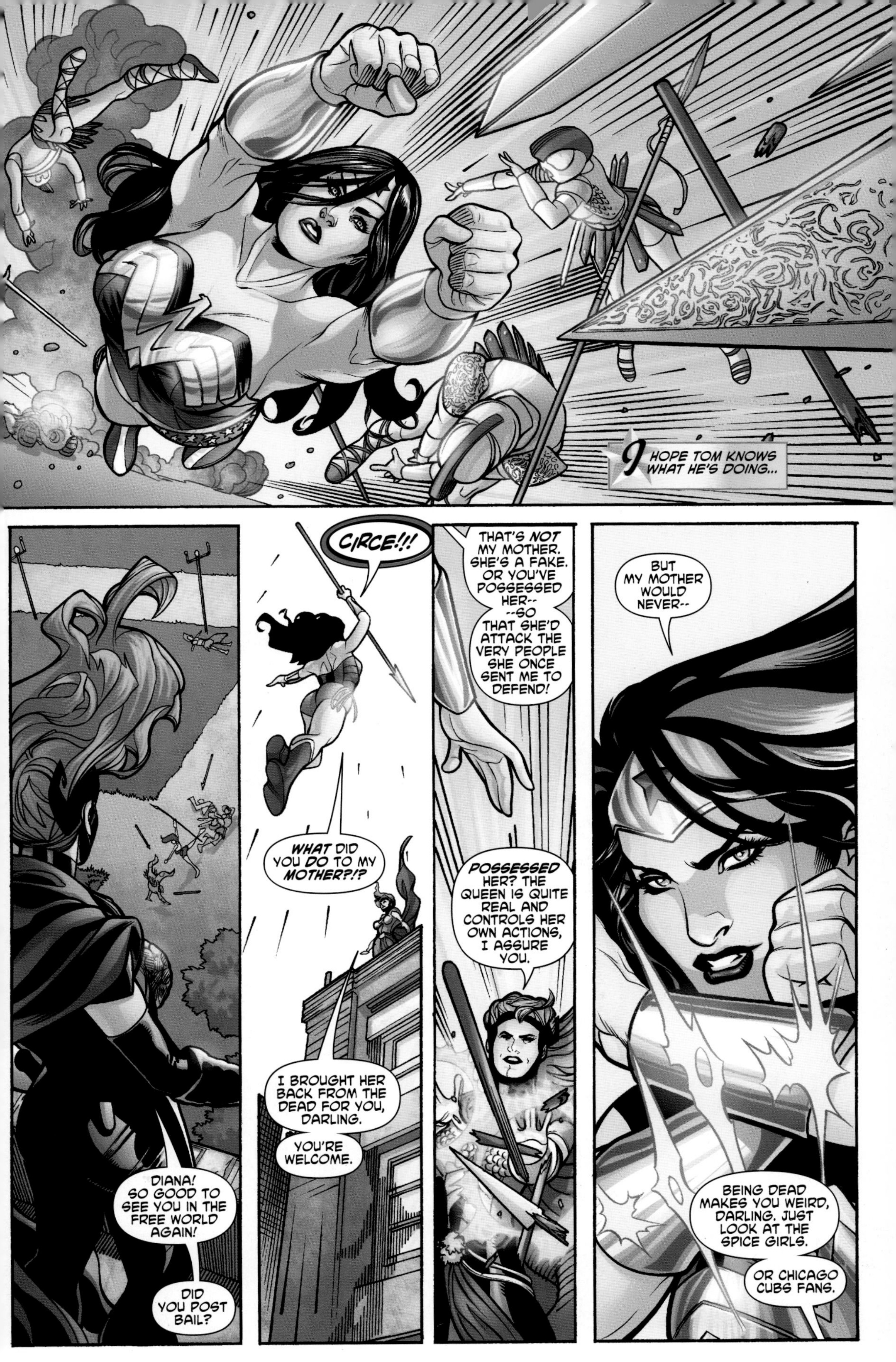
I HOPE TOM KNOWS WHAT HE'S DOING...
DIANA! SO GOOD TO SEE YOU IN THE FREE WORLD AGAIN!
DID YOU POST BAIL?
CIRCE!!!
WHAT DID YOU DO TO MY MOTHER?!?
I BROUGHT HER BACK FROM THE DEAD FOR YOU, DARLING.
YOU'RE WELCOME.
THAT'S NOT MY MOTHER. SHE'S A FAKE. OR YOU'VE POSSESSED HER--
--SO THAT SHE'D ATTACK THE VERY PEOPLE SHE ONCE SENT ME TO DEFEND!
POSSESSED HER? THE QUEEN IS QUITE REAL AND CONTROLS HER OWN ACTIONS, I ASSURE YOU.
BUT MY MOTHER WOULD NEVER--
BEING DEAD MAKES YOU WEIRD, DARLING. JUST LOOK AT THE SPICE GIRLS.
OR CHICAGO CUBS FANS.

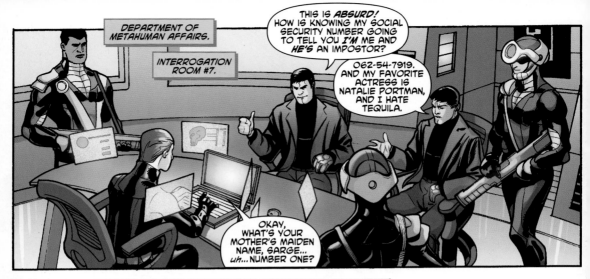

DEPARTMENT OF METAHUMAN AFFAIRS.

INTERROGATION ROOM #7.

THIS IS *ABSURD!* HOW IS KNOWING MY SOCIAL SECURITY NUMBER GOING TO TELL YOU *I'M* ME AND *HE'S* AN IMPOSTOR?

062-54-7919. AND MY FAVORITE ACTRESS IS NATALIE PORTMAN, AND I HATE TEQUILA.

OKAY, WHAT'S YOUR MOTHER'S MAIDEN NAME, SARGE... *uh...* NUMBER ONE?

THIS IS AN OUTRAGE! LOCK HIM UP!

YOU REALLY WANT TO KNOW WHO THE *FAKE* SARGE IS? HAND ME A PEN...

"HOPE I KNOW WHAT I'M DOING..."

A HANDWRITING TEST-- EXCELLENT IDEA.

THREE IDEAS, ACTUALLY. FIRST, ANYONE WHO KNOWS ME KNOWS I LOST MY *HAND*--AND WEAR A *METAL* PROSTHESIS.

FFFIYEEE!!!

SECOND, *METAL* DOESN'T BLEED.

AND LAST OF ALL...

...YOU'RE ALL *FIRED.*

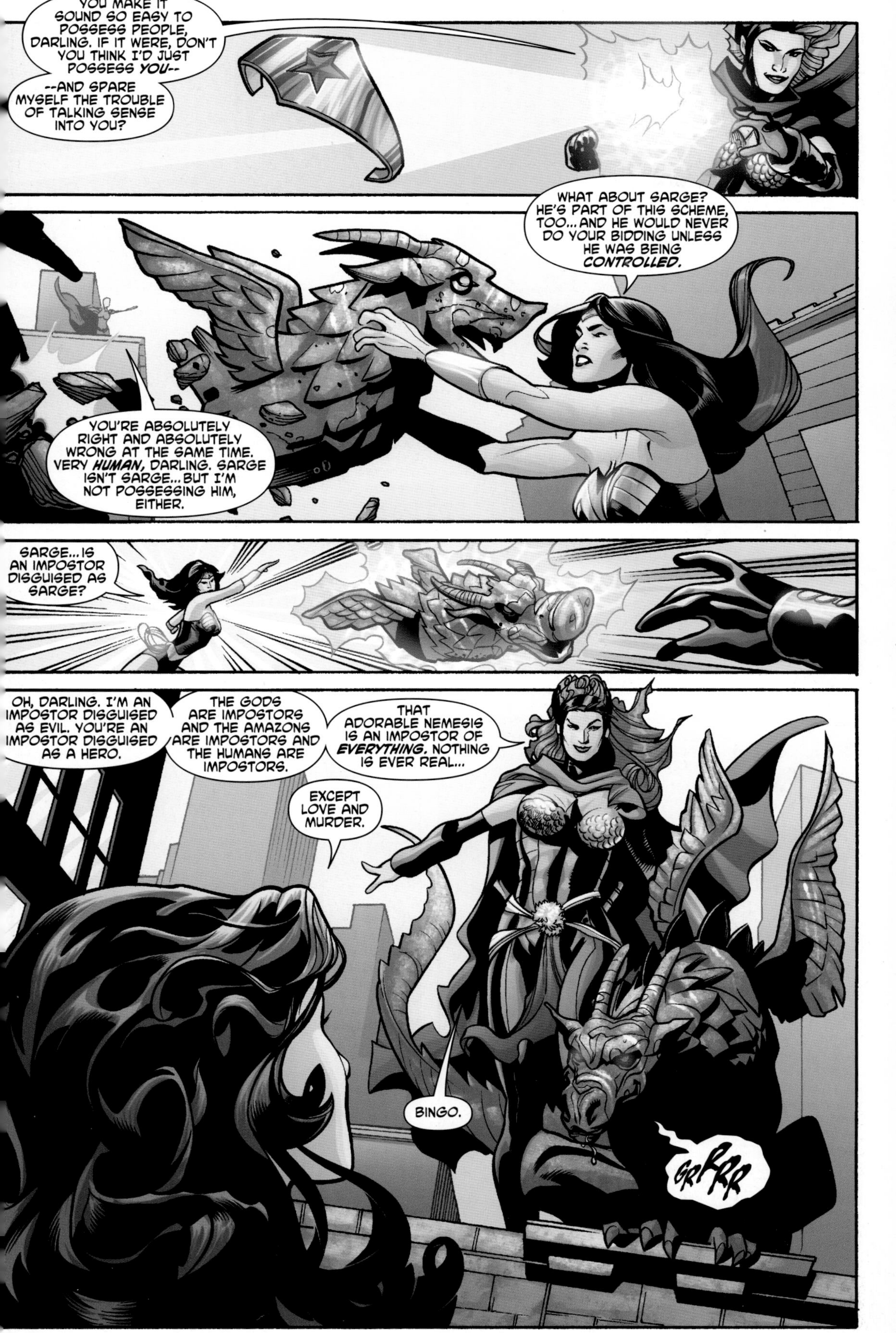
YOU MAKE IT SOUND SO EASY TO POSSESS PEOPLE, DARLING. IF IT WERE, DON'T YOU THINK I'D JUST POSSESS *YOU*--
--AND SPARE MYSELF THE TROUBLE OF TALKING SENSE INTO YOU?
WHAT ABOUT SARGE? HE'S PART OF THIS SCHEME, TOO...AND HE WOULD NEVER DO YOUR BIDDING UNLESS HE WAS BEING *CONTROLLED.*
YOU'RE ABSOLUTELY RIGHT AND ABSOLUTELY WRONG AT THE SAME TIME. VERY *HUMAN,* DARLING. SARGE ISN'T SARGE...BUT I'M NOT POSSESSING HIM, EITHER.
SARGE...IS AN IMPOSTOR DISGUISED AS SARGE?
OH, DARLING. I'M AN IMPOSTOR DISGUISED AS EVIL. YOU'RE AN IMPOSTOR DISGUISED AS A HERO.
THE GODS ARE IMPOSTORS AND THE AMAZONS ARE IMPOSTORS AND THE HUMANS ARE IMPOSTORS.
THAT ADORABLE NEMESIS IS AN IMPOSTOR OF *EVERYTHING.* NOTHING IS EVER REAL...
EXCEPT LOVE AND MURDER.
BINGO.
GRRRR

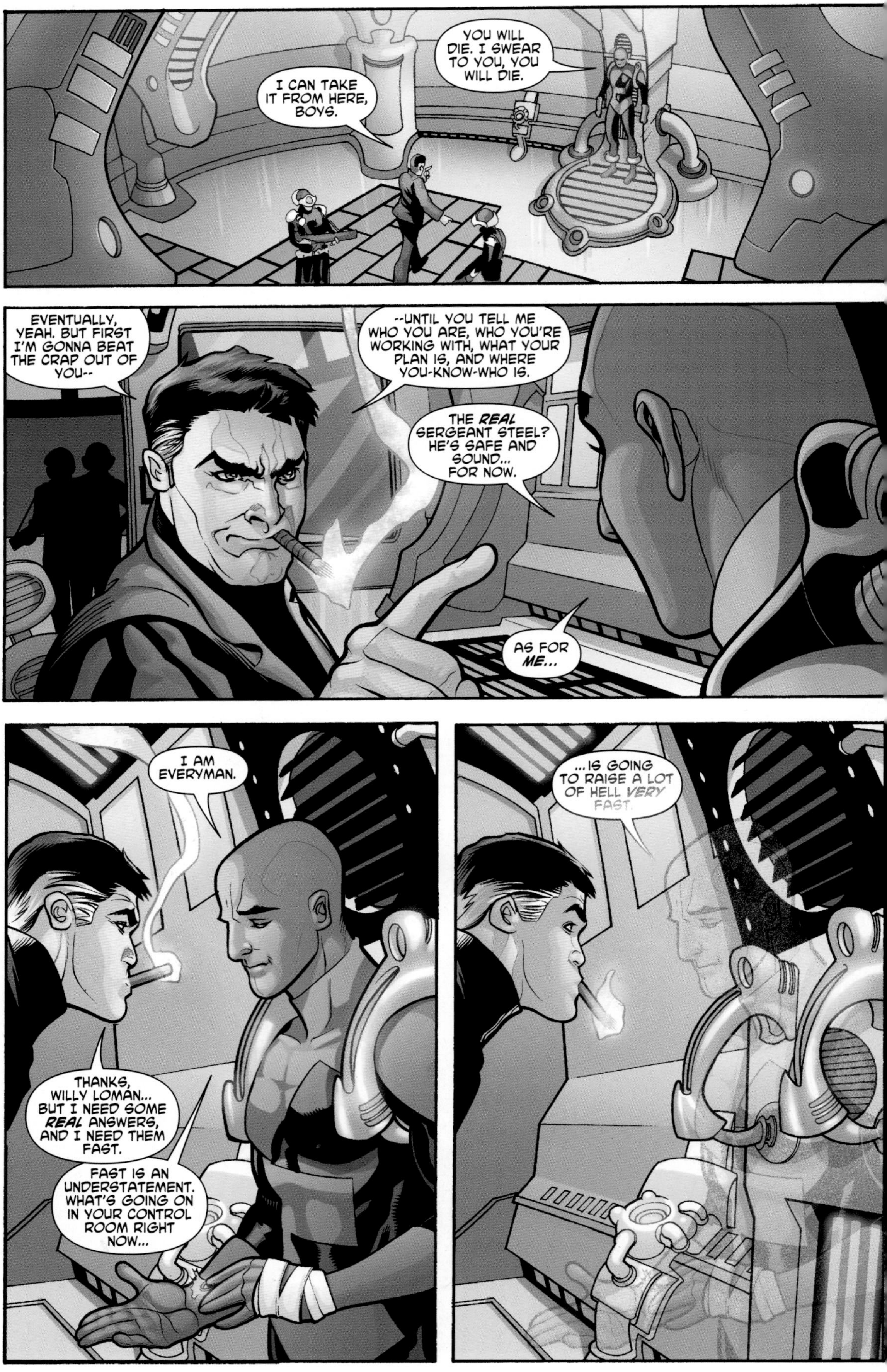
YOU WILL DIE. I SWEAR TO YOU, YOU WILL DIE.
I CAN TAKE IT FROM HERE, BOYS.
EVENTUALLY, YEAH. BUT FIRST I'M GONNA BEAT THE CRAP OUT OF YOU--
--UNTIL YOU TELL ME WHO YOU ARE, WHO YOU'RE WORKING WITH, WHAT YOUR PLAN IS, AND WHERE YOU-KNOW-WHO IS.
THE REAL SERGEANT STEEL? HE'S SAFE AND SOUND... FOR NOW.
AS FOR ME...
I AM EVERYMAN.
THANKS, WILLY LOMAN... BUT I NEED SOME REAL ANSWERS, AND I NEED THEM FAST.
FAST IS AN UNDERSTATEMENT. WHAT'S GOING ON IN YOUR CONTROL ROOM RIGHT NOW...
...IS GOING TO RAISE A LOT OF HELL VERY FAST.

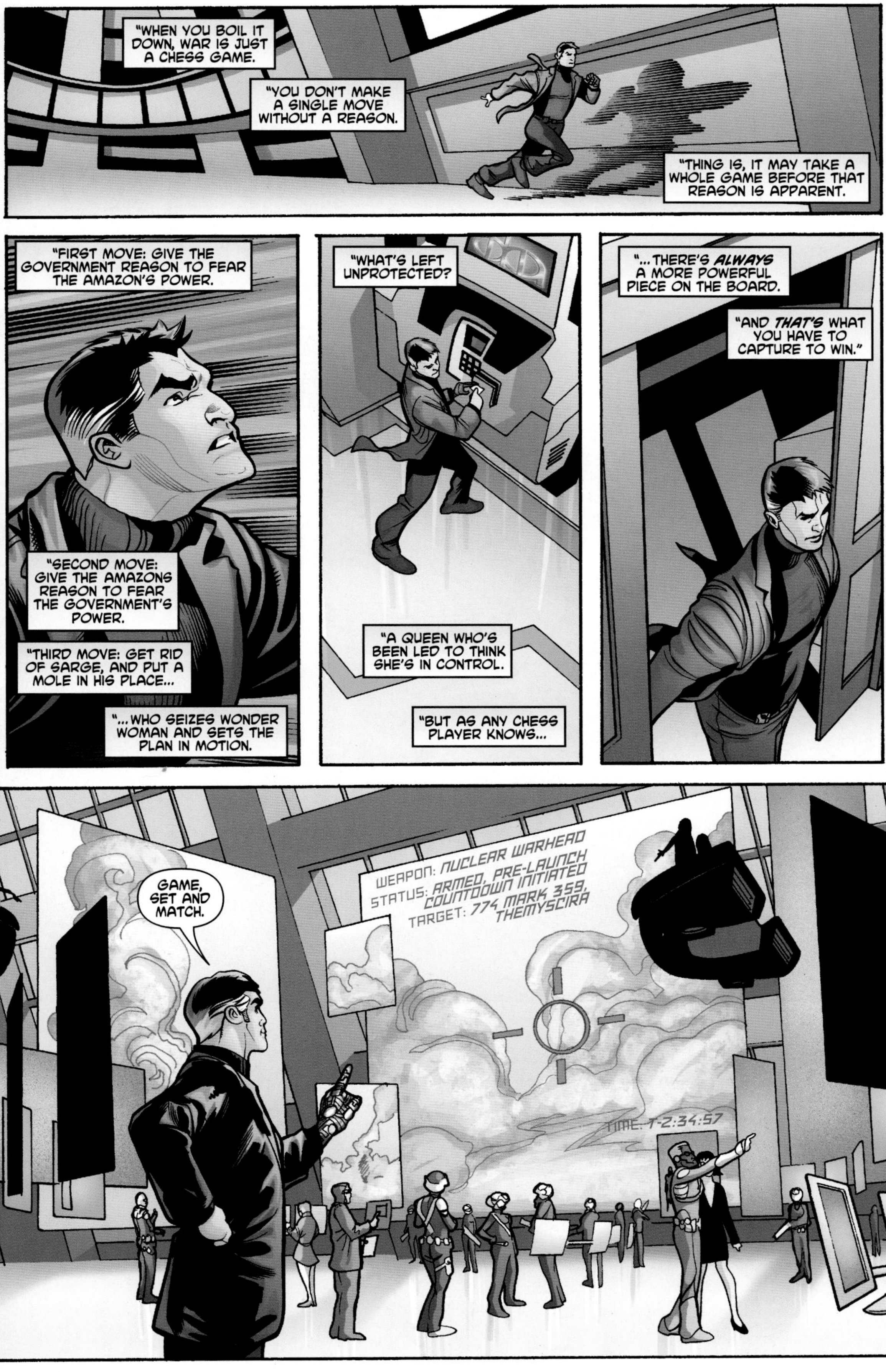
"WHEN YOU BOIL IT DOWN, WAR IS JUST A CHESS GAME.
"YOU DON'T MAKE A SINGLE MOVE WITHOUT A REASON.
"THING IS, IT MAY TAKE A WHOLE GAME BEFORE THAT REASON IS APPARENT.
"FIRST MOVE: GIVE THE GOVERNMENT REASON TO FEAR THE AMAZON'S POWER.
"SECOND MOVE: GIVE THE AMAZONS REASON TO FEAR THE GOVERNMENT'S POWER.
"THIRD MOVE: GET RID OF SARGE, AND PUT A MOLE IN HIS PLACE...
"...WHO SEIZES WONDER WOMAN AND SETS THE PLAN IN MOTION.
"WHAT'S LEFT UNPROTECTED?
"A QUEEN WHO'S BEEN LED TO THINK SHE'S IN CONTROL.
"BUT AS ANY CHESS PLAYER KNOWS...
"...THERE'S *ALWAYS* A MORE POWERFUL PIECE ON THE BOARD.
"AND *THAT'S* WHAT YOU HAVE TO CAPTURE TO WIN."
WEAPON: NUCLEAR WARHEAD
STATUS: ARMED, PRE-LAUNCH COUNTDOWN INITIATED
TARGET: 774 MARK 359, THEMYSCIRA
GAME, SET AND MATCH.
TIME: T-2:34:57

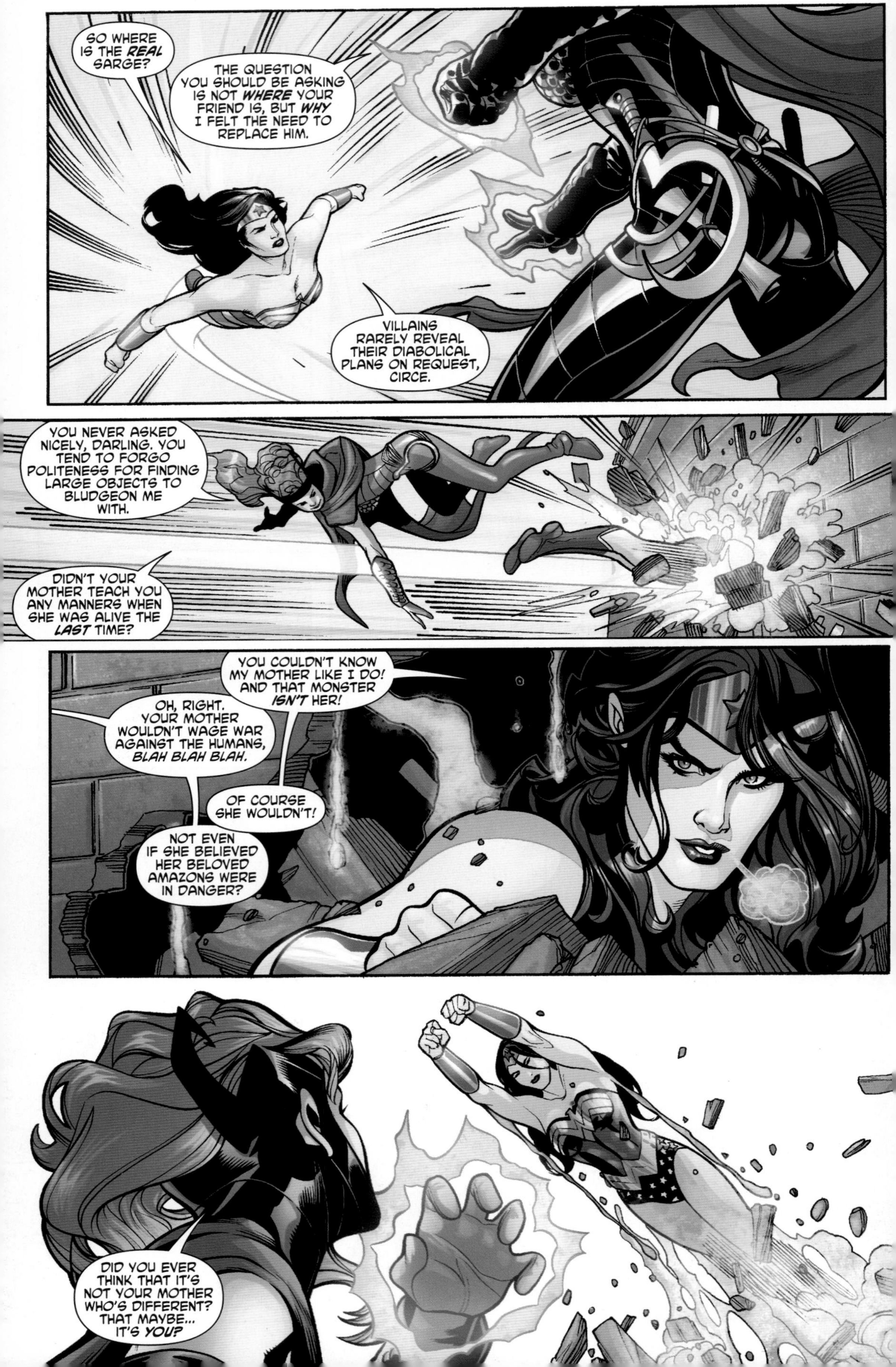
SO WHERE IS THE *REAL* SARGE?
THE QUESTION YOU SHOULD BE ASKING IS NOT *WHERE* YOUR FRIEND IS, BUT *WHY* I FELT THE NEED TO REPLACE HIM.
VILLAINS RARELY REVEAL THEIR DIABOLICAL PLANS ON REQUEST, CIRCE.
YOU NEVER ASKED NICELY, DARLING. YOU TEND TO FORGO POLITENESS FOR FINDING LARGE OBJECTS TO BLUDGEON ME WITH.
DIDN'T YOUR MOTHER TEACH YOU ANY MANNERS WHEN SHE WAS ALIVE THE *LAST* TIME?
YOU COULDN'T KNOW MY MOTHER LIKE I DO! AND THAT MONSTER *ISN'T* HER!
OH, RIGHT. YOUR MOTHER WOULDN'T WAGE WAR AGAINST THE HUMANS, *BLAH BLAH BLAH.*
OF COURSE SHE WOULDN'T!
NOT EVEN IF SHE BELIEVED HER BELOVED AMAZONS WERE IN DANGER?
DID YOU EVER THINK THAT IT'S NOT YOUR MOTHER WHO'S DIFFERENT? THAT MAYBE... IT'S *YOU?*

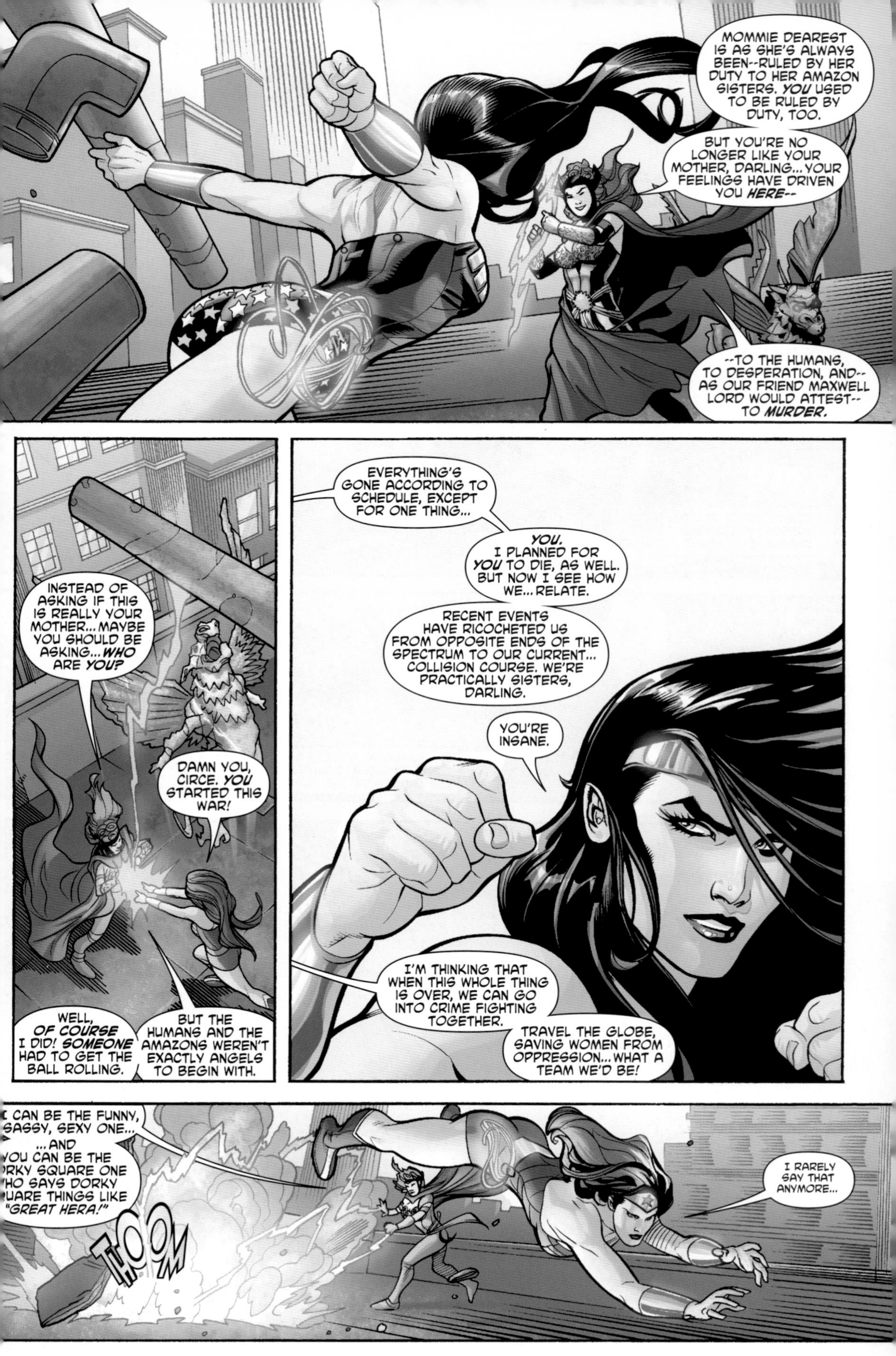

MOMMIE DEAREST IS AS SHE'S ALWAYS BEEN--RULED BY HER DUTY TO HER AMAZON SISTERS. *YOU* USED TO BE RULED BY DUTY, TOO.
BUT YOU'RE NO LONGER LIKE YOUR MOTHER, DARLING... YOUR FEELINGS HAVE DRIVEN YOU *HERE*--
--TO THE HUMANS, TO DESPERATION, AND--AS OUR FRIEND MAXWELL LORD WOULD ATTEST--TO *MURDER.*
INSTEAD OF ASKING IF THIS IS REALLY YOUR MOTHER... MAYBE YOU SHOULD BE ASKING... *WHO* ARE *YOU?*
DAMN YOU, CIRCE. *YOU* STARTED THIS WAR!
WELL, *OF COURSE* I DID! *SOMEONE* HAD TO GET THE BALL ROLLING.
BUT THE HUMANS AND THE AMAZONS WEREN'T EXACTLY ANGELS TO BEGIN WITH.
EVERYTHING'S GONE ACCORDING TO SCHEDULE, EXCEPT FOR ONE THING...
YOU. I PLANNED FOR *YOU* TO DIE, AS WELL. BUT NOW I SEE HOW WE... RELATE.
RECENT EVENTS HAVE RICOCHETED US FROM OPPOSITE ENDS OF THE SPECTRUM TO OUR CURRENT... COLLISION COURSE. WE'RE PRACTICALLY SISTERS, DARLING.
YOU'RE INSANE.
I'M THINKING THAT WHEN THIS WHOLE THING IS OVER, WE CAN GO INTO CRIME FIGHTING TOGETHER.
TRAVEL THE GLOBE, SAVING WOMEN FROM OPPRESSION... WHAT A TEAM WE'D BE!
CAN BE THE FUNNY, SASSY, SEXY ONE... ...AND YOU CAN BE THE ORKY SQUARE ONE HO SAYS DORKY UARE THINGS LIKE "GREAT HERA!"
THOOM
I RARELY SAY THAT ANYMORE...

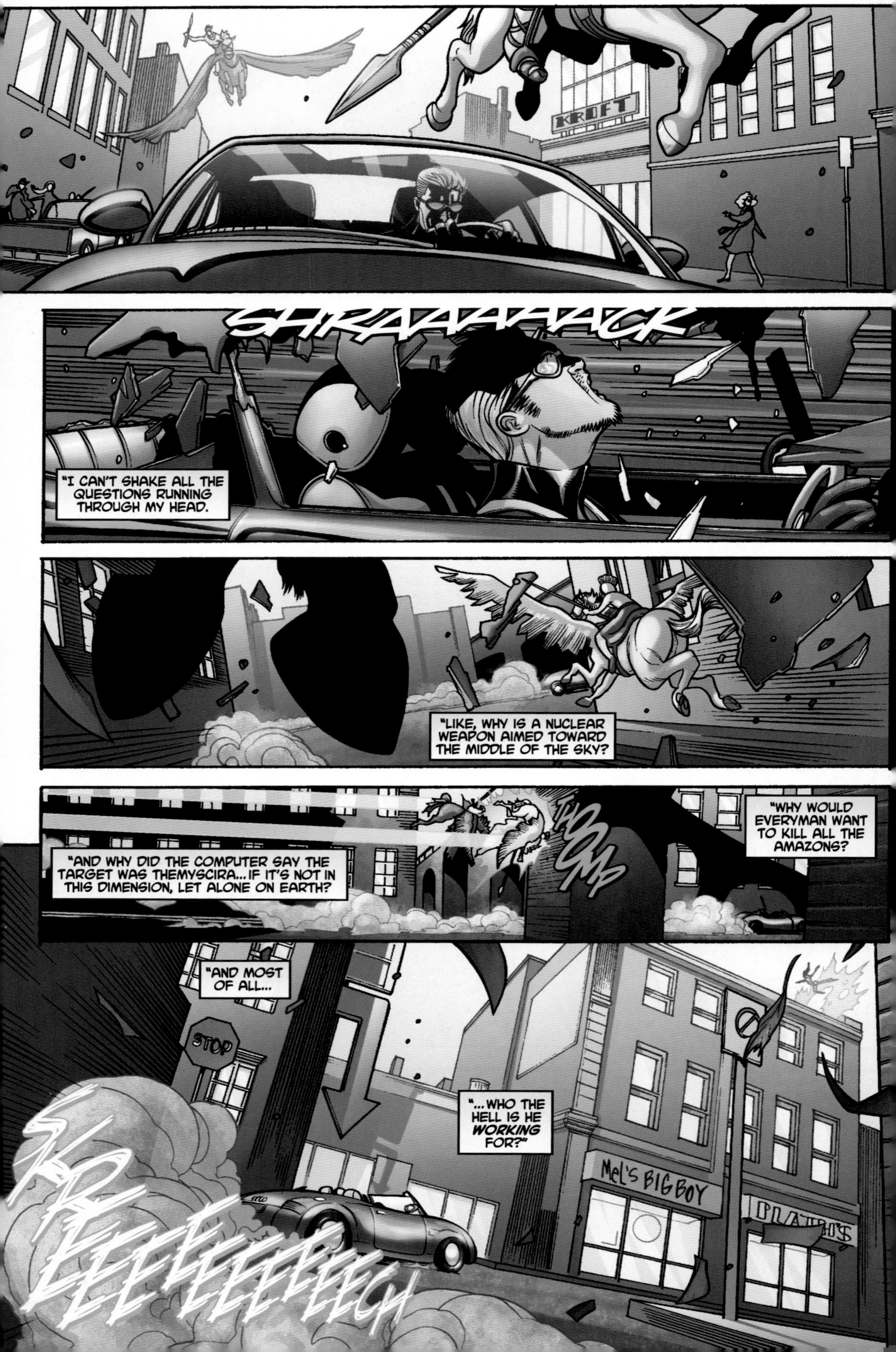
KROFT
SHRAAAAACK
"I CAN'T SHAKE ALL THE QUESTIONS RUNNING THROUGH MY HEAD.
"LIKE, WHY IS A NUCLEAR WEAPON AIMED TOWARD THE MIDDLE OF THE SKY?
"AND WHY DID THE COMPUTER SAY THE TARGET WAS THEMYSCIRA... IF IT'S NOT IN THIS DIMENSION, LET ALONE ON EARTH?
THOOMP
"WHY WOULD EVERYMAN WANT TO KILL ALL THE AMAZONS?
"AND MOST OF ALL...
STOP
"...WHO THE HELL IS HE WORKING FOR?"
Mel'S BIG BOY
SKREEEEEEEEEEEEECH

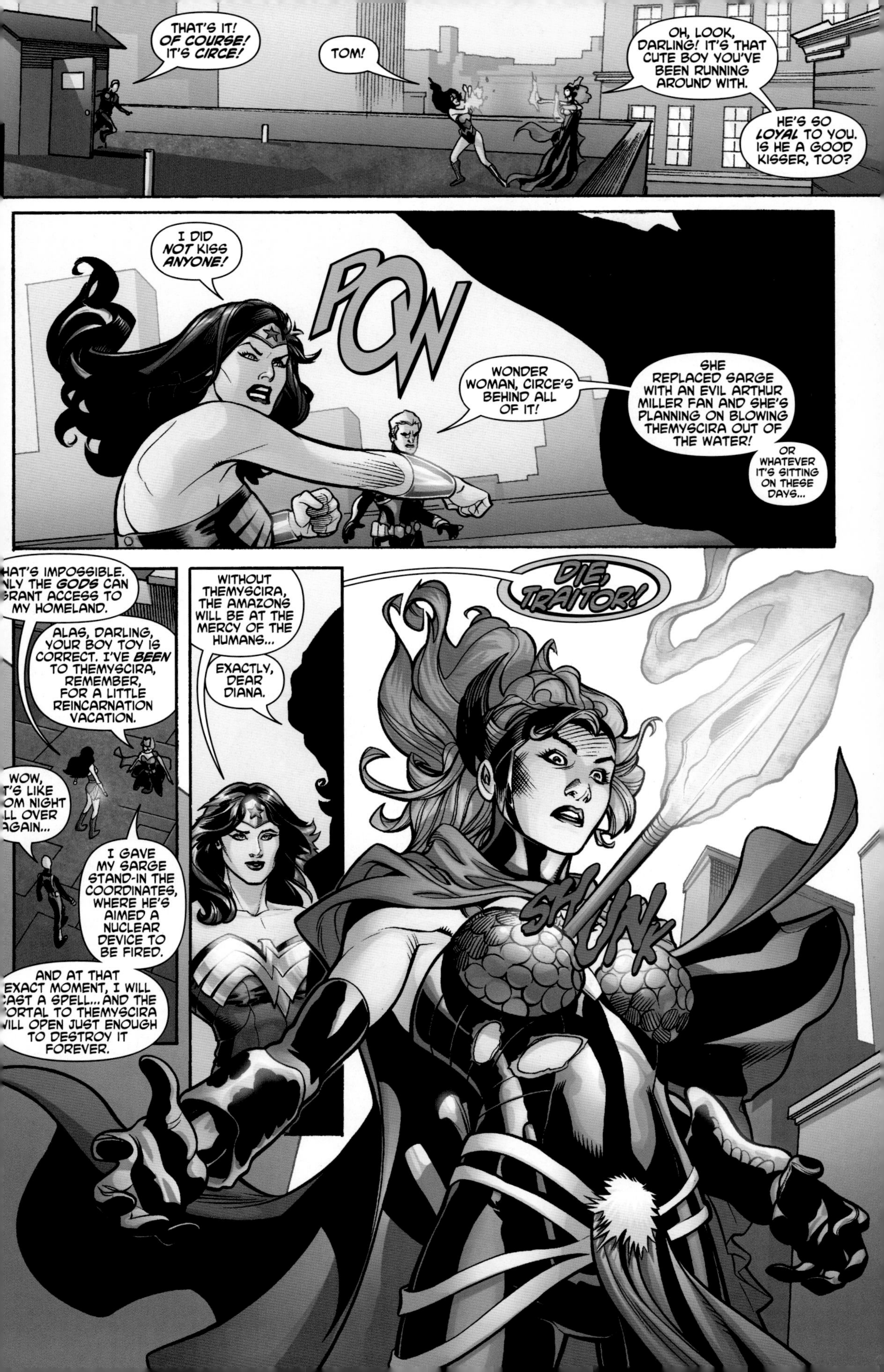

THAT'S IT! OF COURSE! IT'S CIRCE!
TOM!
OH, LOOK, DARLING! IT'S THAT CUTE BOY YOU'VE BEEN RUNNING AROUND WITH.
HE'S SO LOYAL TO YOU. IS HE A GOOD KISSER, TOO?
I DID NOT KISS ANYONE!
POW
WONDER WOMAN, CIRCE'S BEHIND ALL OF IT!
SHE REPLACED SARGE WITH AN EVIL ARTHUR MILLER FAN AND SHE'S PLANNING ON BLOWING THEMYSCIRA OUT OF THE WATER!
OR WHATEVER IT'S SITTING ON THESE DAYS...
HAT'S IMPOSSIBLE. NLY THE GODS CAN GRANT ACCESS TO MY HOMELAND.
ALAS, DARLING, YOUR BOY TOY IS CORRECT. I'VE BEEN TO THEMYSCIRA, REMEMBER, FOR A LITTLE REINCARNATION VACATION.
WOW, T'S LIKE OM NIGHT LL OVER AGAIN...
I GAVE MY SARGE STAND-IN THE COORDINATES, WHERE HE'S AIMED A NUCLEAR DEVICE TO BE FIRED.
AND AT THAT EXACT MOMENT, I WILL CAST A SPELL... AND THE ORTAL TO THEMYSCIRA WILL OPEN JUST ENOUGH TO DESTROY IT FOREVER.
WITHOUT THEMYSCIRA, THE AMAZONS WILL BE AT THE MERCY OF THE HUMANS...
EXACTLY, DEAR DIANA.
DIE, TRAITOR!
SHUNK

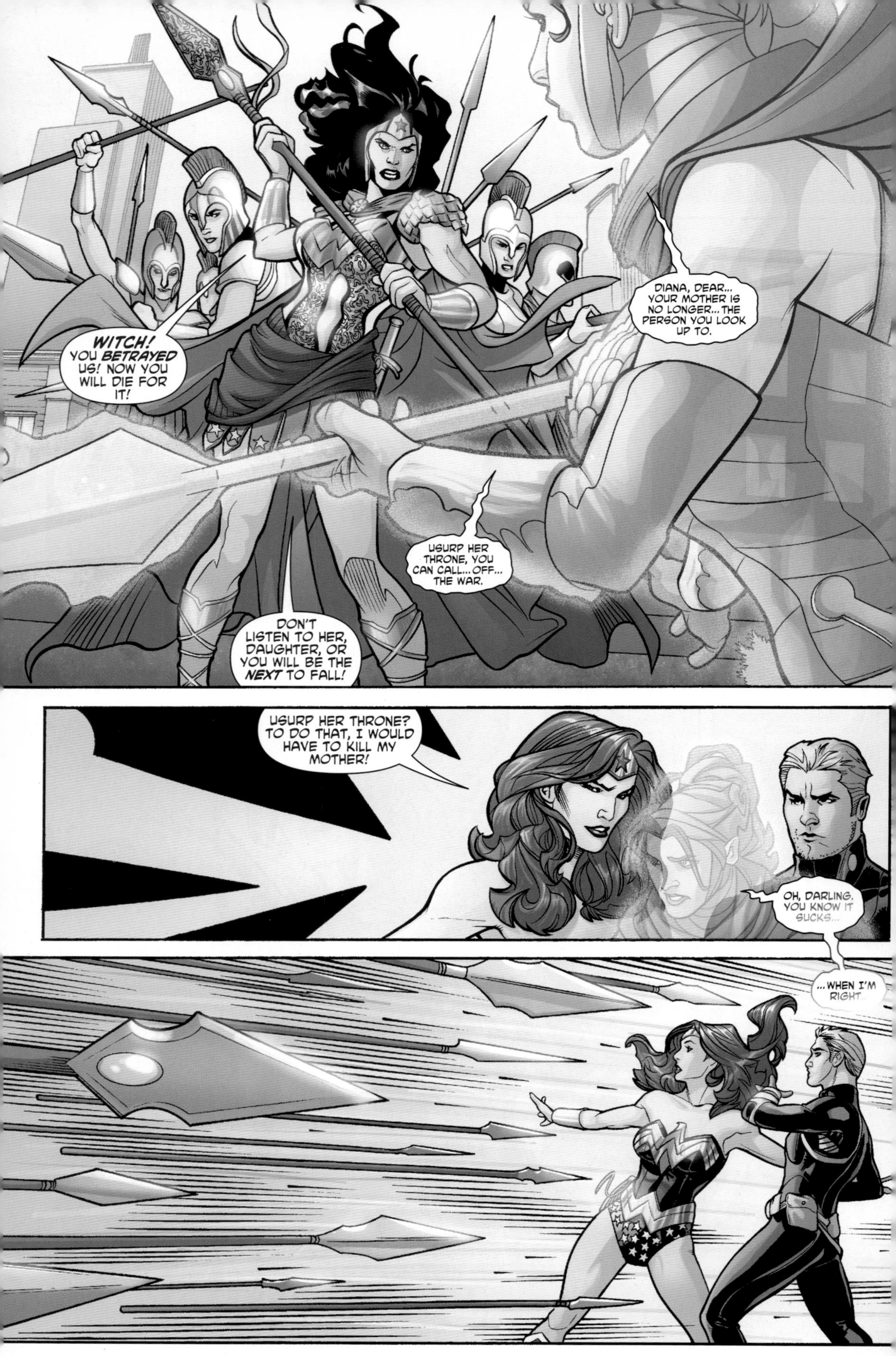

WITCH! YOU BETRAYED US! NOW YOU WILL DIE FOR IT!
DIANA, DEAR... YOUR MOTHER IS NO LONGER... THE PERSON YOU LOOK UP TO.
USURP HER THRONE, YOU CAN CALL... OFF... THE WAR.
DON'T LISTEN TO HER, DAUGHTER, OR YOU WILL BE THE NEXT TO FALL!
USURP HER THRONE? TO DO THAT, I WOULD HAVE TO KILL MY MOTHER!
OH, DARLING. YOU KNOW IT SUCKS...
...WHEN I'M RIGHT.

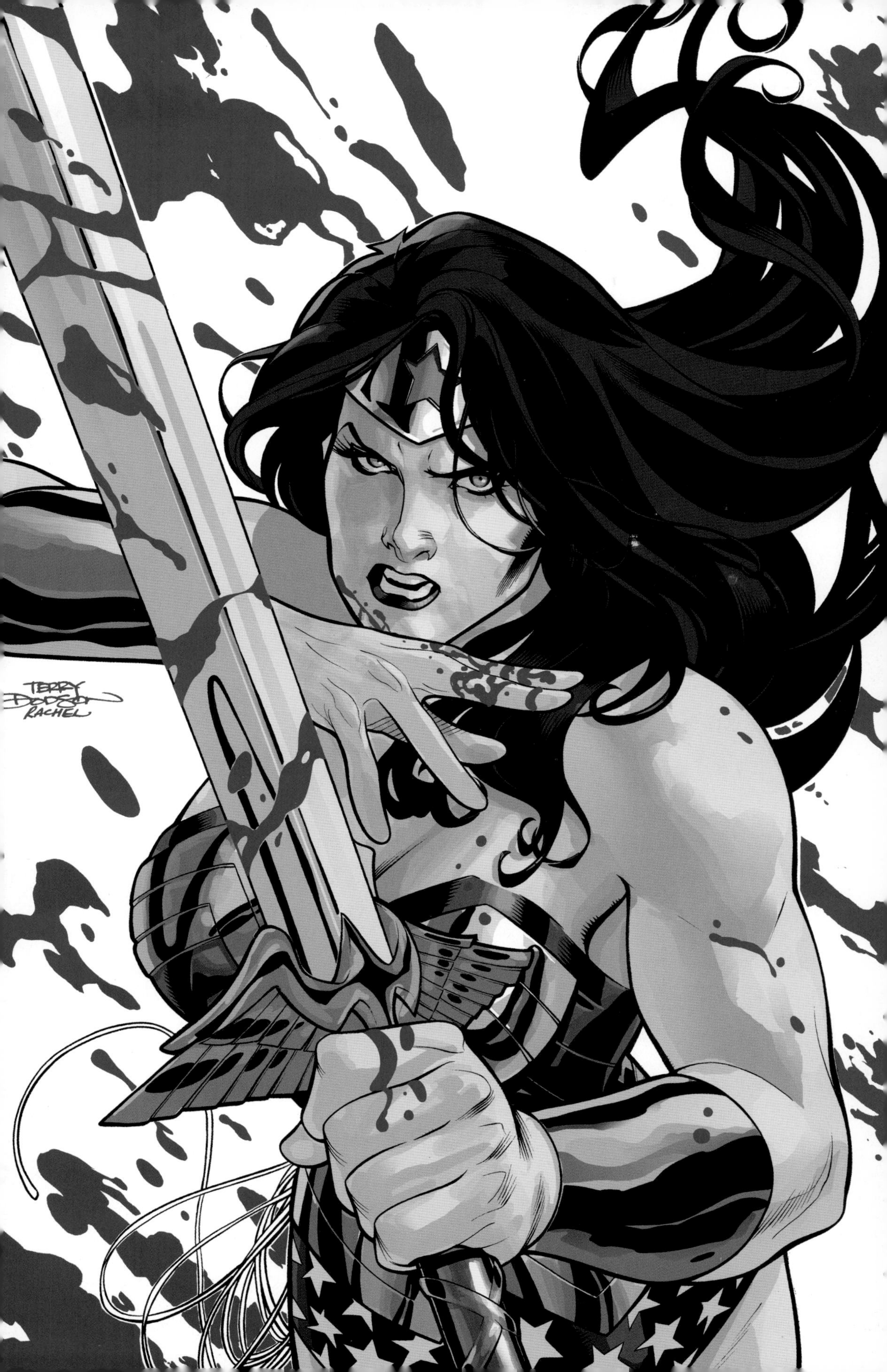
TERRY
DODSON
RACHEL

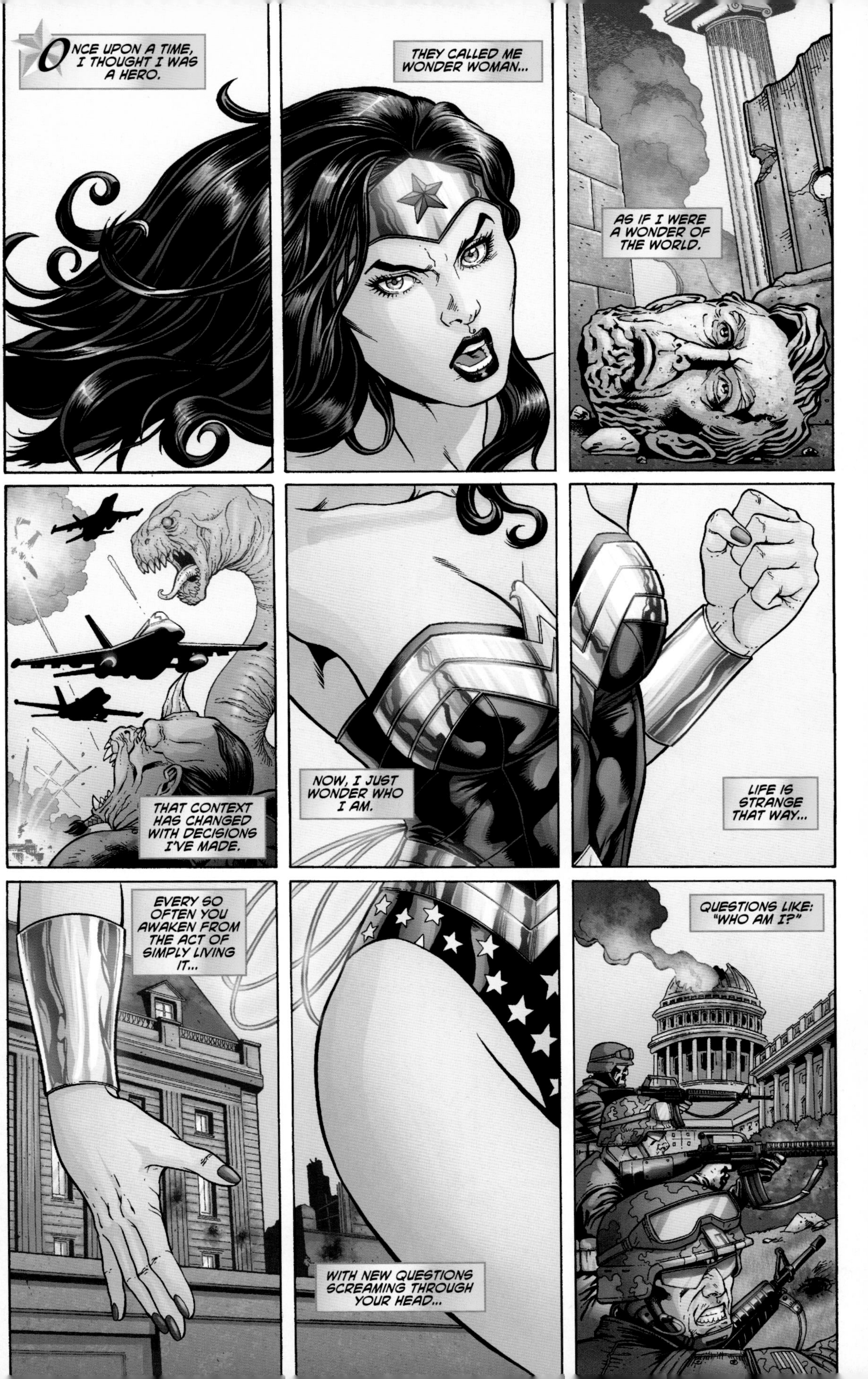
ONCE UPON A TIME, I THOUGHT I WAS A HERO.
THEY CALLED ME WONDER WOMAN...
AS IF I WERE A WONDER OF THE WORLD.
THAT CONTEXT HAS CHANGED WITH DECISIONS I'VE MADE.
NOW, I JUST WONDER WHO I AM.
LIFE IS STRANGE THAT WAY...
EVERY SO OFTEN YOU AWAKEN FROM THE ACT OF SIMPLY LIVING IT...
WITH NEW QUESTIONS SCREAMING THROUGH YOUR HEAD...
QUESTIONS LIKE: "WHO AM I?"

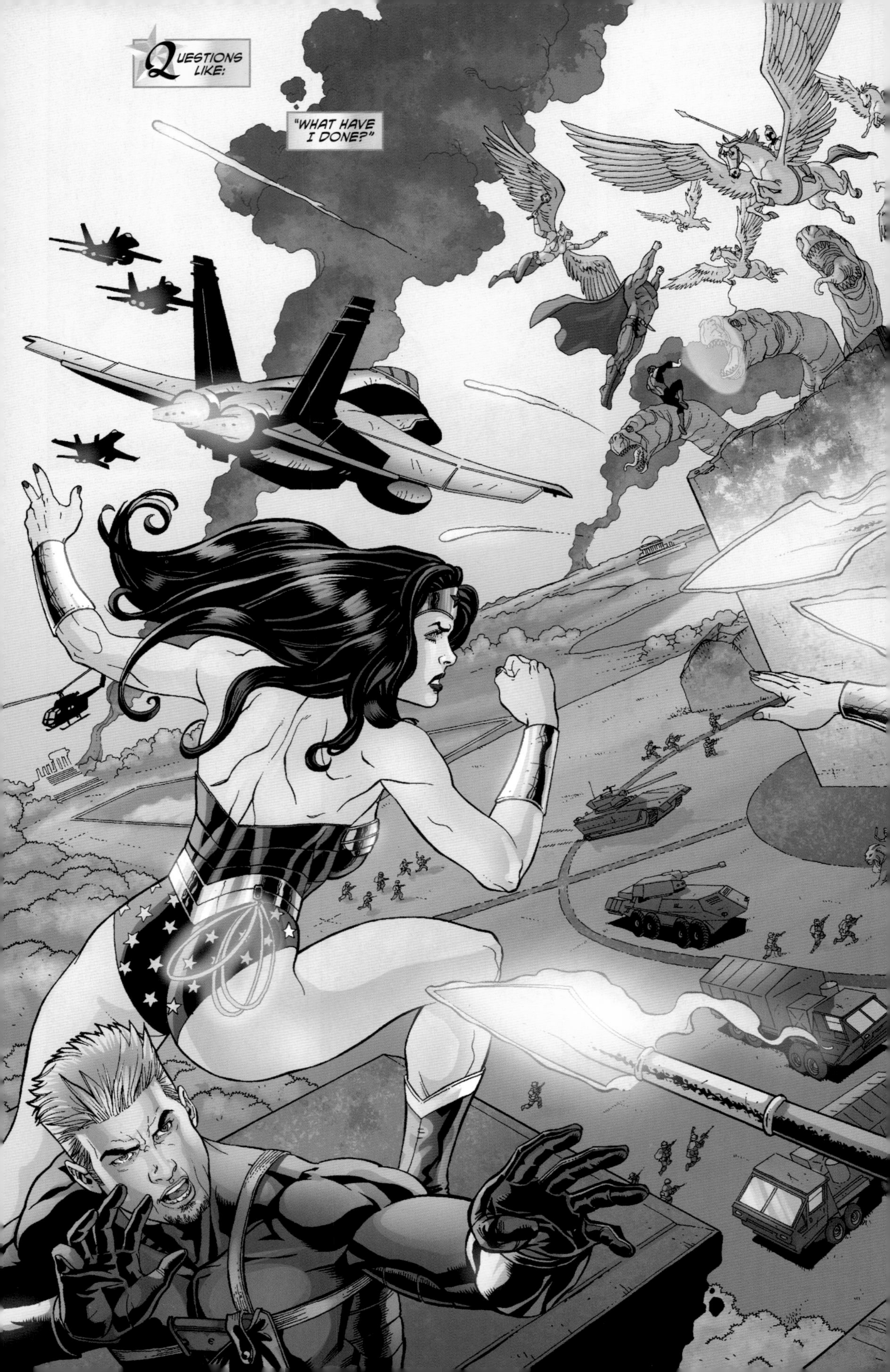
QUESTIONS LIKE:
"WHAT HAVE I DONE?"

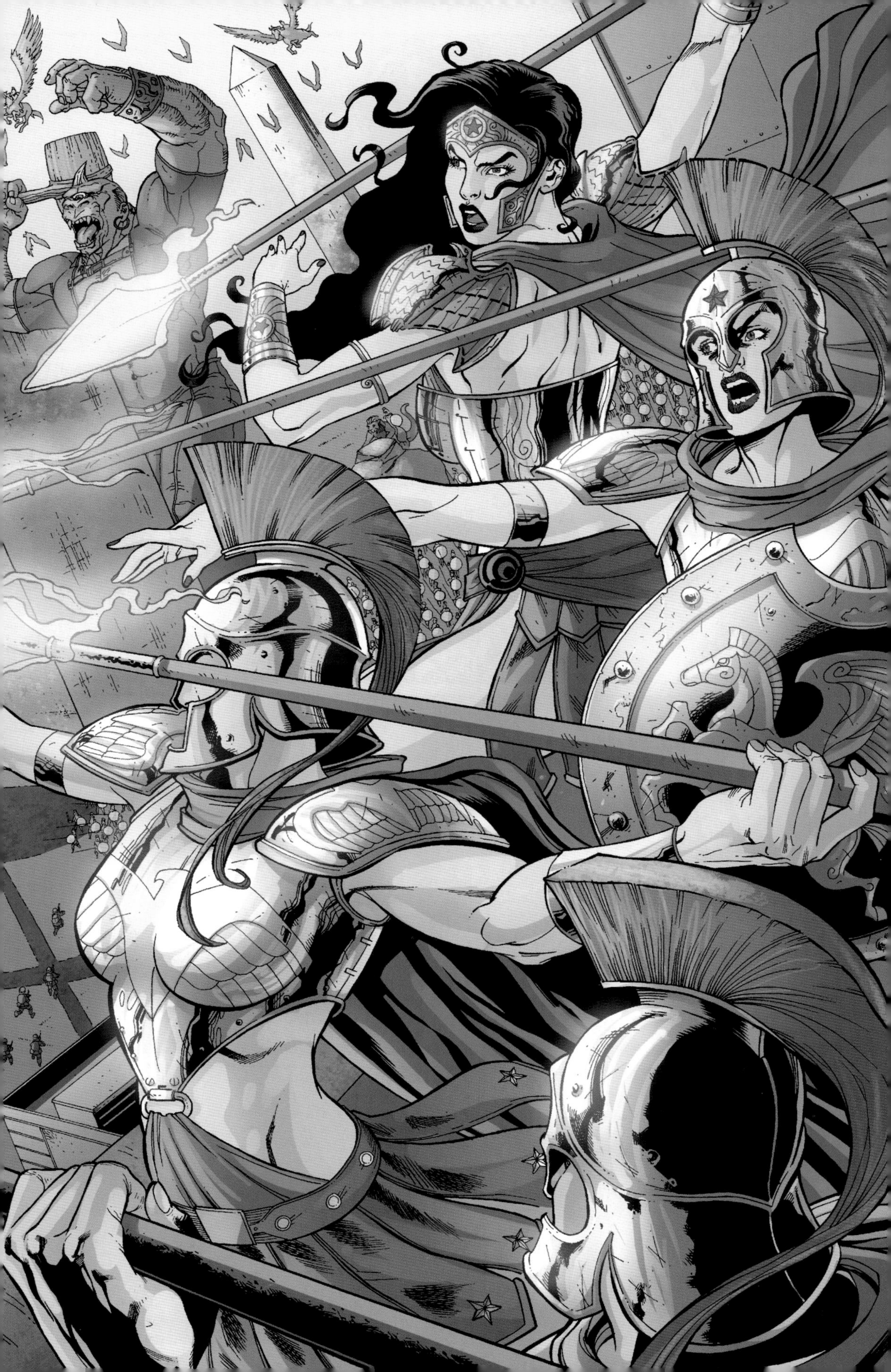

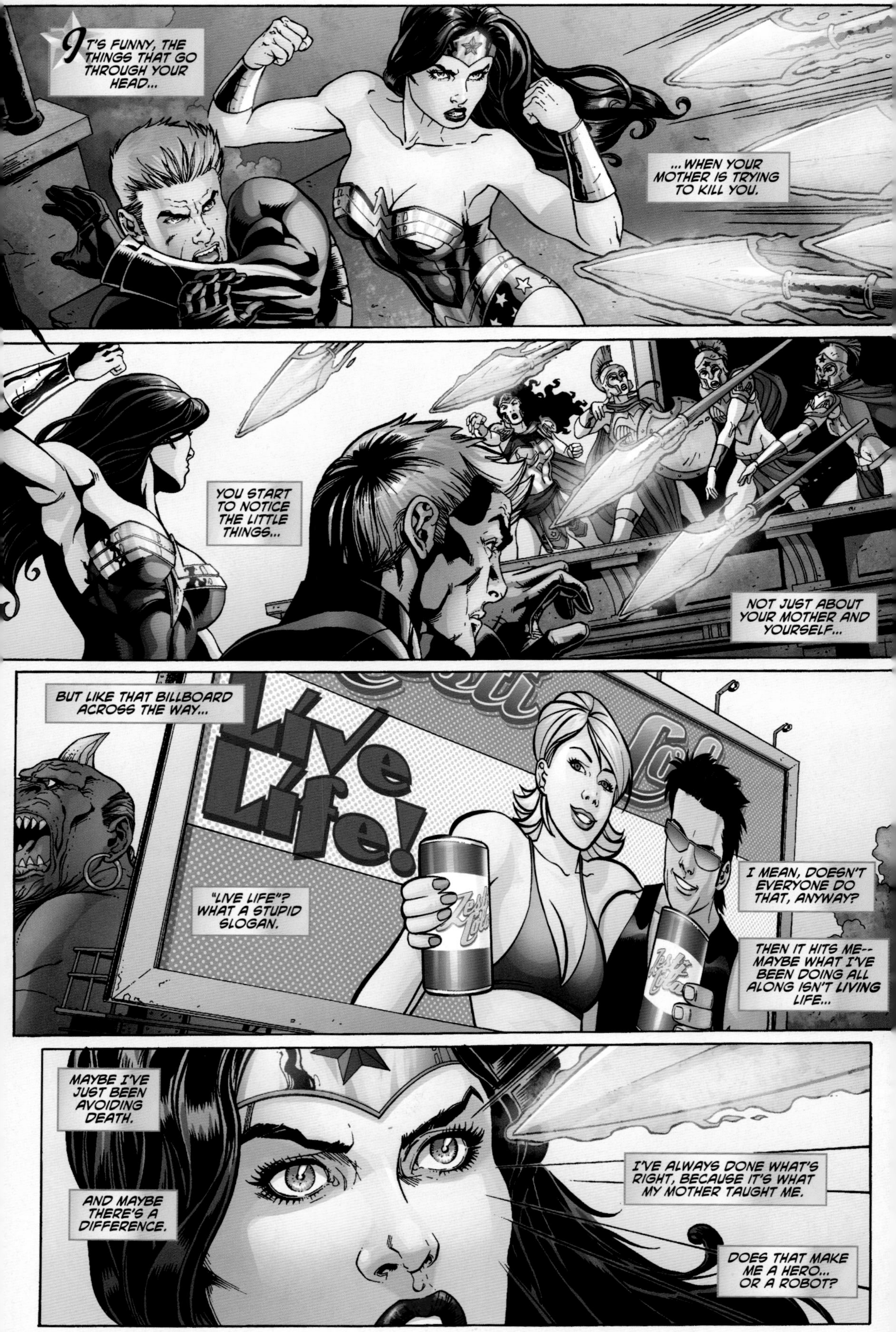
IT'S FUNNY, THE THINGS THAT GO THROUGH YOUR HEAD...
...WHEN YOUR MOTHER IS TRYING TO KILL YOU.
YOU START TO NOTICE THE LITTLE THINGS...
NOT JUST ABOUT YOUR MOTHER AND YOURSELF...
BUT LIKE THAT BILLBOARD ACROSS THE WAY...
Live Life!
"LIVE LIFE"? WHAT A STUPID SLOGAN.
I MEAN, DOESN'T EVERYONE DO THAT, ANYWAY?
THEN IT HITS ME-- MAYBE WHAT I'VE BEEN DOING ALL ALONG ISN'T LIVING LIFE...
MAYBE I'VE JUST BEEN AVOIDING DEATH.
AND MAYBE THERE'S A DIFFERENCE.
I'VE ALWAYS DONE WHAT'S RIGHT, BECAUSE IT'S WHAT MY MOTHER TAUGHT ME.
DOES THAT MAKE ME A HERO... OR A ROBOT?

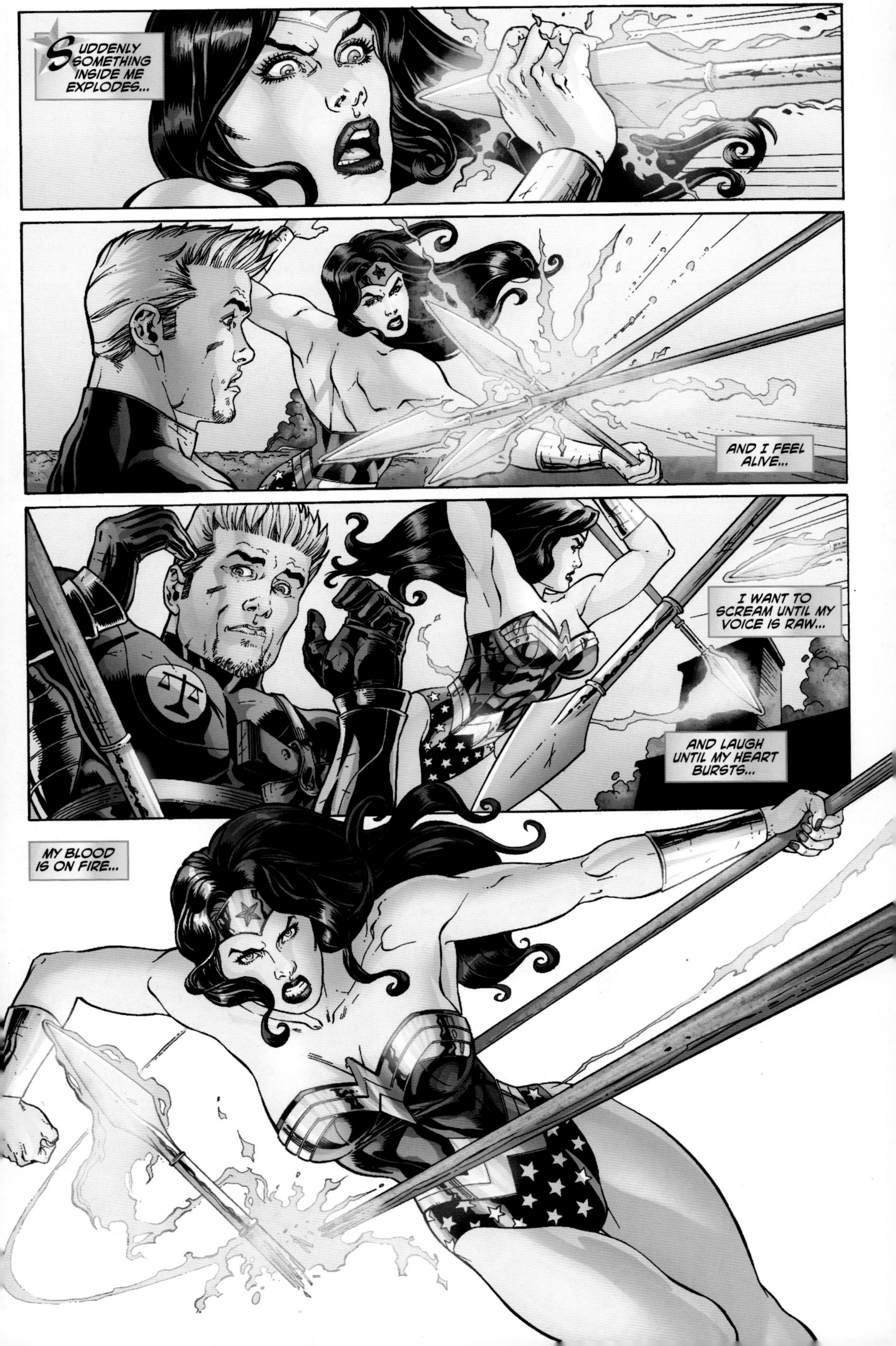
SUDDENLY SOMETHING INSIDE ME EXPLODES...
AND I FEEL ALIVE...
I WANT TO SCREAM UNTIL MY VOICE IS RAW...
AND LAUGH UNTIL MY HEART BURSTS...
MY BLOOD IS ON FIRE...

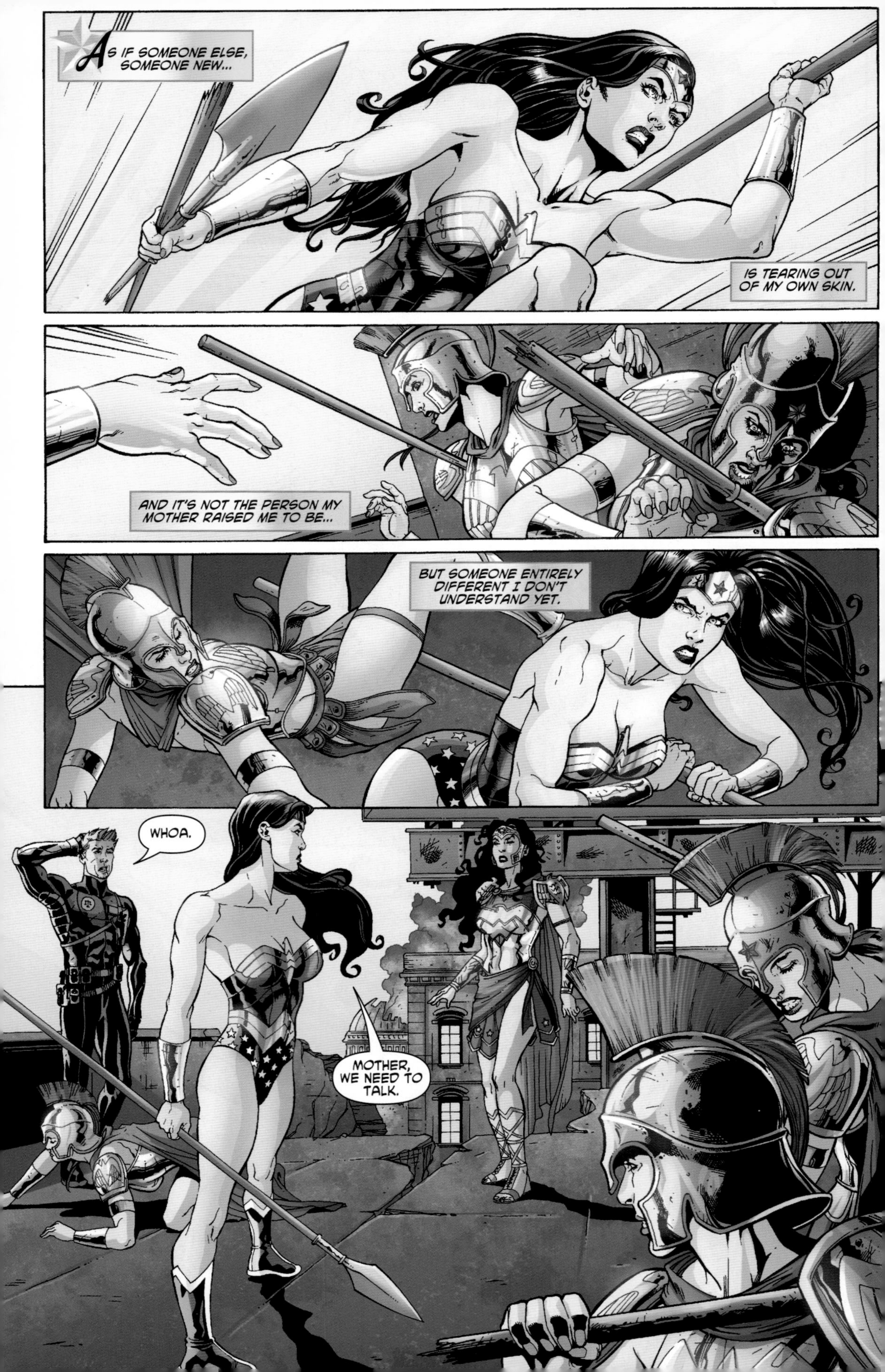
AS IF SOMEONE ELSE, SOMEONE NEW...
IS TEARING OUT OF MY OWN SKIN.
AND IT'S NOT THE PERSON MY MOTHER RAISED ME TO BE...
BUT SOMEONE ENTIRELY DIFFERENT I DON'T UNDERSTAND YET.
WHOA.
MOTHER, WE NEED TO TALK.

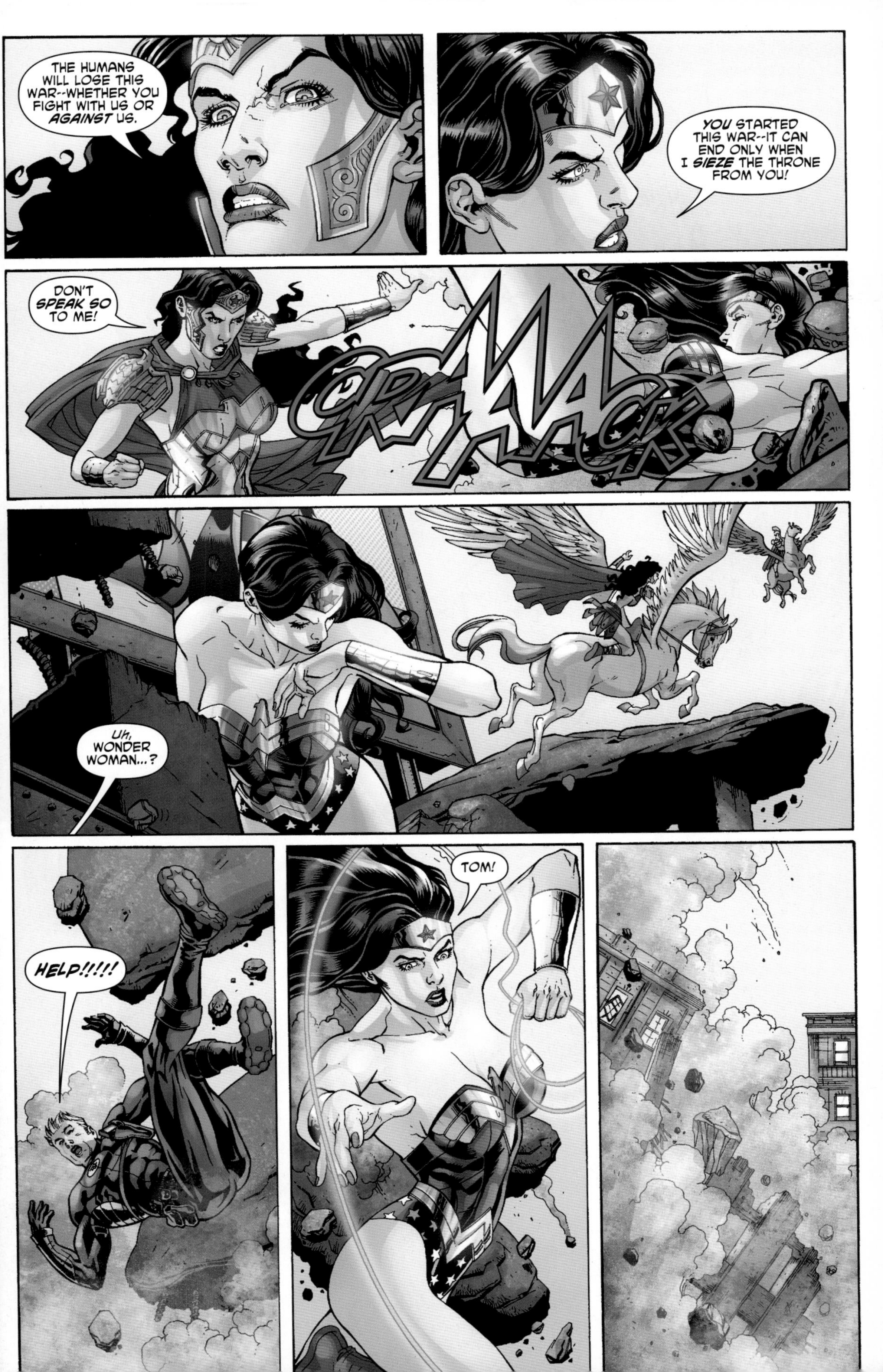
THE HUMANS WILL LOSE THIS WAR--WHETHER YOU FIGHT WITH US OR AGAINST US.
YOU STARTED THIS WAR--IT CAN END ONLY WHEN I SIEZE THE THRONE FROM YOU!
DON'T SPEAK SO TO ME!
CRAAACK
UH, WONDER WOMAN...?
HELP!!!!!
TOM!

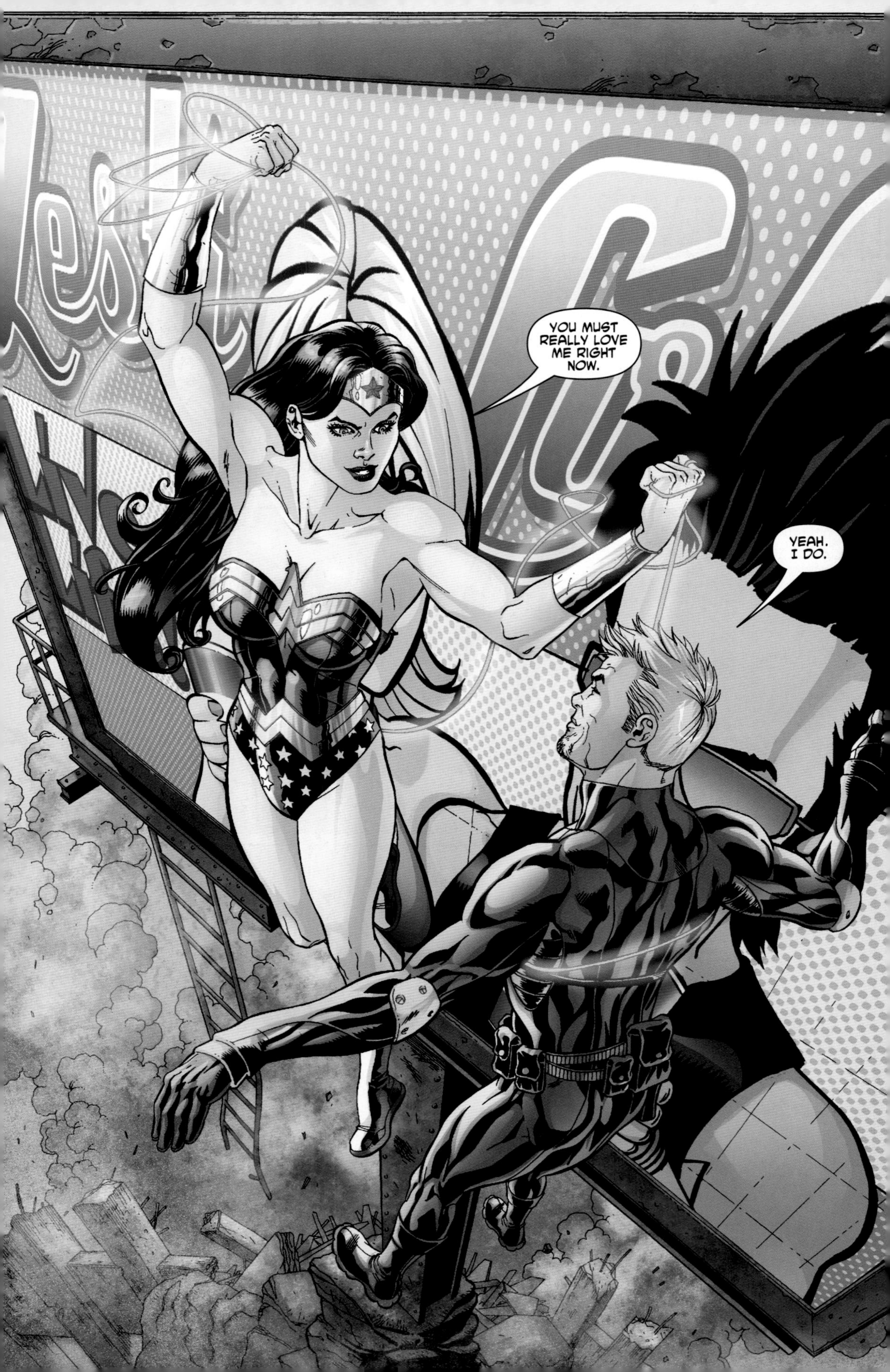
YOU MUST REALLY LOVE ME RIGHT NOW.
YEAH. I DO.

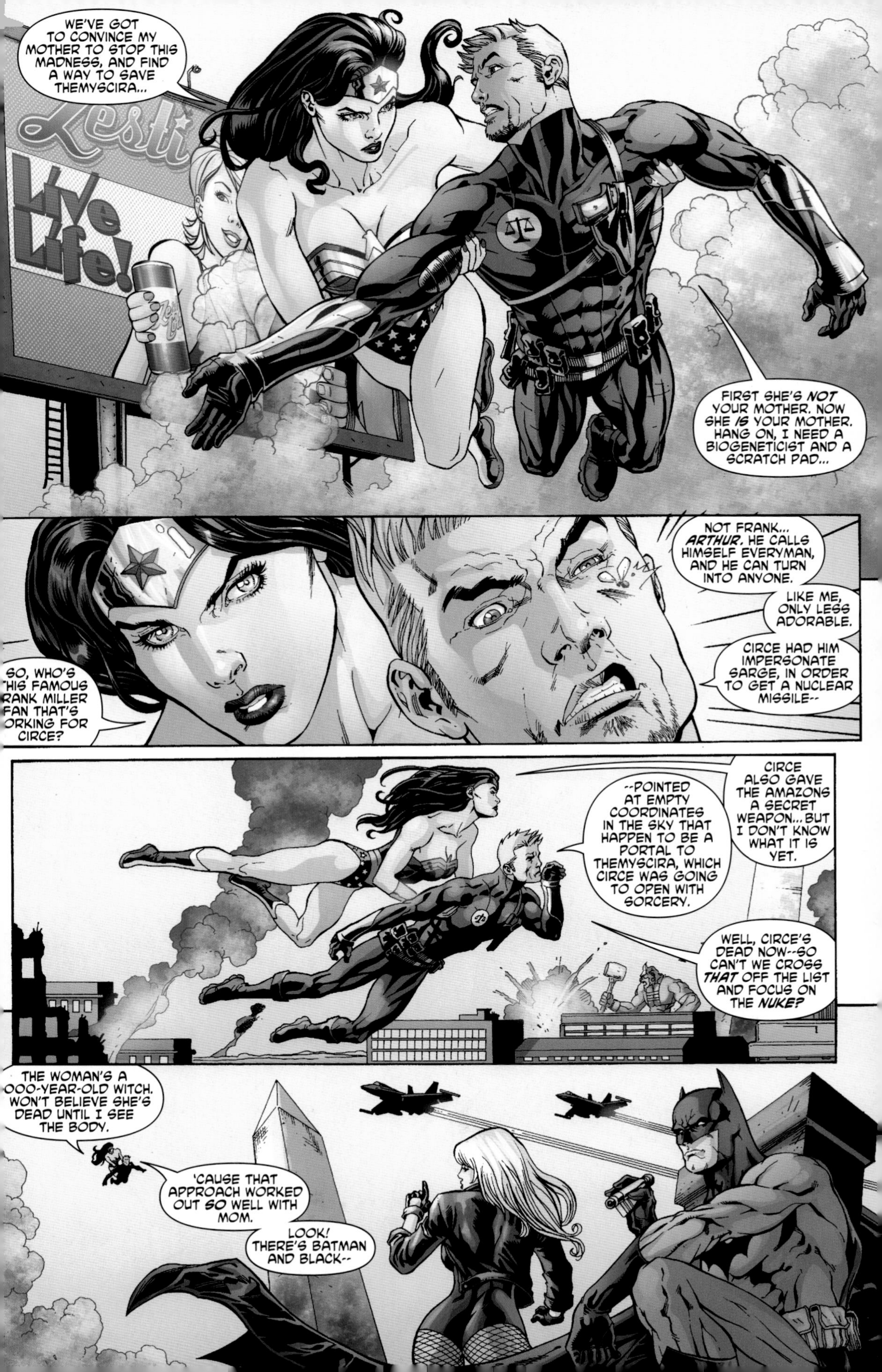
WE'VE GOT TO CONVINCE MY MOTHER TO STOP THIS MADNESS, AND FIND A WAY TO SAVE THEMYSCIRA...
Zesti
Live Life!
FIRST SHE'S *NOT* YOUR MOTHER. NOW SHE *IS* YOUR MOTHER. HANG ON, I NEED A BIOGENETICIST AND A SCRATCH PAD...
SO, WHO'S THIS FAMOUS FRANK MILLER FAN THAT'S WORKING FOR CIRCE?
NOT FRANK... *ARTHUR.* HE CALLS HIMSELF EVERYMAN, AND HE CAN TURN INTO ANYONE.
LIKE ME, ONLY LESS ADORABLE.
CIRCE HAD HIM IMPERSONATE SARGE, IN ORDER TO GET A NUCLEAR MISSILE--
--POINTED AT EMPTY COORDINATES IN THE SKY THAT HAPPEN TO BE A PORTAL TO THEMYSCIRA, WHICH CIRCE WAS GOING TO OPEN WITH SORCERY.
CIRCE ALSO GAVE THE AMAZONS A SECRET WEAPON... BUT I DON'T KNOW WHAT IT IS YET.
WELL, CIRCE'S DEAD NOW--SO CAN'T WE CROSS *THAT* OFF THE LIST AND FOCUS ON THE *NUKE?*
THE WOMAN'S A 3000-YEAR-OLD WITCH. I WON'T BELIEVE SHE'S DEAD UNTIL I SEE THE BODY.
'CAUSE THAT APPROACH WORKED OUT *SO* WELL WITH MOM.
LOOK! THERE'S BATMAN AND BLACK--

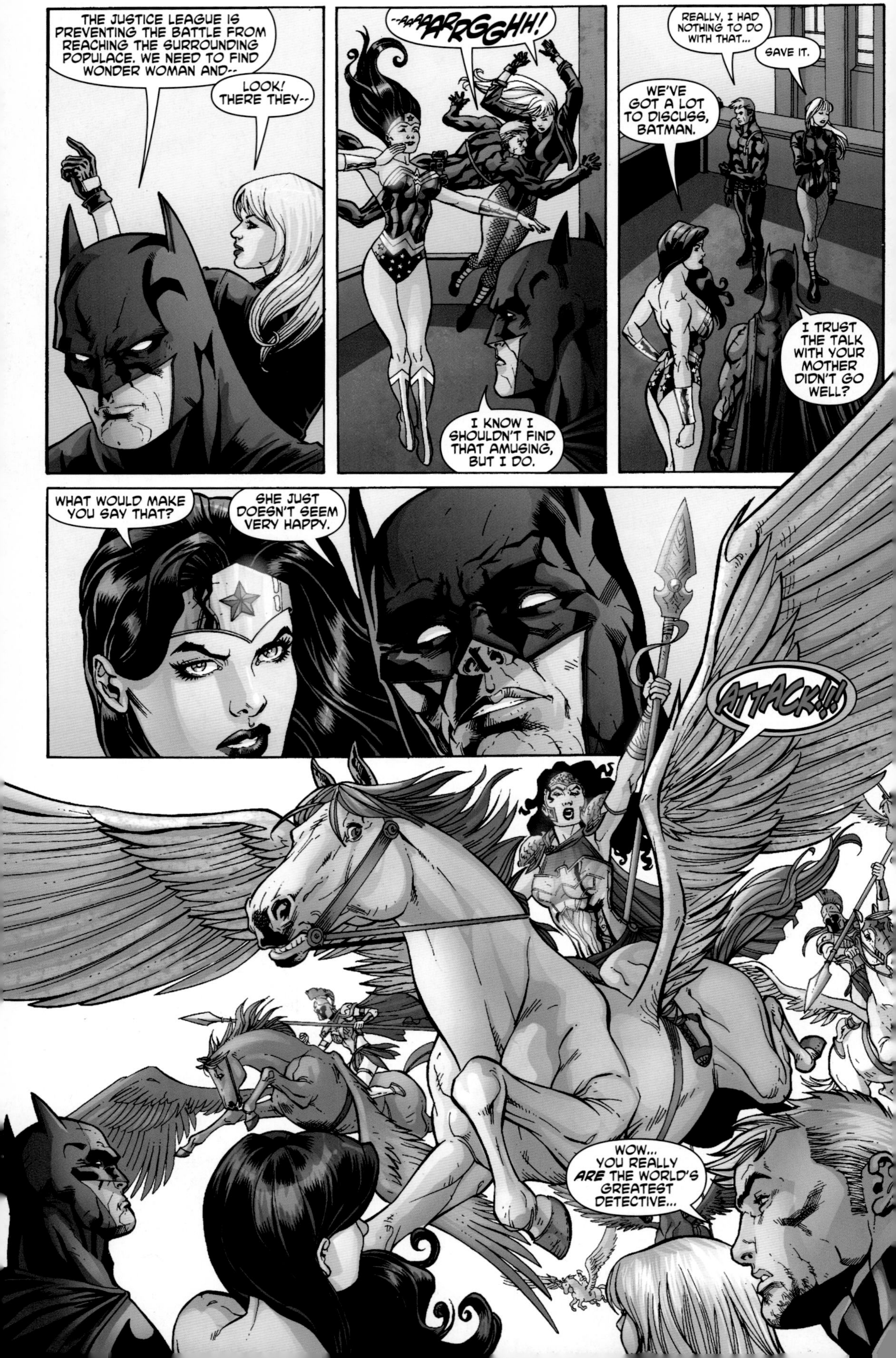
THE JUSTICE LEAGUE IS PREVENTING THE BATTLE FROM REACHING THE SURROUNDING POPULACE. WE NEED TO FIND WONDER WOMAN AND--
LOOK! THERE THEY--
--AAAAARRGGHH!
I KNOW I SHOULDN'T FIND THAT AMUSING, BUT I DO.
REALLY, I HAD NOTHING TO DO WITH THAT...
SAVE IT.
WE'VE GOT A LOT TO DISCUSS, BATMAN.
I TRUST THE TALK WITH YOUR MOTHER DIDN'T GO WELL?
WHAT WOULD MAKE YOU SAY THAT?
SHE JUST DOESN'T SEEM VERY HAPPY.
ATTACK!!!
WOW... YOU REALLY ARE THE WORLD'S GREATEST DETECTIVE...

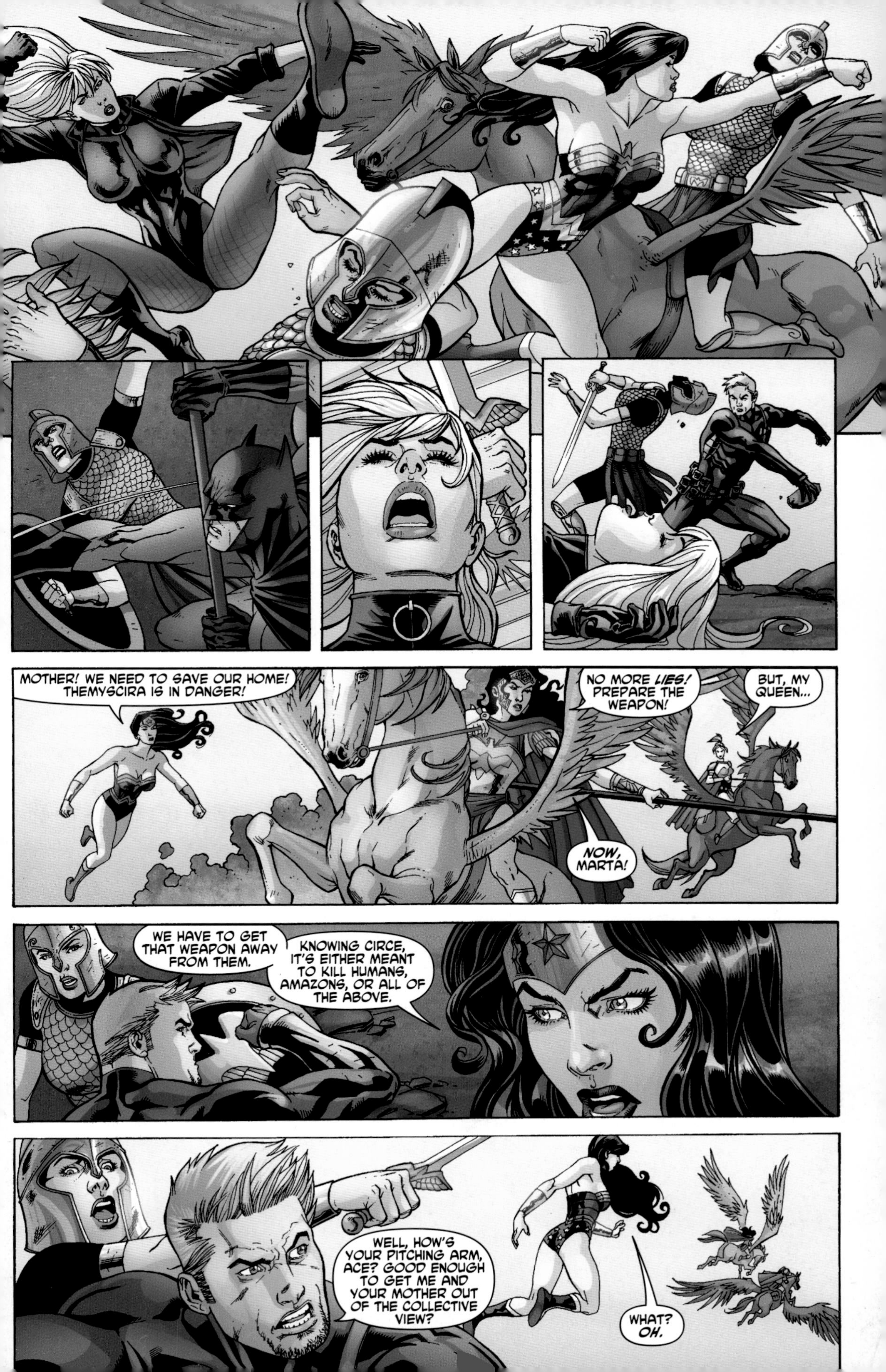
MOTHER! WE NEED TO SAVE OUR HOME! THEMYSCIRA IS IN DANGER!
NO MORE *LIES!* PREPARE THE WEAPON!
BUT, MY QUEEN...
NOW, MARTA!
WE HAVE TO GET THAT WEAPON AWAY FROM THEM.
KNOWING CIRCE, IT'S EITHER MEANT TO KILL HUMANS, AMAZONS, OR ALL OF THE ABOVE.
WELL, HOW'S YOUR PITCHING ARM, ACE? GOOD ENOUGH TO GET ME AND YOUR MOTHER OUT OF THE COLLECTIVE VIEW?
WHAT? *OH.*

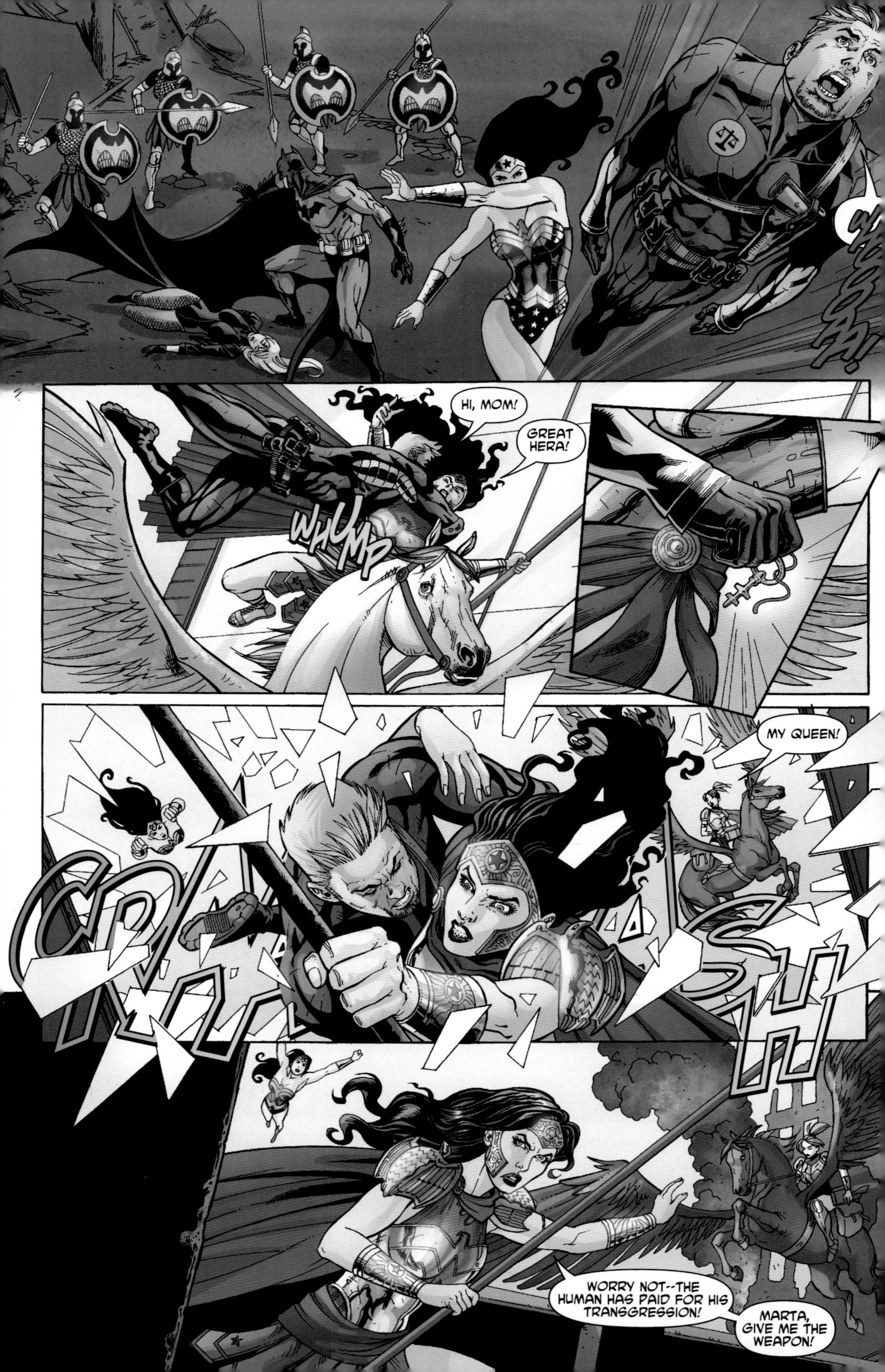

WHOOOA!
HI, MOM!
GREAT HERA!
WHUMP
MY QUEEN!
CRASH
WORRY NOT--THE HUMAN HAS PAID FOR HIS TRANSGRESSION!
MARTA, GIVE ME THE WEAPON!

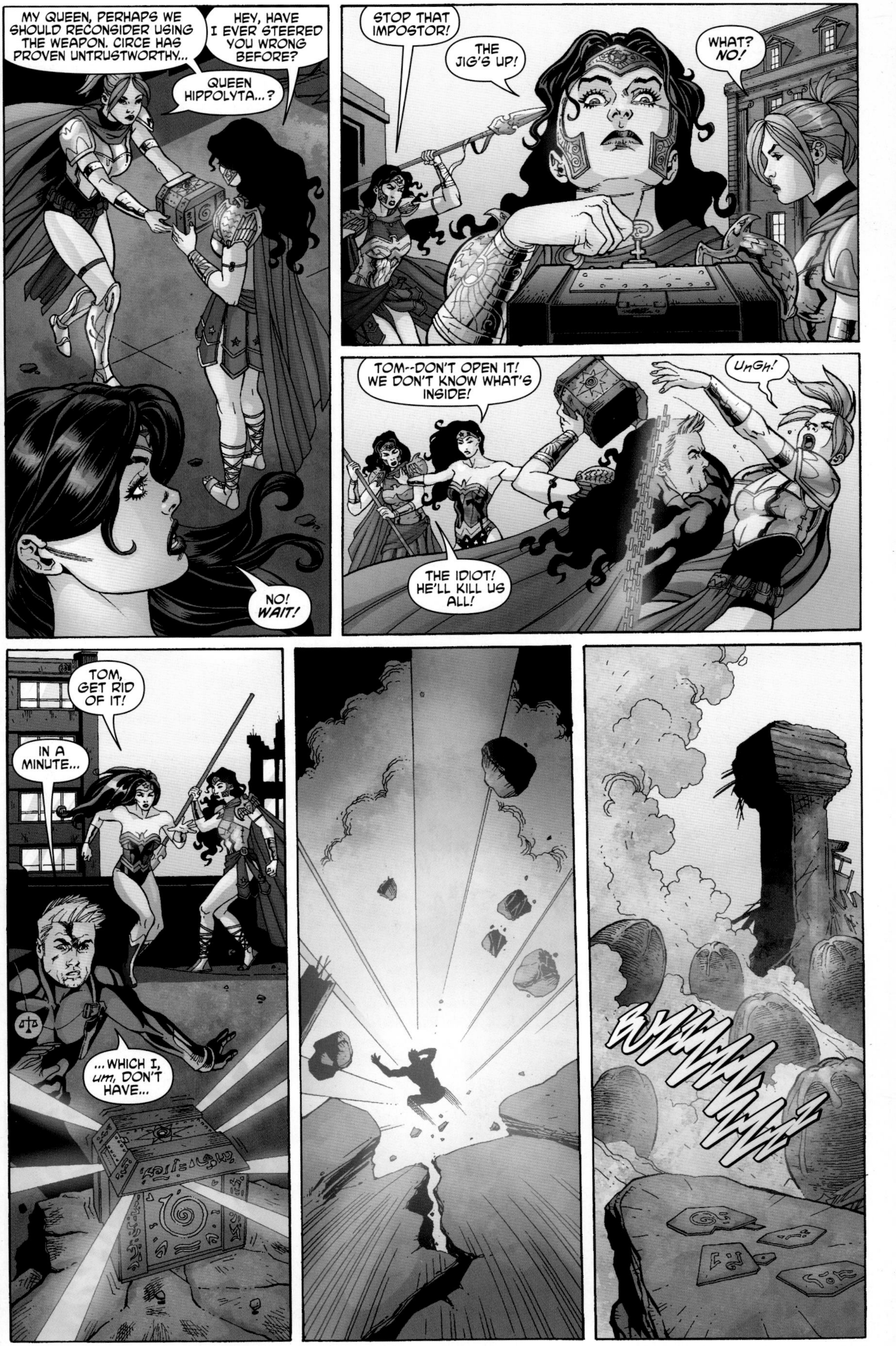
MY QUEEN, PERHAPS WE SHOULD RECONSIDER USING THE WEAPON. CIRCE HAS PROVEN UNTRUSTWORTHY...
HEY, HAVE I EVER STEERED YOU WRONG BEFORE?
QUEEN HIPPOLYTA...?
NO! WAIT!
STOP THAT IMPOSTOR!
THE JIG'S UP!
WHAT? NO!
TOM--DON'T OPEN IT! WE DON'T KNOW WHAT'S INSIDE!
UnGh!
THE IDIOT! HE'LL KILL US ALL!
TOM, GET RID OF IT!
IN A MINUTE...
...WHICH I, um, DON'T HAVE...
BWMMMMM

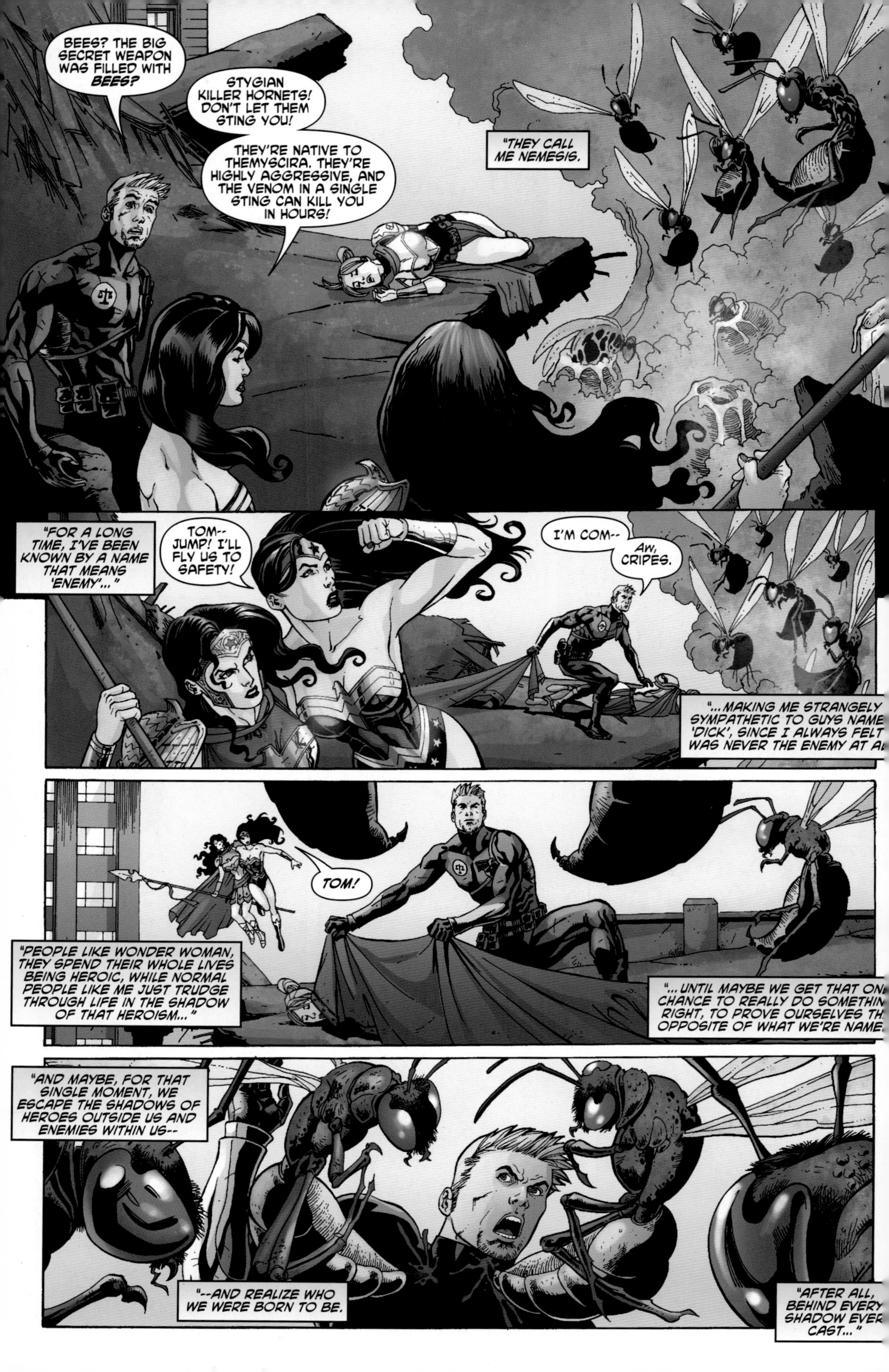
BEES? THE BIG SECRET WEAPON WAS FILLED WITH BEES?
STYGIAN KILLER HORNETS! DON'T LET THEM STING YOU!
THEY'RE NATIVE TO THEMYSCIRA. THEY'RE HIGHLY AGGRESSIVE, AND THE VENOM IN A SINGLE STING CAN KILL YOU IN HOURS!
"THEY CALL ME NEMESIS.
"FOR A LONG TIME, I'VE BEEN KNOWN BY A NAME THAT MEANS 'ENEMY'..."
TOM-- JUMP! I'LL FLY US TO SAFETY!
I'M COM--
AW, CRIPES.
"...MAKING ME STRANGELY SYMPATHETIC TO GUYS NAME 'DICK', SINCE I ALWAYS FELT WAS NEVER THE ENEMY AT A
TOM!
"PEOPLE LIKE WONDER WOMAN, THEY SPEND THEIR WHOLE LIVES BEING HEROIC, WHILE NORMAL PEOPLE LIKE ME JUST TRUDGE THROUGH LIFE IN THE SHADOW OF THAT HEROISM..."
"...UNTIL MAYBE WE GET THAT ON CHANCE TO REALLY DO SOMETHIN RIGHT, TO PROVE OURSELVES TH OPPOSITE OF WHAT WE'RE NAME
"AND MAYBE, FOR THAT SINGLE MOMENT, WE ESCAPE THE SHADOWS OF HEROES OUTSIDE US AND ENEMIES WITHIN US--
"--AND REALIZE WHO WE WERE BORN TO BE.
"AFTER ALL, BEHIND EVERY SHADOW EVER CAST..."

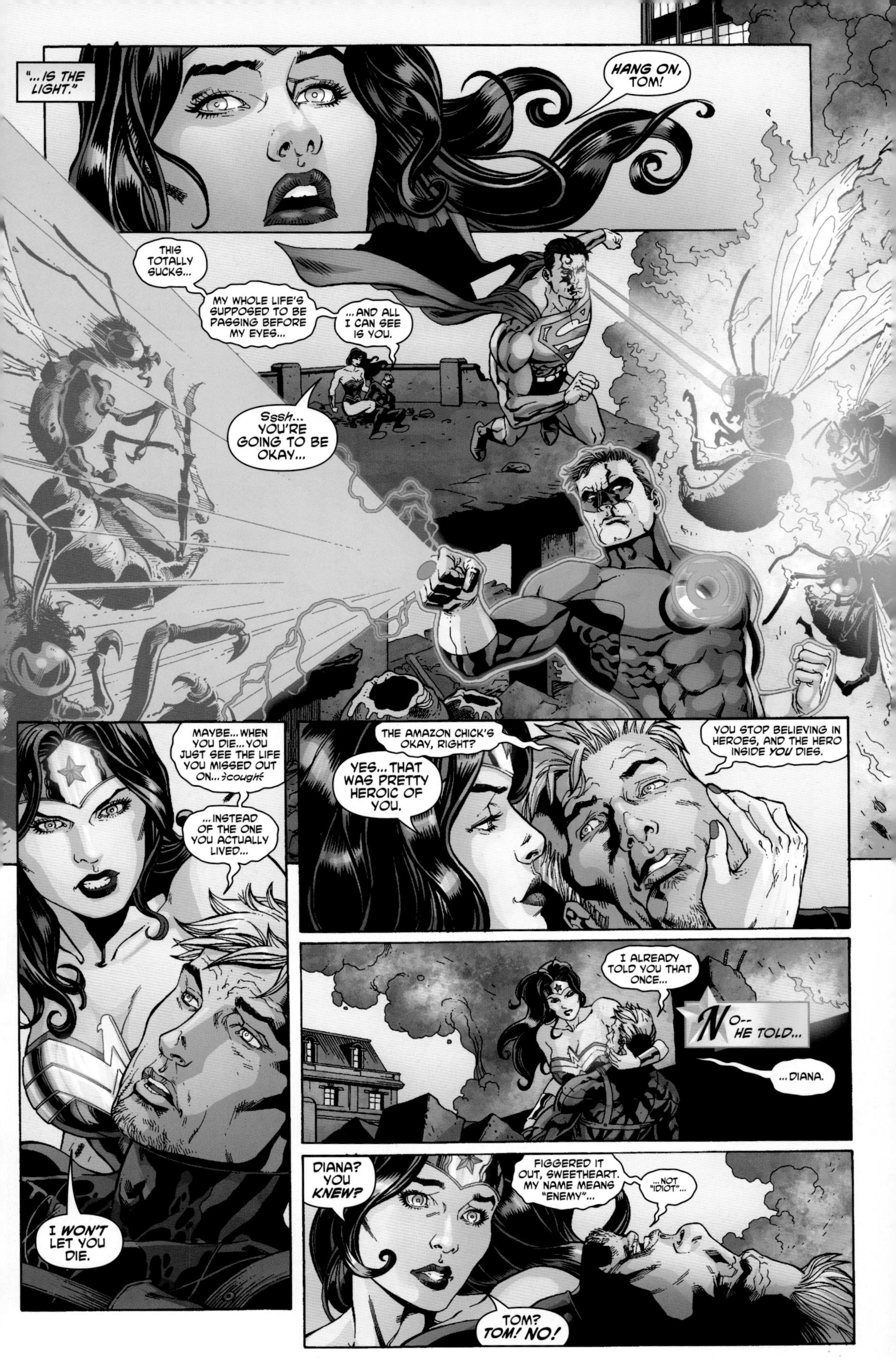
"...IS THE LIGHT."
HANG ON, TOM!
THIS TOTALLY SUCKS...
MY WHOLE LIFE'S SUPPOSED TO BE PASSING BEFORE MY EYES...
...AND ALL I CAN SEE IS YOU.
Sssh... YOU'RE GOING TO BE OKAY...
MAYBE...WHEN YOU DIE...YOU JUST SEE THE LIFE YOU MISSED OUT ON...cough
...INSTEAD OF THE ONE YOU ACTUALLY LIVED...
I WON'T LET YOU DIE.
THE AMAZON CHICK'S OKAY, RIGHT?
YES...THAT WAS PRETTY HEROIC OF YOU.
YOU STOP BELIEVING IN HEROES, AND THE HERO INSIDE YOU DIES.
I ALREADY TOLD YOU THAT ONCE...
NO-- HE TOLD...
...DIANA.
DIANA? YOU KNEW?
FIGGERED IT OUT, SWEETHEART. MY NAME MEANS "ENEMY"...
...NOT "IDIOT"...
TOM? TOM! NO!

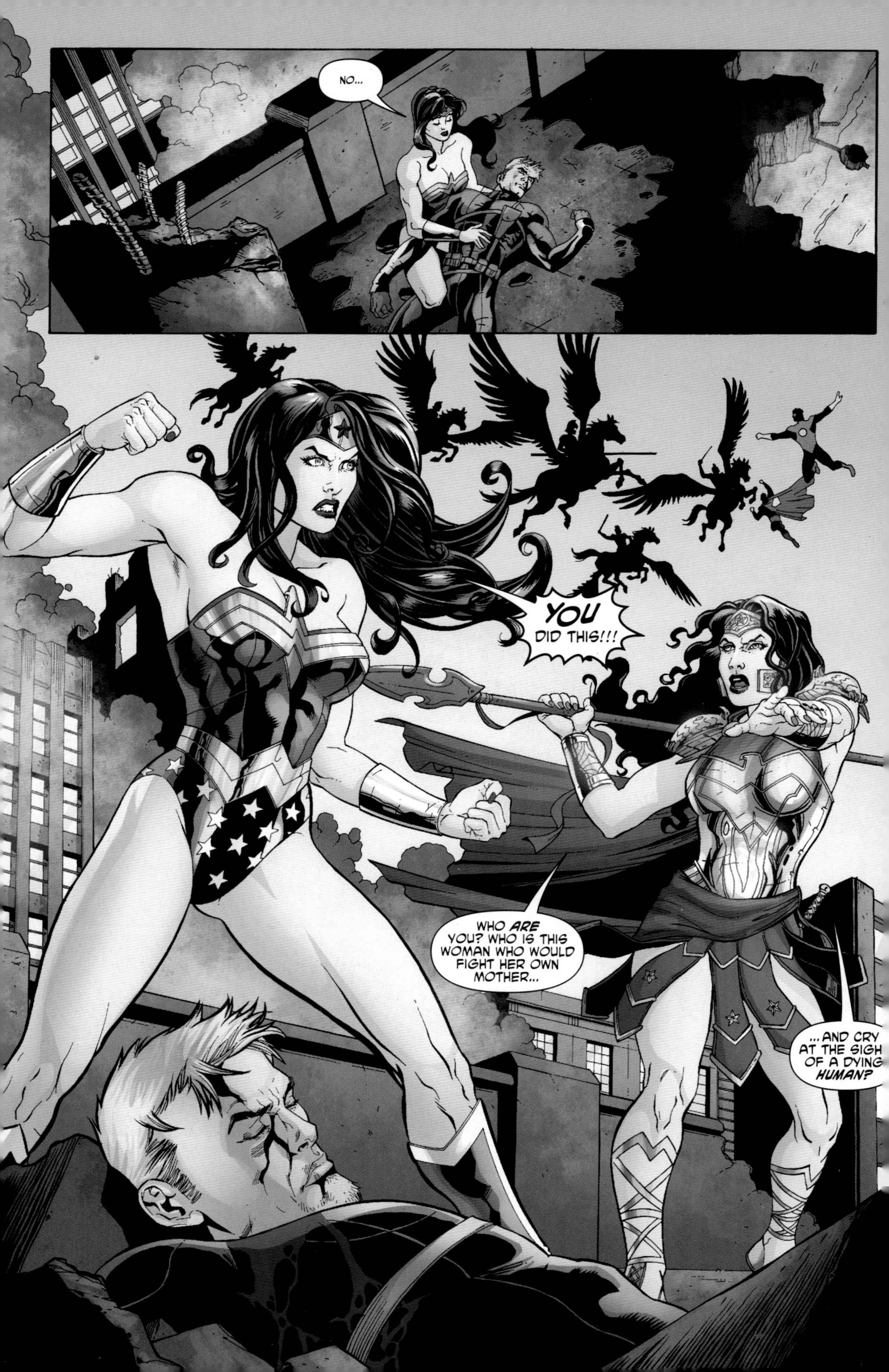
NO...
YOU DID THIS!!!
WHO ARE YOU? WHO IS THIS WOMAN WHO WOULD FIGHT HER OWN MOTHER...
...AND CRY AT THE SIGH OF A DYING HUMAN?

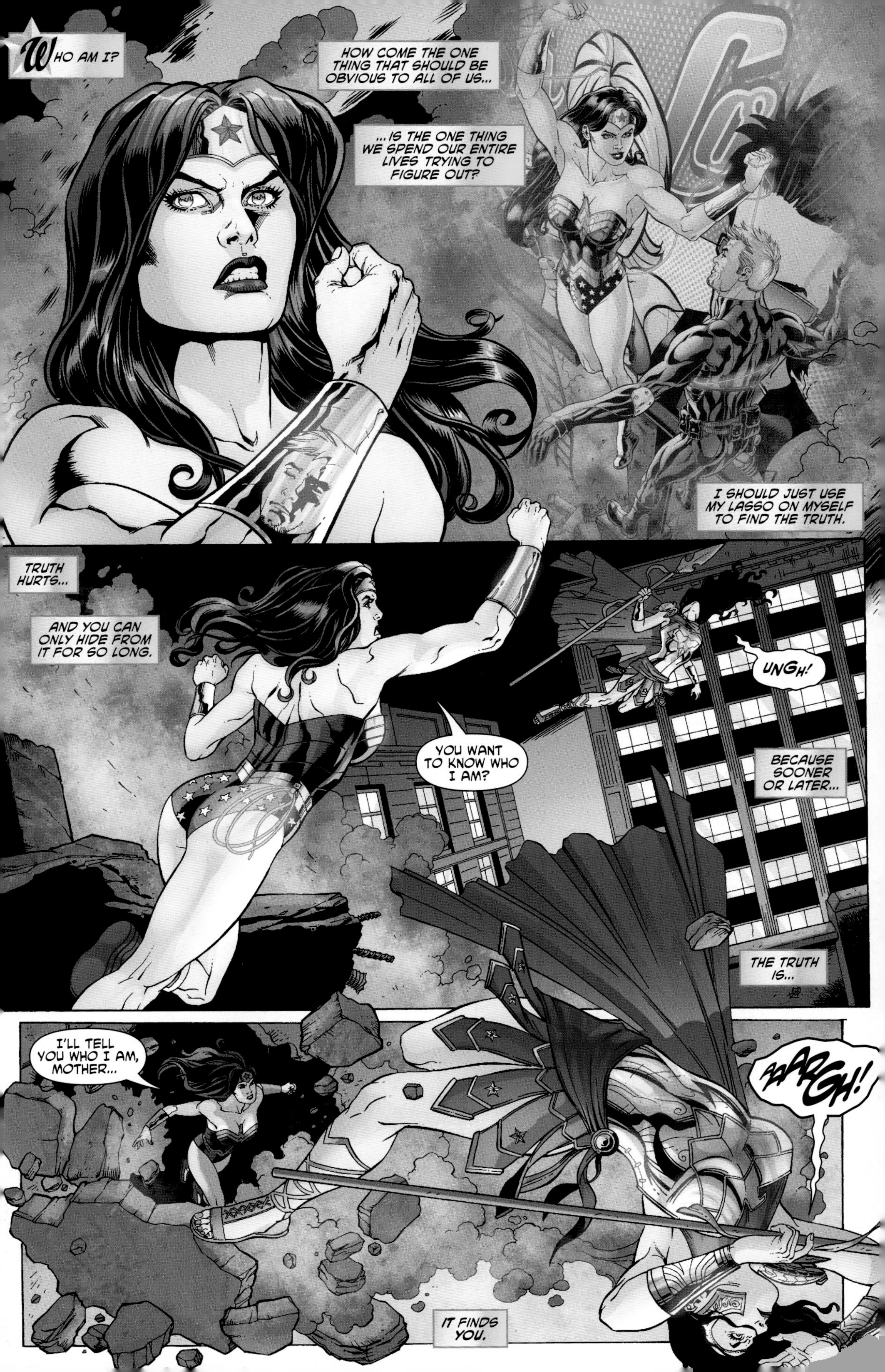
WHO AM I?
HOW COME THE ONE THING THAT SHOULD BE OBVIOUS TO ALL OF US...
...IS THE ONE THING WE SPEND OUR ENTIRE LIVES TRYING TO FIGURE OUT?
I SHOULD JUST USE MY LASSO ON MYSELF TO FIND THE TRUTH.
TRUTH HURTS...
AND YOU CAN ONLY HIDE FROM IT FOR SO LONG.
UNGH!
YOU WANT TO KNOW WHO I AM?
BECAUSE SOONER OR LATER...
THE TRUTH IS...
I'LL TELL YOU WHO I AM, MOTHER...
RAARGH!
IT FINDS YOU.

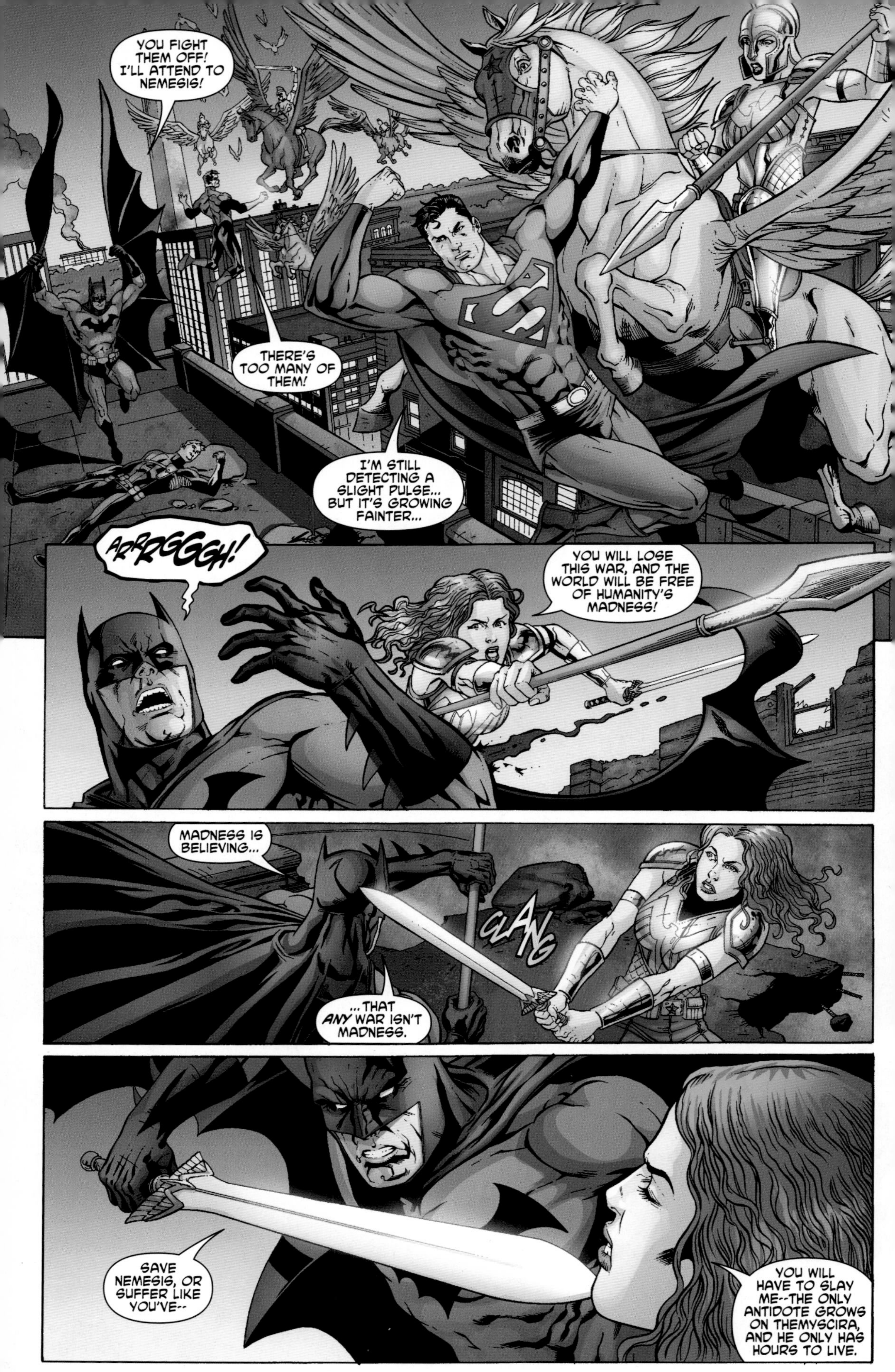
YOU FIGHT THEM OFF! I'LL ATTEND TO NEMESIS!
THERE'S TOO MANY OF THEM!
I'M STILL DETECTING A SLIGHT PULSE... BUT IT'S GROWING FAINTER...
ARRRGGGH!
YOU WILL LOSE THIS WAR, AND THE WORLD WILL BE FREE OF HUMANITY'S MADNESS!
MADNESS IS BELIEVING...
CLANG
...THAT *ANY* WAR ISN'T MADNESS.
SAVE NEMESIS, OR SUFFER LIKE YOU'VE--
YOU WILL HAVE TO SLAY ME--THE ONLY ANTIDOTE GROWS ON THEMYSCIRA, AND HE ONLY HAS HOURS TO LIVE.

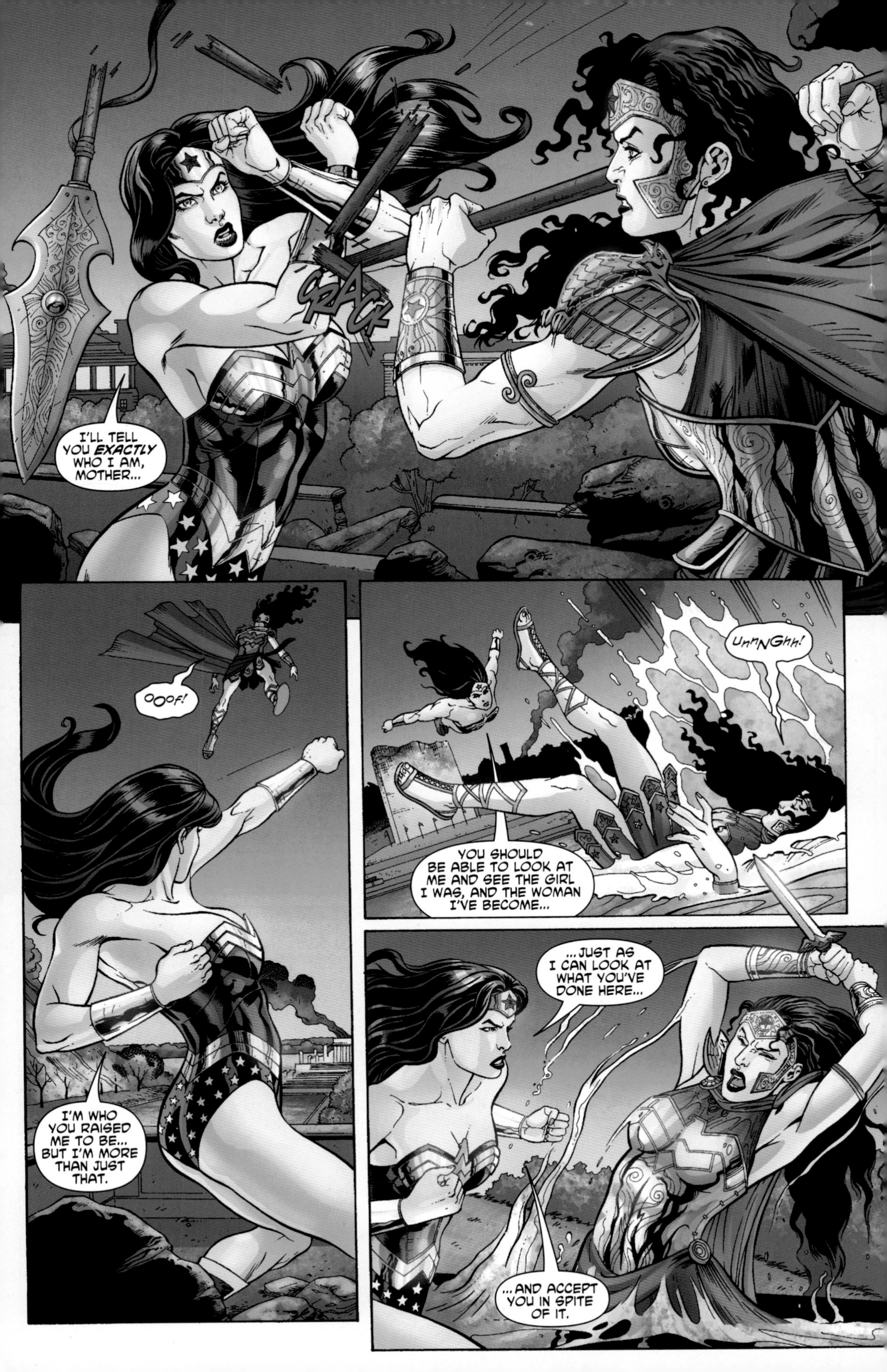

CRACK
I'LL TELL YOU EXACTLY WHO I AM, MOTHER...
OOOF!
I'M WHO YOU RAISED ME TO BE... BUT I'M MORE THAN JUST THAT.
UnnNGhh!
YOU SHOULD BE ABLE TO LOOK AT ME AND SEE THE GIRL I WAS, AND THE WOMAN I'VE BECOME...
...JUST AS I CAN LOOK AT WHAT YOU'VE DONE HERE...
...AND ACCEPT YOU IN SPITE OF IT.

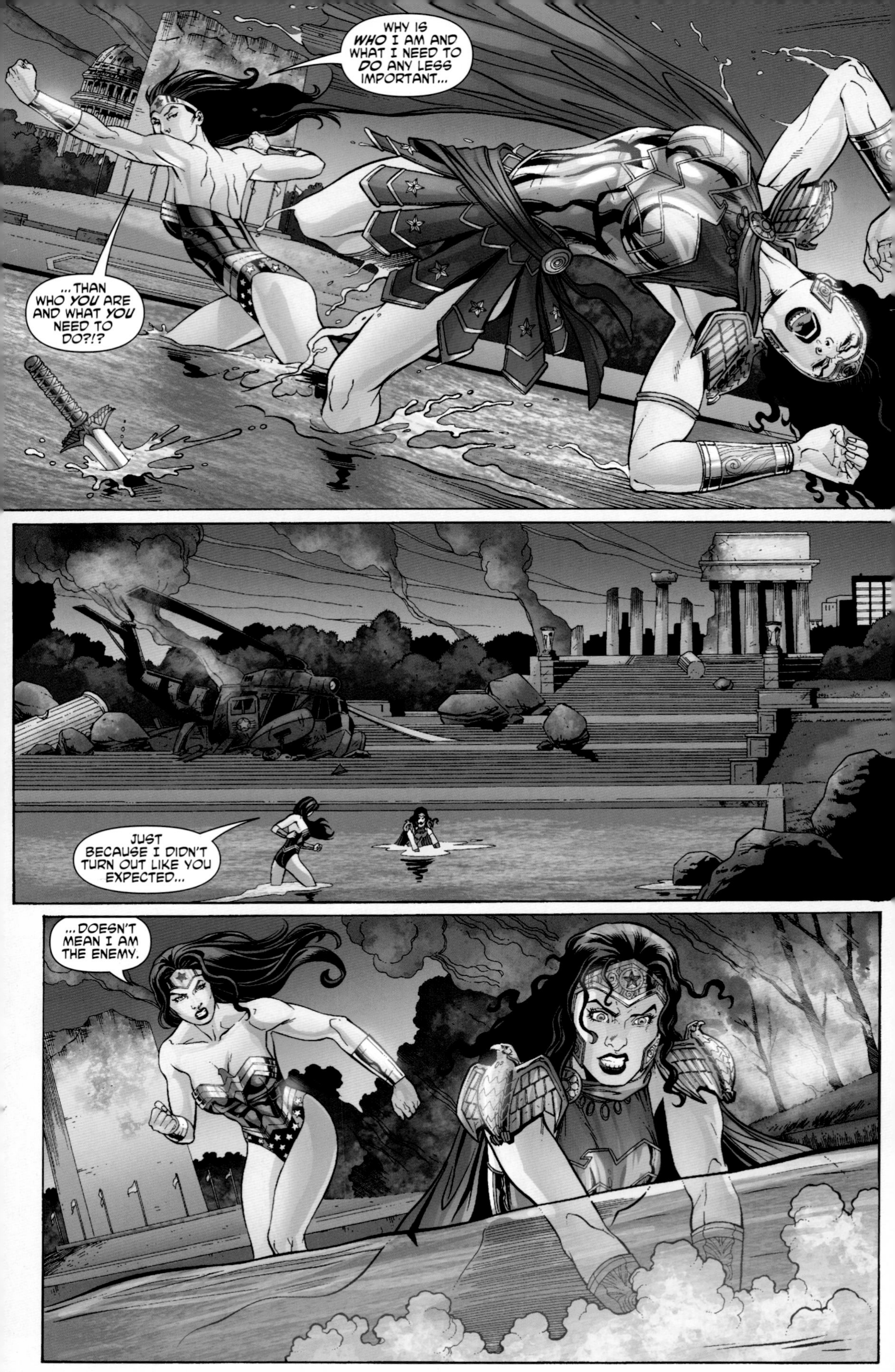
WHY IS WHO I AM AND WHAT I NEED TO DO ANY LESS IMPORTANT...
...THAN WHO YOU ARE AND WHAT YOU NEED TO DO?!?
JUST BECAUSE I DIDN'T TURN OUT LIKE YOU EXPECTED...
...DOESN'T MEAN I AM THE ENEMY.

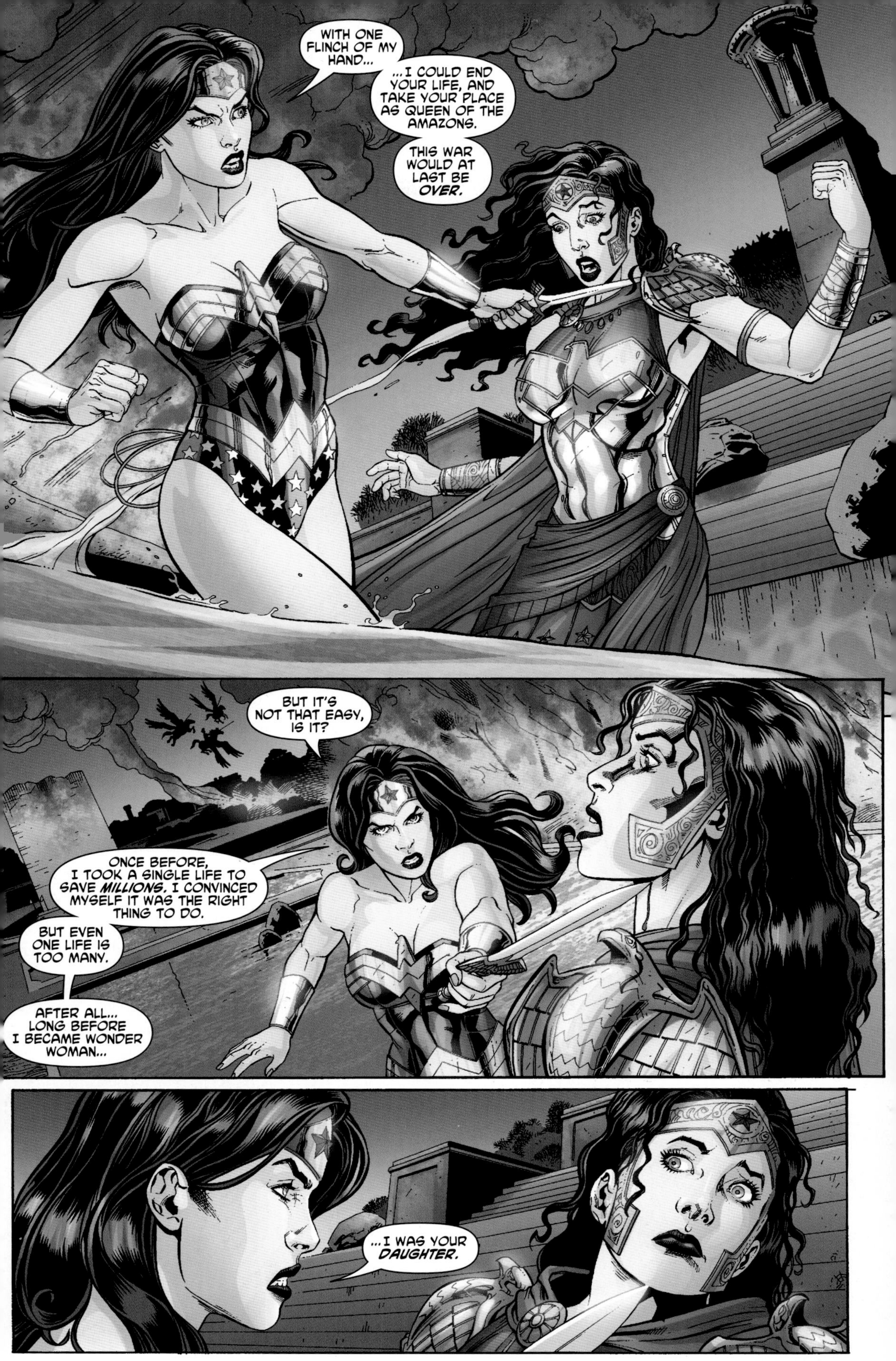

WITH ONE FLINCH OF MY HAND...
...I COULD END YOUR LIFE, AND TAKE YOUR PLACE AS QUEEN OF THE AMAZONS.
THIS WAR WOULD AT LAST BE *OVER.*
BUT IT'S NOT THAT EASY, IS IT?
ONCE BEFORE, I TOOK A SINGLE LIFE TO SAVE *MILLIONS.* I CONVINCED MYSELF IT WAS THE RIGHT THING TO DO.
BUT EVEN ONE LIFE IS TOO MANY.
AFTER ALL... LONG BEFORE I BECAME WONDER WOMAN...
...I WAS YOUR *DAUGHTER.*

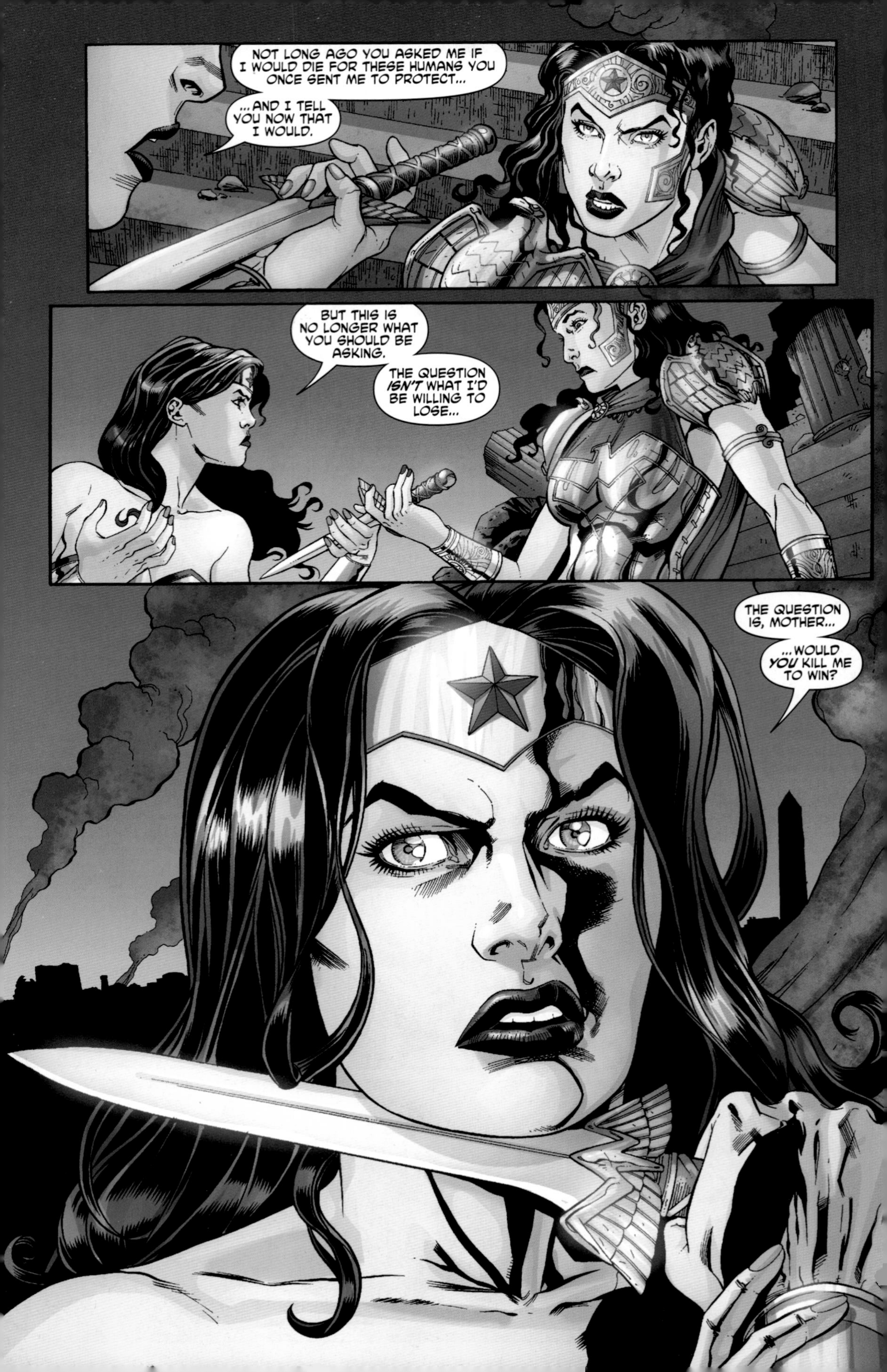
NOT LONG AGO YOU ASKED ME IF I WOULD DIE FOR THESE HUMANS YOU ONCE SENT ME TO PROTECT...
...AND I TELL YOU NOW THAT I WOULD.
BUT THIS IS NO LONGER WHAT YOU SHOULD BE ASKING.
THE QUESTION *ISN'T* WHAT I'D BE WILLING TO LOSE...
THE QUESTION IS, MOTHER...
...WOULD *YOU* KILL ME TO WIN?

Find out what happens next in

WONDER WOMAN
Amazons Attack

WILL PFEIFER ~ PETE WOODS

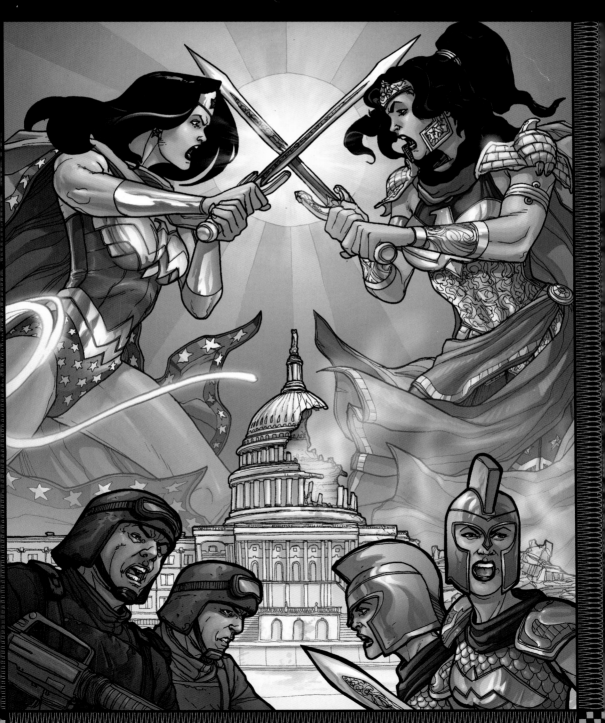

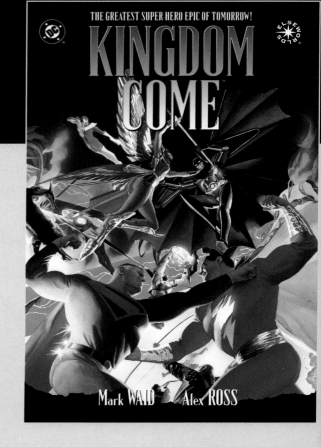
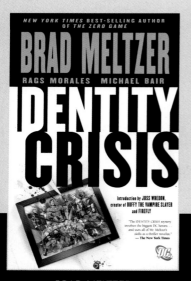